"B.S."

I Love You

B.S.
I Love You

SIXTY FUNNY YEARS WITH
THE FAMOUS AND THE INFAMOUS

MILTON BERLE

McGraw-Hill Book Company

New York   St. Louis   San Francisco   Bogotá   Hamburg   Madrid
Milan   Mexico   Montreal   Panama   Paris   São Paulo
Tokyo   Toronto

1 2 3 4 5 6 7 8 9 D O C D O C 8 7

ISBN 0-07-004913-0

LIBRARY OF CONGRESS CATALOGING-IN-PUBLICATION DATA

Berle, Milton.
    B.S. I love you.
    1. Berle, Milton.   2. Comedians—United   States—Biography.   3.
Entertainers—United States—Anecdotes, facetiae, satire, etc.   4. Entertainers—
United States—Anecdotes, facetiae, satire, etc.   I. Title.
PN2287.B436A3 1988   791.45′028′0924 [B]   87-17337
ISBN 0-07-004913-0

Book design by Patrice Fodero

This book is dedicated to the many Friars who are dedicated. It also pays tribute to my wife Ruth who made me what I am today—feeble but happy! And it nods deferentially to the many entertainers and public figures, famous, infamous, and otherwise, with whom I broke bread at the Friars Round Table.

And How About a Hand

For all of the people who helped turn this labor of love into a feast:

What can I say to Milt Rosen? As a scribe, Milt waded through thousands of my notes, some written sixty years ago, transcribed a hundred miles of my audio tapes, researched dates for me, and asked questions that put my memory cells to work. My debt cannot be measured in dollars and cents, which is why I intend to pay Milt with an autographed copy of the book.

Tom Miller, my editor, who proved over the many months that Harvard and Broadway can mix, also deserves more than thanks. He gets a free autographed eight-by-ten color glossy.

A verbal ovation goes to the Executive Directors of both branches of the Friars, Jean-Pierre Trebot in the East and, in Beverly Hills, Nick Uricchio. Both offered files, copies of rare Friars publications, and even the pictures off the walls.

Jonie Taps was invaluable in helping me out with a refresher course on the start of the Beverly Hills Friars. Jonie provided pictures of the period, each of which was worth more than a thousand words. Payment here too must take the form of an autographed copy of the book. Unfortunately, Jonie doesn't want an autographed copy of the book. He'd rather have a watch. When I write a book about watches he'll get a watch.

To Irving Fein, master producer, and my agent, Arthur Pine, who had faith in this project from the beginning, and to Gladys Justin Carr, Editorial Director of McGraw-Hill, who had trust in that faith, I will with royalties build monuments. Their support deserves no less.

Contents

Introduction

While still a congressman, Lyndon Baines Johnson visited the New York Friars and joined us at the Round Table. To demonstrate an absence of favoritism, Congressman Johnson also came to the Friars in California once.

Johnson enjoyed most, on both occasions, the banter at the Round Table. In New York he was witness to a Groucho Marx–Maurice Chevalier encounter. Chevalier had just done *Gigi*. Groucho outdid himself with a description of Chevalier making love to Hermione Gingold. Chevalier took off on Groucho's lady friends.

In the Beverly Hills Friars, Johnson heard us assemble a list of the horniest politicians. For dessert, he listened as Gene Kelly was torn apart for his role in *Marjorie Morningstar*.

Johnson told us that there were places in Washington, D.C., where barbs and put-downs prevailed, but nothing that could compare to what went at the Friars. We rode hard, he told us, and went at it wet.

Soon after Congressman Johnson became President, he held one of his spectacular Texas barbecues at the Johnson ranch. My wife and I were lucky enough to be among the guests.

Halfway through my third helping of ribs, I happened to find myself at the President's side. Johnson said, "Milton, I'll be out in California next month."

I said, "Mr. President, would you like to come up to the Friars?"

Johnson said, "It's too darn complicated. There's all the Secret Service men and there's the route. Too darn complicated. It's a damn shame too. The way you carry on, you fellows B.S. each other so sweet. It's sweeter bullshit than you'd hear from a steer trying to take on a blue-eyed cow."

Foreword from a
Friend

Usually I don't write forewords, but I don't mind doing this one for Milton Berle. Milton's a very close friend of mine; I see him at least twice a year.

Nobody is more qualified to write a book about the Friars than Milton Berle. Milton has spent more time at the Friars than any man who ever lived. That's not a great commendation, it's a statement of fact. When you write a foreword you should at least be truthful.

I remember a great deal about show business in the last seventy years. Milton Berle remembers *everything* about show business in the last seventy years. He can tell you the names of each act on the bill at the Olympia Theater in New Bedford, Massachusetts, on October 5, 1919.

I can recall only one act, my own. It was a singing act, and I was rehearsing it Monday morning. The manager heard my rehearsal and canceled me. I was the only act in show business who was canceled before he opened.

But why am I knocking myself? I should be knocking Milton Berle—it's his foreword. Milton Berle's head is a storehouse of show business details. Why not? There's nothing else in there.

I feel better; I'm doing my job.

I'll tell you another thing about Milton Berle you may or may not want to know. He changed his name and nose once. I changed my name a dozen times in one year. I never changed my nose; everything I have is my own—unfortunately.

This book was read to me by a twenty-year-old dancer. It was the most interesting thing we did together. Don't go by what I say—I lie a lot. But she did read it to me. I dozed off for a few minutes in the middle of the last chapter, but the parts I did hear reflected very accurately Milton Berle's love for entertainment, entertainers, and the Friars, where for seventy years performers have gathered to relax, eat well, compare notes, gossip, and talk dirty.

I'm sure you'll enjoy reading Milton's book. It's a good book—worthy of this foreword.

I really should finish this with something funnier than that. But it's Milton's book, let him finish it.

George Burns

Prologue

Milton Berle has produced a treasure of a book, a cornucopia of laughter and show business reminiscences that will be read and reread over the years. It is filled with humor, but it is not a joke book. There have been numerous collections of joke books, but except for a few dealing with the famed round table at the Algonquin there have been, to my knowledge, no books that have dealt with pure wit. *B. S. I Love You* fills that lacuna. There is a great difference between jokes and wit: Jokes are deliberately contrived bits of humor ranging from the simplistic good news–bad news jokes, to elaborately contrived stories ending with unexpected twists. Wit, on the other hand, is spontaneous—an instant extemporaneous response to a situation.

B. S. I Love You is a collection of anecdotes that involve members of the round table of the Friar's Clubs in New York and California. The cast of characters is astounding. It includes Lyndon Johnson, Groucho Marx, Babe Ruth, Errol Flynn, Humphrey Bogart, Warren Beatty, Al Jolson, Orson Welles, and a hundred others.

Someone once remarked that Milton Berle has a witty ear, and he uses it here to eavesdrop on some of the funniest and quickest minds in show business. The wit is often barbed and cutting, and there are no sacred cows. Everybody is a target, and the more important the person, the more biting the attacks.

Milton Berle has done a superb job of capturing the feelings, the insecurities, the insanities, and the joys of being an entertainer. He is a survivor, a man who, if he will forgive the cliché, is a living legend himself.

They say that laughter is the best medicine. Read this book and get well.

Sidney Sheldon

Funny Life

Welcome to My World

I don't know what I'd do without you guys, but I'd rather!

Frank Fay

I never knew you could have so much fun sitting up!

Hugh Hefner

Why am I here? I could be home with bursitis!

Groucho Marx

Lunch is such great fun here at the Friars. Why did I show up for dinner?

Mayor Jimmy Walker

Part of a phone conversation in 1957:
Thanks for the invitation to brunch, but I think our comedians in Congress are funnier than yours!...And where are the Havanas you promised me? Indian giver!

John F. Kennedy

The world-famous Friars Club is a fraternal organization with a mother branch in New York and a lusty offspring in Beverly Hills, California.

For eighty years members of the Friars, by organizing and entertaining at thousands of shows, dinners, stag roasts, and tributes, have helped to raise millions of dollars for worthy causes. In times of war, Friars have and will entertain wherever and whenever asked. In World War Two, a group of us entertained servicemen and servicewomen a hundred and fifty times in one year.

Because the basic thrust of the club is social, it offers many of us a home away from home, a roof under which fellowship and brotherhood sit as guests at every table or booth.

The daily lunch is an opportunity for some of the older members to reminisce about the "good old days." We have a few members who reminisce clear back to the beginning of the twentieth century. Lunchtime presents an opportunity for the passing on to new and younger members many of the show-business wisdoms and truths older members have learned. Not quite a theatrical Socrates, I lunch with new comedians once a week or so. We all learn.

Show business has become largely "business." The bottom line seems to be the bottom line on the accountant's printout. Show business is computerized. Its middle name is electronics. Soon, if it's possible, geneticists will isolate the genes that make people funny or give them incredible voices. The dangers are right out there for all of us to see. Somehow, I don't panic. As long as there's a Friars Club, its cadre of entertainers, and a me to show that footlights and maybe even mike feedback can keep the adrenaline flowing, I'm not ready to write a eulogy for the only way of life I've ever known. I'm not sure there is any life anywhere else. Since my first day at the Friars in 1920, I don't think I've really been anywhere else.

Noon has found me at the Friars Round Table in New York or California over nine thousand times. If a day breaks and I haven't made the obituary column, I'll be at my home away from home—the Friars Club.

Red Buttons caught me one lunchtime at the Round Table in the Beverly Hills Friars after I'd been away. He asked me why he hadn't seen me at lunch the day before. I explained, "I was in Boston. My plane back was delayed by the worst snow storm in a century."

Red said, "Excuses! Always excuses!"

Similarly, after my bypass surgery, I returned to the club only to encounter Joe Vitrelli, a Friar who'd been away for the several weeks of my operation and recovery. Vitrelli mentioned that he hadn't seen me all week. I explained that I'd had a bypass. Norm Crosby shrugged. "Okay, that explains Monday. What about Tuesday and Wednesday?"

In my brief time on earth I've exercised great affection for women, children, especially a son, a daughter, and two brilliant grandsons, audiences, applause, and the smell of greasepaint. But passion, base and boiling, I've had only for the Friars.

Ruth, my wife, because of a temporary short circuit in her taste buds, believes sincerely that if the waters were rising and there was room in the lifeboat for no more than one customer, I'd haul a Friar aboard. He'd probably be one who likes to ask show-business questions. He'd certainly be somebody fond of reminiscing. I'm not about to chance a long drift without somebody who would want to know how I got to know Marilyn Monroe. Or some innocent who'd ask, "Milton, how'd you get to be called 'The Thief of Badgags'?" And a glutton for punishment—"Milton, act out every sketch ever written!"

I'd be free to play show business, past and present, because I wouldn't have to worry about Ruth's safety and comfort. She certainly would have contingency plans of her own for the flood. She'd take along the trench coat she wore in the Gestapo and the phone book with the numbers of all the ladies she could have lunch with to discuss the next Share show, a major West Coast charity event.

My lust for the Friars goes unquestioned because Ruth isn't the jealous sort. She once found powder on my sleeve and accused me of going bowling!

As my Friar and I'd sail out to sea, Ruth would wave good-bye fondly. She might even be happy to see *Kon-tiki* take off again. She knows where the safe-deposit boxes are. She has keys for them. (When she takes her key chain out of her purse, she looks like the warden at San Quentin. Due to her mother's teaching, she has bank accounts I don't know about. When Ruth and I were first married, her mother, Genghis Khan, said, "My darling daughter, your husband is a spendthrift and a gambler. Start saving on the side!" Ruth started saving on the side during the wedding ceremony. At present she has bank accounts in a hundred and sixteen countries. Much of the money that filtered between Iran and the Nicaraguan contras, no doubt, went through Ruth's private Swiss account with no help from Oliver North.)

When a number of press agents formed the Friars in 1907, give or take a few versions and other starting dates, they had no hint that I'd be along soon, loaded down with candy and roses, to pledge my troth.

I wasn't even born yet. Mr. and Mrs. Berlinger didn't even like one another at the time. They'd had some other kids and weren't thrilled with the crop, each blaming the other for some kind of familial genetic bankruptcy. That's only partially true. My mother craved more Berlingers. Pa took her aside, pointed to my brother Phil and asked, "Do you really want more kids like that?"

Mama must have said "Maybe," because I got here. In the background, Ruth's mother cheered them on. She knew that someday she'd need me.

One minute after I was born, Pa slapped the doctor, two nurses, and a passing delivery boy who was taking flowers to a lady with advanced gout. I think Pa's last words to the doctor were "I'll get you for this!" Pa also stopped strangers in the street and said that blood tests would show that I was another "immaculate conception."

And I started my inevitable march to the Friars!

Small Fry at the Friars

In 1920, I was twelve years old. Taller than most sixteen-year-olds in my neighborhood, I was ninety percent knees, elbows, and other assorted bony parts. Famous within about a block radius of the Berlinger railroad flat, I was still not able to live up to what a *Variety* reviewer would say of me in 1926: "The boy borders on the precocious."

But I was on my way. My mother said that I was on my way. My mother knew. Nobody challenged her anyway. At Coney Island a tide tried to challenge my mother. She had it deported. After a family meal once, my mother went into the bedroom to lie down. Pa explained that the food might have disagreed with her. My Uncle Dave said, "It wouldn't dare!"

The highlight of 1920, according to the kids who hung out at the corner candy store, was the sale of Babe Ruth to the Yankees. The Red Sox fans thought that Colonel Ruppert, the owner of the Yankees, who'd made his money as a brewer, was crazy to part with $125,000 for a ball player with skinny, bandied legs, a head that didn't fit, and, in between, a beer paunch. The Red Sox took the money.

A few people thought that the coming in 1920 of a little thing called Prohibition might have some historical value. I personally didn't lose much sleep over the banning of hard drink. From the action around Manhattan, it looked as if *nobody* lost any sleep!

What really put 1920 into the record books and motivated this book was a happening that until now has never been made public—1920 was the year I went to the Friars for the first time! You now know something that Will and Ariel Durant never learned. Arthur Schlesinger probably didn't know either. My wife didn't find out until very recently. Overwhelmed by the discovery, she wondered if we could have 1920 bronzed and put next to her army rifle, electric cattle prod, and whip.

Already a big star and a family friend because he liked my work and his wife, Ida, liked the way my mother lost to her at poker, Eddie Cantor decided in 1920 that it was time for me to visit the Friars and go up against the big boys. "You won't be such a wise guy big mouth when the men at the club cut you down to size," Cantor said, only half-joking. (I wasn't always meek, shy, retiring, and self-effacing. Hard as it is to believe, when I was twelve I was brash. I knew it all. I had the nerve of two porcupines making love! I won't say that I had a big head, but Sears wouldn't have painted it for a hundred and a quarter. I was the kind of kid my mother told me not to play with!)

My life consisted of three meals a day—sometimes, performances— and a hundred gags. I did anything for a laugh—funny makeup, funny clothes, funny walks, funny props bought for pennies at a magic store on Sixth Avenue. I hocked my soul for copies of joke magazines— *Captain Billy's Whiz Bang, Jim Jam Jems, The Calgary Eye-Opener,* and *College Humor.* Some kids saved stamps and coins. I collected "insults," which I doled out with a vengeance. All somebody had to do was ask me, "How's the meat loaf?" and I'd start a run of "bad cook" jokes that lasted until the next meal. My mother wasn't bothered by my "bad cook" jokes. My father did most of the cooking. He didn't get hurt as long as my mother and I came back from a tour with more money than we had when we left. I never talk about my father much. The truth is that I loved Moses Berlinger! He laughed at my jokes.

Eddie Cantor was only slightly impressed by audience reaction to me offstage, especially the laughter that would follow a cutting one-liner. He wanted the best for me and honestly believed that the road to show-business hell was paved with insult jokes and toppers from young squirts. It was okay for Cantor and Jessel and my mother's good friend Sophie Tucker to whip people with words. They'd paid their dues, had themselves been slaughtered a few times, and earned the right.

Cantor was certain that a few minutes at the Friars Club would pare about ten layers from my ego. Aware that I needed a modesty bypass, he often tried to nudge sense into me gently and with his own jokes—"Kid, you got more gas in you than a Boston diner!" "You got more cheek on you than a Coney Island blanket!"

When he ran out of lines that applied to a situation, Cantor threw lines that didn't. The "cheek" joke could be followed by a reference to my nose—"Your nose is so big you're still breathing yesterday's air!" The trick was to keep going until the curtain came down. (Years later Dick Shawn took from the same well. Losing his way in a sequence during a Friar's roast, Shawn blasted through until he came to a natural stop. He explained to the audience that he had no idea of what he was saying. But the important thing, he confessed, was to keep talking. The audience will forgive you as long as you finish the sentence!)

For our junket to the Friars, Cantor insisted that I wear long pants. He didn't want to see and hear my knees clanging together nervously in the presence of the greats who gathered at the Friars.

The trick was to get my mother to release the long pants. As warden of my wardrobe, she was tough. Her philosophy regarding long pants was basic: In the hunt for stardom, my attention was never to be diverted. Women, the result of long pants, would be a diversion. Nothing threw off timing more than a fantasy about a pretty lady in the third row. Glands made a performer forget rhythm, the words to a song, and the exact reading of a joke. My mother didn't want to turn me into Mildred Berle. She would step aside and unleash me at every chorus girl, soubrette, dancer, and actress on any and all stages of the world—but first I had to become a star!

For twelve-year-old Milton, long pants was costume. As long as I remained in knickers and shorts, I was safe from the ravages of sex. No female with active loins would dream of searching for companionship behind the facade of my knickers and short pants.

Thus the long pants, both the dark gray worsted and the blue serge, were available for interviews, auditions, and callbacks. And nothing else! (Cantor's mother felt the same. Until he was sixteen, Cantor thought he was a Fauntleroy.)

My mother didn't know that her list of diabolical side functions for my long pants was anachronistic. I had already been deflowered by a show girl in *Floradora*. Alas, the moat my mother had built around my closet and the alligator that patrolled hourly were useless. Moreover, the loss of my virginity was followed by a series of booster shots. Sadly, this affair, which I believed to be secret, wasn't so secret. Foolish for a moment one evening, I mentioned to Walter Woolfe, the star of *Floradora,* that I had seduced this young lady. Woolfe answered, "It's very hard to find somebody who hasn't!"

That I was an innocent is reflected in an anecdote that has become an oft-told joke: On our first dalliance, I stood naked before my lady love. Breathlessly, she looked at a certain part of my anatomy and asked, "Do you mind if I kiss you?" I said, "Are you supposed to?"

I had two pairs of long trousers in Miss Kiss-It's apartment on Forty-seventh Street. She had bought them for me in an attempt to camouflage my youth. We often took walks before and after our dalliances. Promenading with a Cub Scout might have caused some talk. Also, she didn't feel so much like a cradle snatcher when we went from milk and cookies to our nuptial bed.

I considered borrowing a pair of the long pants my paramour had under her guardianship. I could have pled an audition of some sort, but she knew that my mother had longies for these special occasions. The request, she would have concluded, could have come only from the fact that another woman had entered my life. I had to spare her this hurt and the rage that would come down on me like bolts of lightning. Not that my show girl was smitten with me. I was a mechanical device by which she could find gratification. Being young, I had a hell of a warranty. I never needed oiling and parts didn't break down. Modestly, I must admit that I wasn't the Don Juan I became later, the Lothario of whom my dear wife said, twenty years into the marriage, "With practice he'll get better!" (Ruth is an incredible boudoir companion and has been known to bolster my ego with statements like "When you're finished, cover me up!" To cap one of our anniversaries, I promised Ruth an unforgettable night of romance. I swore to achieve heights never before attained by mortal man. In the morning at the breakfast table, Ruth looked at me and said, "Oh, yeah, how'd you make out last night?")

The long pants didn't come easily for me the day of my first trip to the Friars. My mother was a tough nut to crack. Cantor was known to be a cutie. With his distorted sense of humor, he probably intended, she felt, to take me out on the town to meet some wild wild women.

Cantor crossed his heart seven ways. He was thinking of my career. The Friars, he avowed, was worth a hundred auditions. The biggest producers filled its hallowed halls—Daniel Frohman, David Belasco, Oscar Hammerstein, Sr., and Sam H. Harris, to name merely a few. Among them the four had only produced everything on Broadway but the blind newsboy.

My mother wasn't overwhelmed with the parade of names or Cantor's logic. She asked, "Eddie, with all these big shots hanging around, how come you and Jessel aren't working?" Actually, Cantor worked a great deal. My mother merely believed that *one* day off was the end of a career. My mother brought to show business the acuity that made her a great store detective. She was a store detective, honest! Assigned to watch out for shoplifters, she managed to wangle an assignment in the piano department. During her tenure not one Steinway disappeared!

Disregarding my mother's barb at his momentary unemployment, Cantor swore that he'd lead me by the hand straight to the Friar monastery on Forty-eighth Street. He'd have me back in the apartment right after lunch. My mother agreed finally, but with one codicil. If there was the slightest dent in my libido, she'd tell about Eddie and the girl in the balancing act at the show that had just closed at the Winter Garden.

Practicing on our family, my mother raised guilt to a religion and threats to poetry. Both arts were present in her admonition to Cantor. My mention of my mother's skill in these areas at the Round Table, many years later, brought a challenge from Bill Cosby. Cosby said that his mother could give mine cards and spades. His mother was the "guilt" and "fear" distributor for all of eastern Pennsylvania and parts of New Jersey. Cos swore that his mother had read *Portnoy's Complaint* and sent it back with corrections.

Cantor and I walked into the Friars on my world premiere visit a few minutes before noon. I pretended nonchalance, but I was as impressed as all heck. I felt a little like Joe E. Lewis must have felt when he was invited to the White House. Walking up the few steps, he looked around, awed, and said, "I don't have my library card!" (Awe also had a field day when W. C. Fields was invited to the mansion of Louis B. Mayer, the movie mogul. Fields looked at the impressive house front and asked, "Do you think they have a gift shop?")

Yes, I was impressed.

And soon overwhelmed.

Within an hour of my arrival for the first time on that spring day in 1920 at the Friars Round Table, I'd met George M. Cohan, already a big Broadway star, Gentleman Jim Corbett, one of my favorite fighters, Enrico Caruso, the opera star by whom singers are still measured, and Daniel Frohman, one of the major producers Cantor had promised to deliver. Frohman didn't sit with us long, but I marked him down as present and accounted for anyway. We did exchange several words.

The membership of that premiere Round Table grew as men started to come in for lunch. Billy B. Van joined us. A reporter for the New York *World* who also wrote material for shows and performers, he was co-starring in a Broadway show with Corbett. Fred Allen sat down with us. And finally Irving Berlin. I was glad that President Coolidge and the Pope hadn't decided to show up. We wouldn't have had room for them. With my luck, *I* would have had to tell them that the table was overbooked.

Wisely, I sat and listened. Cantor and Van threw most of the lines, with Allen sneaking in at every fifth or sixth opening for a score. The first time I opened my mouth, and not even to offer a joke, war broke out. I hoped it was in fun, although I wasn't a hundred percent sure.

Caruso had just said something to the waiter in a language that defied linguistic classification. Cantor said, "Enrico, you speak English like your boat won't dock until next Thursday!"

Allen said, "That's my joke."

Not too bright, I said, "It's Willie Howard's joke."

Pretending to be hurt, which was easy because even in those years he looked as if pain was his natural state, Fred Allen said, "Cantor, the next time you honor us with the presence of a protégé, make sure he's an idiot! This table is saturated with intelligence just with *my* being here!"

Cohan said, "Cantor, we don't even like having you here. As for you, Mr. Beale or Bell or Bill, whatever your name is, have some respect for your elders. Unless it's Jim Corbett. Nobody has respect for him!"

Berlin asked, "Why are we insulting Corbett? I like it when you insult Cantor!"

Billy B. Van said, "Enrico, this is all your fault!"

Caruso responded with a burst of Italian, gestures and all, indicating, I supposed, that he believed everybody at the table to be stark-raving mad. His words came fast and furious and went on for sixteen bars.

Allen pointed to the tenor and said, "Milton, never forget that!"

The comic war and my first lunch at the Friars Round Table

came to an end. Getting up to leave, Cantor said, "I wish I had a good exit line."

Forgetting myself, I said, "I'm saving mine for an *important* lunch!"

Allen said, "That was good, young man. Do we credit it to your wit or dumb luck?"

Cantor grabbed me by the collar and started to drag me out of the room before I could answer. Cohan waved at us. "Come up and see us again, Milton."

Corbett said, "But not too soon!"

I wondered if tomorrow was soon enough.

In the Beginning Was Delight

Thank you for your kind invitation to become an honorary member of the Friars Club. I must decline. I have enough trouble being a member of the Bull Moose Party! I might add that I think your roast chicken is Bully!

Theodore Roosevelt

To his press representative Charles Emerson Cook: I know that you would very much like to see my name on the roster of the Friars. I would like to see my name in any of the fourteen newspapers in this city.

Lew Dockstader, the Minstrel Man

Show people like to be with their own. Physicians join medical associations, but don't run with other doctors socially. Unless one is a heck of a patient referrer, then the whole AMA is his pal.

Show people pal around together. The cluster urge may come from the abuse entertainers took for a long time. It was "life on the wicked stage." For years no respectable hotel would accept actors. A decent club wouldn't have anybody that smelled of greasepaint. At the turn of the century, a certain young lady dreamed, more than anything else in the world, of becoming an actress. Sarah Glantz was pretty, talented, and eager. Her parents wouldn't hear of it. She'd bring undying shame to the family name; Glantzes everywhere would have to jump off bridges. Miss Glantz married Moses Berlinger. Mama decided to make it through me. If I hadn't succeeded, she probably would have had another kid when she was sixty and given it dancing lessons. Once when I became a headliner as a single, Mama said, "I'm glad you're a star, Milton, I was getting tired." (Of course she was really tireless.)

Whether it was due to social pressure or merely the desire to revel together, the publicity men who founded the Friars went at it with gusto. A proper club needs a proper name. Somebody suggested calling it the Friars. Cheers went up and the name was accepted. Everybody had a drink, maybe two drinks, and saluted the appellation. The next morning, when everybody was sober again, somebody asked why the name was chosen and somebody else said, "Who cares!" and the Friars it remained.

The name hints at a monastery with dark halls, bare benches, and always the echo of constant Latin prayers. However, none of the original Friars were religious. They were boozers and hellions of the worst sort.

Wells Hawks, the first abbot, which is a cute word for president and another pious term, hadn't seen the inside of a house of prayer since his first communion. It was rumored that at his baptism Hawks had put an olive in the holy water and gulped down the concoction with one flick of the wrist.

The first honoree at a Friar function was the brilliant actor Clyde Fitch. The mere thought of entering a monastery of any sort must have shocked him no end. The well of his appetites was bottomless. Moreover, the libidinous spring that fed it flowed in all directions.

It's possible that the name "Friars" was chosen because the members believed in wining, dining, and the carefree life. Somehow a connection was made with the life led by one Robin of Locksley and his band of merry men, among whom was a Friar Tuck. The good Friar believed in wining, dining, and the carefree life. On a rare occasion Friar Tuck didn't mind cudgeling a foe, but mostly he had a good time and "wish you were here."

This latter theory is a six-to-five favorite, as the face that shines forth from the club emblem is closer to Sherwood Forest than it is to a saintly priory. The symbolized Friar is round-faced, jolly, probably lusty, and almost certainly would love to stay up all night playing poker. His ample sleeves could hide enough aces to man the Israeli Air Force. (Ruth has never liked the whole Sherwood Forest notion. What was Maid Marion doing while the guys frolicked around? Ruth may be a descendant of the Sheriff of Nottingham anyway. I know that we went to see the original *Robin Hood* together. When the Sheriff threatened to hang Robin from the highest limb of an oak, Ruth rooted for the tree.)

Friaring isn't without its risks. In our stag roast for Phyllis Diller, Sammy Shore, the comedian turned novelist, wore a monk's outfit as part of his being a singing trio. The next day Sammy reported in, "That outfit was so heavy and it rubbed my skin. Did monks really wear those things in the old days?"

Red Buttons said, "That's why they were always praying." Buttons lowered his head and went into the singsong of prayer: "Lord, send me something for prickly heat! Lord, send me calamine lotion! Lord, let somebody invent polyester!"

The Friar pioneers of 1907 seemed to have a good idea going, but at first they had no place to call home. They roamed from restaurant to restaurant, meeting wherever a bar and kitchen were available. Finally, after wandering around the desert for two million drinks and many a side of beef, they settled in their first monastery on Forty-fifth Street in Manhattan.

The gaiety attracted actors who in turn provided more gaiety. Actors begat more actors, and soon those who trod the boards outnumbered those who trod the streets and beat the drums for their clients.

With a move into larger quarters eight years later, it taking that long because some of the members were glued to the dark pine bar, the sense of the organization changed. The surroundings became too good for the poor and the civilian. The monastery became a hostel almost purely for entertainers. A few prosaic types were allowed in because they were wealthy, claimed good friends in the ranks, or, for sentimental reasons, had something to do with publicity. Otherwise, in the lavish friary, with its theater, dining rooms, card rooms, and well-appointed nooks, only the likes of Jerry Cohan, George's dad, John Philip Sousa, and William Morris, founder of the talent agency, could be found. Mayor Walker and Governor Al Smith were given memberships because their politics seemed to be closer to theatrical comedy than they were to the truths of the political process.

Firmly rooted after 1920, the Friars looked as if it was going to be a joy ride forever. Sadly, events got in the way.

A Wall Street crash later, a Depression later, and an executive secretary absconding with the rent later, and a few bad business decisions later, fate played havoc with the Friars' home address for about fifteen years. Zeppo Marx, the good-looking Marx brother, described by his brother Chico as "the unfunniest Marx since Karl," complained about the club's wanderlust, "We didn't stay in one place long enough to become 'occupant'!"

An extremely funny man, another of my idols and mentors, and a gem because he kept telling me how good I was, Walter C. Kelly said, "During the bad days we were evicted so often we had dishes to match the sidewalk!" Also thinking back many years later, Groucho Marx said, "One time we were thrown out on the sidewalk and there was no sidewalk!"

Reacting to the news that we were broke in 1935 and had lost everything—building, sugar bowls, two hundred decks of cards— Joe Frisco, the stuttering comedian and a man who dedicated his life to losing wagers, asked, "Who p-p-placed the b-bet?" He didn't get a laugh because at the time he wasn't a member of the club. When the times turned good, he was voted in. Always consistent with his love of losing, he bet against being voted into the club. He asked for a recount too!

William Degan Weinberger, the executive director of the Friars at the time, swore that Joe Frisco came into his office one day and tried to borrow some money on his unpaid dues.

Weinberger told Frisco, "You can't borrow on your unpaid dues!"

Frisco said, "W-w-why not? N-n-nobody el-l-lse is b-b-borrowing on them!"

The Western branch of the Friars came about because of two bad middleweight fights. Firmly Californian by the fifties, George Burns, Jack Benny, and Al Jolson, along with some buddies, had a Friday-night ritual. They met at the Brown Derby for dinner. Jolson liked to tell the others what to order. They ignored him. After dinner they went to the fights at the Hollywood Legion, a block and a half away.

This one week, the fights ended quickly. It wasn't ten o'clock yet. There being no place to go at that time, the night was over. Sighing, Burns said, "We need a Friars Club out here."

Jolson said, "Let's start one." He turned to Jonie Taps, a biggie with Columbia Pictures: "You know how to organize." More than hinting at what should be ordered from the menu, Jolson liked to delegate.

Taps happened to be an astute organizer. Not a Friar in the East, he had been in the music-publishing business. His ability to smell out a coming cowboy and country-music trend made a potful of money for his company. Brought out to head the music department at Columbia, he soon became indispensable to Harry Cohn, his boss and one of the most powerful men in Hollywood.

Taps called a meeting in his office. Bob Hope, Bing Crosby, Pat O'Brien, Robert Taylor, and the usual too-numerous-to-mention showed up. Because it involved the Friars, George Jessel sat on the throne. Since 1926 nobody breathed Friars air without his permission. One time, a little perturbed, Benny Fields, an early crooner and the partner of Blossom Seeley in a top vaudeville act, objected to a Jessel dictum, "George, you're not God!"

Jessel said, "I didn't say I was God. But this group better listen to me while I spake unto them!" (Ruth spakes to me quite often.)

Jessel conducteth the first meeting. Because of, or in spite of him, a stellar group of officers was chosen: Abbot—George Jessel; Dean—Bing Crosby; Prior—Robert Taylor; Proctor—Bob Hope; Herald—Jimmy Durante; Secretary-Treasurer—William L. Penzer. The last, the only one in the group who could add, fit in nicely. Penzer held the lease on the building and had signed the necessary notes.

Upon being chosen for his post, Durante was delighted. He said, "I never won nothing before!"

Harry Cohn was not one to be unaware of what was going on in his bailiwick. He summoned Jonie Taps later.

What was going on? Was Taps planning a big move of some sort? Taps explained, "We're forming a branch of the Friars out here in California."

"Am I in it?" Cohn asked.

"You're the president," Jonie Taps said.

Cohn had one further question: "Do I have to pay dues?"

Jonie Taps's response reflected his innate executive ability.

New York was petitioned. By then I was the Charlemagne of the New York Friars and helped California obtain its franchise. I'm glad I did, as I moved West not too long after that. Without the Friars I would have had to go out and rent an audience somewhere.

Moving about as often as its parent, the California Friars finally settled down in Beverly Hills. On the way it managed to attract a few celebrities as members. One of them, a willing applicant, was an actor named Ronald Reagan. He was a cute guy, but nobody got all excited about him. At lunch one day, Jack Haley, the "Tin Man," told him, "You've got a future, Dutch, but it's not in our business!"

Among other things, such as becoming the honcho of the club and getting his portrait on our wall of fame, Ronald Reagan became the second Friar to recite *Casey at the Bat* as a closer. The first was De Wolfe Hopper in New York. Hopper became famous for his rendition in theaters everywhere. Ronald Reagan did it at Las Vegas's Last Frontier Hotel in 1954. Reagan must have been fairly good, as he was held over for the second show.

Many of the Friars flew to Las Vegas to see the act. They don't talk about it much anymore. Most of the critics are still in shock from *Bedtime for Bonzo*. A regular at the Round Table, his co-star in the picture and now the lonely Maytag man, Jesse White says, "It was a good little film. It was very good for Reagan. Playing with the chimp gave him practice for his real kids."

Now out of show business, Reagan has never forgotten his big number. It was rumored that at a summit meeting he offered to recite the entire poem if the Russians would remove their missiles from Europe. It was also rumored that the Russians said that the recital would be tantamount to a declaration of war.

Friar Reagan doesn't come around to the club anymore. With the battering he's been taking, I have the feeling he'd like to.

Where the Boys Are

(Talking about Pretty Amberg, a short hoodlum)
He's so damn small he's a waste of bail.

Three Finger Brown

My brother Ralph is so dumb he'd freeze to death
outside of a whorehouse waiting for the light to
change!

Al Capone

If Kefauver don't stop bothering me I'm gonna
have to lay off some cops!

Frank Erickson

This Friars is nice. How come I don't own it?

Owney Madden

I'm a polite guy. If I was an arrow I wouldn't
point!

Sam Giancana

This guy had a Mafia hot tub. It was four feet
across and five thousand feet deep!

Pat McCormick

It wasn't the fancy clothes the young gangsters wore in 1924. The clothes were impressive, but many of the young entertainers wore smart outfits that seemed to send out waves of class. Nor was it the money that Gyp the Blood or Mrs. Rosenberg's boy, Lefty Louie, tossed around. They had big wads. My brother Phil told me he saw Ice Pick Feder with a wad so big "you'd kill yourself if you jumped off it!" What the young hoodlums had was—a car! As soon as they looked old enough to drive, they came around in sleek touring cars, advertising the value of a life in crime. The life was appealing. You got places fast. I was at an age when I wanted everything fast. I wanted to be somebody right now!

I was saved by two things—I was going to be a star in show business! And, second, my Uncle Dave had a car. I started to drive his Reo when I was thirteen. By the time I was sixteen I looked as if I owned it. One other factor might have contributed to my remaining licit—I don't like to bleed. Getting shot sometimes leads to bleeding.

The temptations were there for many youngsters.

I didn't pal out with the hoodlums. I had no time to hang out with them. I had no time to hang out with the rabbinical students and priests either. I was show business.

Strangely, show business brought the "boys" to me. Any star who's played big clubs, Las Vegas, and probably even concerts at pretty theaters-in-the-round has rubbed shoulders with many a Nunzio and Vito. We've all worked for nightclub owners without necks. They get that way from shrugging at grand juries and saying "I don't know."

One afternoon at the Round Table we had a very select group—Sinatra, Pat Henry, Jilly Rizzo, and Jerry Vale. Jan Murray came in and, sitting down, said, "I have the feeling that everybody at this table knows where Jimmy Hoffa is!"

No performers condone the evils doled out by the "boys." They had their own selfish reasons for starting Las Vegas, but start it they did. They took a desert crossroads and turned it into the most unique entertainment center in the world. There were weeks in the fifties and sixties when visitors saved Belafonte for the fourth night. Sinatra, Sammy Davis, Joey Bishop, Peter Lawford, and Shirley MacLaine were only the third night.

The "boys" financed and shaped today's Broadway. The Irish, at the beginning of this century, and the Italians and Jews later on, were the audiences. Without these minorities Ziegfeld's extravaganzas would have been one-man shows with maybe one knock-kneed girl dancer in a torn sweater and sneakers.

The "boys" backed plays, hired the best writers, musicians, and talent. When nobody was looking, some of them undid the whole thing putting their helpless girlfriends into the show. One of Longy Zwillman's lady friends had a mind like a sieve. She could remember one line and that with effort. John Murray Anderson, the revue director, said about her, "Her memory is so bad, every two minutes it's a new show!"

A truly sad story came out of one of the "boy" and "girl" relationships. Artie Dann was a rising young comedian. His nose was rather large, and, like Danny Thomas, Dann got big laughs from nose jokes. The minor infirmity didn't get in his way when he proposed to a beautiful chorus girl. Truly magnificent, the young lady had a minor problem of her own. She was unable to go ten minutes without sex. It was possible that her right knee hadn't seen her left knee in ten years. While Dann was onstage she managed to calm herself with any man in sight.

Dann was booked into the Roosevelt Hotel in New Orleans. For the first show his wife sat in the audience. Also in the audience was a top hoodlum of the area. He was primo. Glancing around, the hoodlum saw Mrs. Dann and fell in love. It was more than love and beyond passion.

After the show the hoodlum went to congratulate Dann for his performance and also to tell him, "You're going to have to get a divorce."

Dann said, "You're crazy. I love my wife."

The hoodlum said, "I like her too. Get a divorce."

Dann said, "You're absolutely nuts!"

The hoodlum said, "Do you want to play any more clubs? Do you want to play Pittsburgh? Cleveland? Big theaters? Get a divorce."

Bookings not easy to come by, Dann divorced his wife.

The hoodlum and his new bride took off on a honeymoon to Italy. In Rome the hoodlum noticed that his wife was never in the room. Following her, he learned the truth of her affliction. Bellhops, busboys, waiters, bakers, anybody was a likely partner for her.

Feeling that his co-workers would laugh themselves sick if he were to make a public display of any sort, the hoodlum started to rearrange his plans, change times for meetings, check into hotels other than those on his itinerary, and in any way possible make it difficult for his new bride to set assignations.

The couple returned to New Orleans. Again, pride reared its

ugly head. The hoodlum was unable to air his complaints. A divorce might have indicated that he himself was at fault. The marriage lasted several years. When the situation became unbearable, the hoodlum swallowed his pride and divorced his shame.

Shortly thereafter, Artie Dann was playing the Roosevelt again. The hoodlum burst into his dressing room and started to scream at the comic. "I'm gonna kill you," the hoodlum threatened. "Kill you and dump you into Lake Pontchartrain. Son-of-a-bitch, why didn't you tell me she was a nympho?"

Artie Dann said, "She never mentioned it to me!"

The "boys" built the nightclubs. Owney Madden paid for the Cotton Club, the Elks didn't. Larry Fay put Texas Guinan into his various clubs, and from the various stages came Ruby Keeler and Barbara Stanwyck. The Embassy Club, where Helen Morgan sang her torch songs, was built by Dutch Schultz.

Yup, the "boys" weren't saints, angels with dirty faces. Yet, as far as performers were and are concerned, they used some of their ill-gotten gains wisely. They happened to make the mistake of falling in love with what they created. From the smallest to the biggest, diamond-studded in Chicago to plain checkered tablecloths in Pittsburgh, the "owners" kept an eye on the stage.

When we gathered at the Round Table to review engagements and "owners," we found ourselves talking with relish and about peers. Membership applications in hand, the Friars didn't go into dark alleys chasing down dudes with scars on their cheeks and a floating crap game in their back pocket. We weren't hypocrites. When I talked about Big Jim Colissimo, I never threw salt over my shoulder to ward off the evil spirit.

Naturally, we didn't throw a daily brunch for the gangster of the day. Mad Dog Coll didn't stop off at our bar for a belt after chewing up somebody with a machine gun. Some gangsters came to the Friars. Others came to our affairs. We didn't ask for birth certificates or job descriptions. A thorough screening might have entrapped a few judges who were on the take, a businessman with a scam working, or a performer with a mild prison record. If we'd screened with a fine mesh, we'd have caught Errol Flynn. He was a kleptomaniac. He stole things when he visited friends at home. He once stole diamond cuff links from Bogart. Bogart never mentioned it.

We might have had to think about allowing Al Capone to sit down at the Round Table. (I don't know who was going to ask him to leave.) We were saved a possible early death because Capone never showed up at the Friars. On several trips to New York, he made the rounds. He neglected us. Once when he wanted a favor, he sent up his brother Ralph to invite us up to the ribbon-cutting ceremonies at the Cotton Club. I was to be Capone's good-luck gift to Owney Madden. Since I was working, I tried to beg off. There wasn't enough time between shows. Ralph said, "I understand, but I can't tell Al. There'll be a car."

As soon as my first show ended, Ralph beckoned me and my mother into a waiting car. We drove to Harlem in ten minutes. (My mother said it was more because "I pee'd twice. I never pee twice in only ten minutes!")

Later, at the Friars, I was trying to relax when a box of Havana cigars was brought to me—a little gift from Capone. A little uncertain, I started to open the box slowly. Lou Holtz asked, "What's in there?"

I said, "Now it's cigars. An hour ago it could have been me!"

In 1934, Capone went to jail for income-tax evasion. Irving Berlin said, "He's got a good accountant...didn't he?"

We could survive without imports from Chicago. We had our own "friends." Many of them were brought around by George Raft. At one time a ballroom dancer who hung around Owney Madden looking for a chore that would earn him a few dollars, Raft became a Mae West favorite and then a movie star.

George Raft never shut the door on his old pals. He sponsored some of them when the going got tough for them. Ben Siegel asked him to wangle a membership in the Friars. George tried, knowing that Siegel's background and reputation would keep him out of everything but membership in the public library.

When George Raft brought Ben Siegel around, we kidded the gangster with the same sharp digs we had for the ordinary citizen. One afternoon Siegel ordered a brisket sandwich and was told the kitchen was out of brisket. Jack E. Leonard asked, "What kind of flowers do you send a dead chef?"

Raft cautioned us to stop kidding his friend. Siegel was sensitive. Naturally, we couldn't wait for the next visit. Relaxed, just a few days before he was set to go to California, Siegel asked if there was anything he could do for us on the West Coast. George Jessel said, "Get Jack Warner. I still hate him from 1927!"

Raft said, "That's a dumb thing to ask Ben!"

Jessel said, "For a crate of oranges we don't need Siegel!"

Siegel told us about his plans to go to Las Vegas, the sleepy town in the Nevada desert. Jesse Block said, "Take water!"

On October 25, 1957, Albert Anastasia went into the Park Central Hotel. In the basement barber shop he sat down for his regular shave. Two men walked in and Anastasia was no more. At the club we looked at pictures of this top hoodlum and Red Buttons said, "I'm telling you—a dime isn't enough of a tip!"

One evening we sat around trying to figure out which comedian we would go see bomb. A call was put through. The voice was coarse and raspy. "We're having a little party for Dean Martin at the Copacabana after the late show. If you have plans, you don't have to come." The voice went on to ask us to call back when we knew how many would be in our group. Phil Silvers asked, "Who called us—was it Proser or Costello?" Monte Proser was the "owner" of the Copa. Frank Costello was the OWNER.

Danny Thomas said, "What's the difference?"

Silvers said, "If it's Proser, we'll need a table for ten. If Costello called, we need a table for two hundred and thirty!"

The garment-center tycoon, the well-dressed Joe Kipness, was a good friend of the "boys." A big gambler, he was in tight with the top bookmakers. Having taken over Arnold Rothstein's business and in partnership with Meyer Lansky, Frank Erickson was the biggest. Every bet over sixteen cents went through him. For banking big bets he took a little "vigorish," a percentage. Arriving to have lunch with Kipness, Erickson was invited to sit with us. Once comfortable, he pointed to a house phone. "I have to leave a number. What's this number?"

Ben Bernie asked, "With or without your vigorish?"

Because of the Kefauver investigation, Mr. E. ran out of luck and went directly to jail without passing GO. Kipness and his buddies were in tears when the decision came down. How could the government do such a thing to a nice guy like Mr. E.? The man had never hurt a fly. He was really performing a public service.

"Don't worry about Mr. E.," Eddie Davis, Cantor's writer said. "He's already laying off license plates."

Also jailed, because of three ladies of the evening who resented being called "whores," was Lucky Luciano. One of the bosses, nose and nose with Frank Costello, Luciano ran hookers. The famous madam Polly Adler, whose book *A House Is Not a Home* was often placed on the how-to shelves in bookstores, worked for him after a brief apprenticeship with Waxey Gordon. Asked to buy a table for ten at one of the Friars' charity functions, Gordon said, "I'll give you ten girls. You could own the hotel!"

In a moment of upset when Polly Adler was arrested, Luciano called his girls "gutless whores." Hurt to the quick, three of them gave the evidence that put Luciano behind bars.

At the club, sadly picking at his food, Jimmy Durante said, "Lucky wasn't!"

A lot of other gangsters were lucky. Many moved on to bigger and better things. Some have become pillars of society and leaders of the community. It's hard to find a tough god-father type anymore. Some time ago Marty Allen, the Brillo-headed comedian, and Slappy White showed up for lunch after having worked a huge benefit the night before. I asked, "Who was honored?"

White said, "Frank Nitti's nephew."

Frank Nitti was Al Capone's enforcer.

Allen said, "I was afraid not to work good."

The Round Table

*The Duke of Bedford is my guest during a
sweltering summer's day in 1955 and the
air-conditioning isn't working:*
"Sir, why don't you take off your coat?"
*"Milton, my father didn't take off his tie
during World War I!"*

By the fifth time I came to the Friars, I was already possessive about
the Round Table. It was where I wanted my birthday parties held,
where I wanted to vacation, and where, upon my marriage, con-
summation would take place. It took me a long time to realize that
it wasn't the only such gathering place in the history of mankind.
I would have bet my soul that it was the *best* one. It was with reluctance that I allowed recognition of other Round Tables. At most,
it owes only some minor debts to Round Tables of the past.

There's an old Sid Caesar routine in which he plays the nutty
professor discussing transportation. Asked if the man who invented
the first wheel was a genius, Sid, as the professor, says, "the guy
who invented the first wheel was an idiot. The guy who invented
the other three wheels, *he* was a genius!"

The guy who invented the first Round Table, he was okay. But
the one who started *our* Round Table, *he* was the genius! For years
Ruth has wondered why I carry on so much about the R.T. She'd
die if she knew I had its picture in my wallet!

The first Round Table at which knights gathered after a hard
day's jousting wasn't exactly famous for laughs. Most of the conversation was taken up with discussions of the proper way to kill a

29

dragon and the ten best ways to rescue a fair maiden. I might have enjoyed this latter topic, although I would have liked it to come about by Merlin asking, "Milton, do you remember the first damsel you rescued?"

As bright as he was reported to have been, there isn't one account of a funny line from Sir Galahad. What a picnic Johnny Carson could have had there: "My new armor didn't get here yet, so I called up about it. They said, 'Your mail is in the mail!'" Jack E. Leonard would have looked at a suit of armor and said, "I've heard of permanent press, but this is ridiculous!" I would do my Guinevere impression. I do a great Guinnie. My Guinevere is so good Robert Goulet sends me flowers! (If he really liked me he would have sent me a better joke!)

For those who faced the previous bravely, here's a bar bet that can make you rich. Richard Harris to the contrary, King Arthur never sat at the Round Table. It was only for knights. He wasn't a knight. He and Merlin sat off to a side pouting. This bit of trivia was unearthed by a fair crooner named Crosby as he got ready to shoot *A Connecticut Yankee in King Arthur's Court.* Crosby had an incredible store of useless information, which he doled out at the rate of three facts a year. Ed Wynn once told him, "I like when you talk, Bing. You're not singing!"

The second Round Table of note was at the Algonquin Hotel in New York. Officially, it was the Thanatopsis Upper West Side Inside Straight and Literary Club. The owner of the hotel, Frank Case, had a thing for writers, thinkers, and all-around smart-talkers. If you had two college degrees and could speak eleven languages, you were in with Frank Case. The sum total of schooling at *our* Round Table was about seven years. Phil Foster liked to brag, "I've got three college degrees. I also have a year of high school."

Frank Case adored British accents. Discussing his snobbishness while on a two-week hate of the Algonquin, Noel Coward told me, "One of Case's ancestors was the concierge at that inn when Mary and Joseph showed up."

Coward was generally impish. On the opening night in *Lady in the Dark* Coward sent Gertrude Lawrence a wire: "Hope you get a warm hand on your opening."

Case set a round table down in the Rose Room at the Algonquin. In this salon some years earlier an ingenue from a Harrigan and Hart show had discreetly taken on most of the Seventh Regiment in an early attempt to set a Guinness record for orgasms while leaning back, and, in addition, to repay the regiment for marching downtown in full regalia each time a Harrigan and Hart show opened. Learning of the hanky-panky, which Alexander Woollcott called "indiscreet behavior," Case had the wall repainted a pristine rose.

The years passed, the indiscreet behavior forgotten, and the Round Table at the Algonquin was brought in. Chairs were offered to the elite—Robert Benchley, Lunt and Fontanne, Harpo Marx, Groucho, George S. Kaufman, Wilson Mizner, Alexander Woollcott, Tallulah Bankhead, no mean orgasm slouch, Dorothy Parker, and a whole glitter of lights that have gone out since then—Franklin P. Adams, a great columnist, and Heywood Broun, a crusader, writer, and would-be actor. Broun was pure venom. Benchley said that he had a perfect opening for Broun's autobiography, "Attila the Hun had a son."

Vitriol wasn't exactly a debit at the Algonquin. Woollcott and his crowd were mean. How mean were they, Johnny? They were so mean they'd give half their money to piranha research! They'd send mud to hurricane victims! They're so devious they can stab you in the back from the front! They pick their friends...to pieces! They don't have many faults but they make the most of the ones they do have! (Can you guess I love "vicious" jokes?) And I can't leave out my favorite—They'd throw a drowning man both ends of the rope!

Even the departed weren't safe from the anacondas of the Algonquin. Commenting on the passing of a rather loose-moraled stage star, Benchley, unable to let sleeping bitches lie, said, "She sleeps alone at last."

Harpo Marx reaffirmed, "At least they're together?"

Another card-carrying member, his brother Chico, asked, "Who? What do you mean—at least they're together?"

Harpo said, "I was referring to her legs!" And another great joke joined the roast file!

An English agent brought a play for George S. Kaufman to read, hoping that it would spur an American production. The author of many smash shows and a top director, Kaufman had huge clout on Broadway. After reading two scenes of the play submitted by the English agent, Kaufman said, "Sir, the Colonies are prepared to fight again!"

The Thanatopsis group had its share of laughs. It didn't have longevity. *My* Round Table is the longest-living round table in the world.

Because I'm a child of truth, I have to admit that the Friars Round Table hasn't always been round, or even a table. At times it has been a group of chairs clustered together. It has been a line of hand-made leather chairs leaning against a wall. In Beverly Hills it has often looked like a district carved out by politicians. It starts as a booth, tables are added as people arrive, more tables are added. Sometimes people at one end have to phone their punch lines in to the other end. A guest one afternoon, Tommy Lasorda, looked down at the end of the gathering and said, "I wish I had somebody who could hit that far." I said, "Tommy, the trouble is you have twenty-five guys who hit that far!"

Whatever its shape, the Friars Round Table remains.

A Round at the Round Table

Harry Delf was the dean of the Friars for a while. Delf wrote *Here Comes Mr. Jordan*. However, he refused to accept the onus of authorship as he was involved in a lawsuit at the time. Stemming from a traffic accident, the suit could, if won, set Delf up for life. Knowledge that Delf was the recipient of big Hollywood bucks could have prejudiced the sum of the award. Delf, therefore, had to plead a lack of resources. Thus, when the cheering started for *Here Comes Mr. Jordan*, none of it was for Harry Delf.

This one afternoon, we were sitting around discussing Raymond Massey's revival of *The Father*. In the play was an ingenue named Grace Kelly. Sam Levenson was on our panel. A schoolteacher turned comedian who became rich talking about poor people and their daily lives, Levenson was not above an appreciation of beauty. He gave the young lady excellent grades, even if she was unlucky enough to be from Philadelphia. Ted Lewis, his memory kept alive today by any performer who puts on a top hat, picks up a cane, and starts strutting, considered Miss Kelly a world-class beauty.

Spurred by the discussion, Delf asked, "Who's the most beautiful woman in the world?" I loved Delf's question. When I'm at the Round Table, I pray for an inquisitive soul nearby. I kvell when I'm asked a question that can start me down memory lane or on a list of the ten best, ten tallest, the ten anything. I relish ransacking my mind for the names of ten Armenian jugglers. Or the ten acts with the most toes. I can't wait for someone to ask me to name the ten weirdest acts in vaudeville. How else could I get Swain's Cats and Rats into the conversation? Or Lady Alice's Pets? Lady Alice's Pets had Jean, the only trained eagle in show business. It was a terrific act until Jill swooped down and ate several of his co-stars. (Ruth and I often play "tens." On our last flight to New

York we worked on a list of ten men Ruth would date if I bit the dust. When she got to two hundred, I decided I didn't like the game. She got to a hundred and forty-one before we took off.)

When Delf asked about beautiful women, my day was made. I led the Round Table on an impromptu safari to the beauties of show business. Wives and mistresses weren't eligible.

Phil Silvers was hurt. "If they have to be in show business, I can't count Sylvia Pearlman."

"Who's Sylvia Pearlman?" Delf asked.

Lou Holtz, the monologuist, jumped up. "You threw him a feed line. A man waits a whole lifetime for a feed line like that. In forty years in the business nobody ever gave me such a feed line."

Silvers explained, "Holtz doesn't like me to talk about Sylvia. He adored her. He worshiped her. But you know she loved me!"

I said, "We're running out of time. I have to be on the set in June."

Silvers said, "In deference to Milton, I'll begin. Garbo! We must start with Garbo, especially in *Flesh and the Devil*."

Levenson said, "I'll accept that."

Silvers continued, "I can't omit Hedy Lamarr. In *White Cargo* when she comes through that beaded curtain and says, 'I'm Tondalayo!'"

I said, "Frieda Merse, the girl Ed Wynn was married to."

A fresh addition to the group, George Jessel said, "Mark Hellinger's wife, Gladys Glad."

Ted Lewis offered Jinx Falkenberg for our consideration. Falkenberg was a show girl and a heartbreaker who became a radio star.

Silvers stuck with his movie ladies. "Loretta Young in *The Crusaders*. Remember when she first looks out of the window as Henry Wilcoxon rides by? Do you men know that Loretta Young was the only gentile girl my mother wanted me to marry? She turned down Jane Wyman twice!"

"What kind of name is that—Wilcoxon?" Jessel asked. "It sounds like a salve for erections."

Levenson said, "Barbara Stanwyck's gorgeous."

Jessel said, "You can't count anybody who married Frank Fay."

"My sister loved Frank Fay in *Harvey*," Levenson said.

"Your sister we could count," Jessel said.

Holtz said, "I'll give you some beauties—Barbara LaMarr. Nevada Smith. And can I throw in a charity vote for Fanny Brice? Not pretty, but funny."

I said, "Dorothy Knapp! Catherine Waugh! Beryl Wallace, not bad!"

"They're all Earl Carroll girls," Lewis said. "Are you trying to make up with Carroll?"

I said, "I could have mentioned Lillian Lorraine. Billie Dove. Suzanne Fleming. Irene Dunne, not one of the beauties of the world?"

"How'd you come up with a practicing Catholic?" Jessel asked.

A few names later the safari ended with a good catch. Since then, from other lineups at the Round Table, other names have been added and seconded—Lana Turner, Elizabeth Taylor, Linda Evans. A big push for Sophia Loren got her into the select circle. Gina Lollobrigida missed by two votes. Early on, when nobody was looking, *I* added Diahann Carroll. I'm sure I wasn't the only sneak. Phil Silvers couldn't be trusted. I once heard him mumbling about Catherine Deneuve. And a few of his ex-wives.

At the last meeting of the beauty pageant committee, after Maureen O'Hara was added, I said, "I don't care who you pick. I just want to live long enough to see who winds up with Brooke Shields!"

A Taste of Funny

His ad-libs aren't worth the paper they're written on.

Steve Allen

You're all talking at once and I can't hear a thing. Let's all talk at once in order.

Danny Kaye

One thing about Jack E. Leonard—he's never lost an enemy!

Henny Youngman

Milton, you have very witty ears!

Fred Allen

Jan Murray promises you nothing...and he delivers!

Alan King

Working as a single in 1924, I discovered that comedy is a lonely art.

Comedy is also fragile. *I* can't define it even though I give college seminars on humor. My ignorance is in good company. My pal Sigmund Freud didn't know what humor was. He wrote a long monograph on it that concluded he didn't know what he was talking about. Freud went through life unable to answer two questions—"What is humor?" and "What do women want?" I have a third unanswerable question—"Where do all the wire coat hangers in the closet come from?"

Steve Allen thinks comedy is—tragedy plus time. I'll accept that. In the late twenties, when we used to sit around schmoozing, some of us had other answers. A young redheaded kid named Skelton believed that comedy was—getting even. I'll buy that definition too. It seems to make sense because most of the comedians I grew up on and worshiped—the Morans and Macks, Rae Samuels, the "Blue Streak of Vaudeville," Willie and Eugene Howard, Smith and Dale, the Avon Comedy Four—these mentors were all members of minority groups. Comedy on a stage could have been the way they got even with the mainstream. Comedy may have been the boxing gloves that helped them pummel their way out of whatever ghetto was trying to confine them.

Larry Gelbart, the creator of the series *Mash*, waxed philosophical at one of our lunches. "All comedians and comedy writers," Larry insisted, "were born in a Bronx or Brooklyn ghetto. As soon as they made some money, they divorced the nice little Jewish girl from the catered wedding, moved West, married a shiksa, moved into a sprawling ranch house with room for horses or a mansion with nine bathrooms, and named their children Stacey, Belinda, and Cameron. In 1966 several other names were added—Jamie, Heather, and Trevor."

Whatever comedy is and whatever its sources, comedy is the air I breathe. My comedians have kept me young. There certainly has been a slew of them across the Round Table.

The thirties belonged to some largely forgotten today, undeservedly forgotten. Richy Craig, Jr., a gentile alien in a Semitic world, was slender and always well-groomed. He wore a fresh carnation in his lapel. One day he came sans flower, and Joe Frisco said, "D-d-didn't you run into a f-funeral today?"

The son of a burlesque comedian, Craig played the Palace when he was nineteen. He didn't brag, but Bing Crosby went at him anyway: "Charles the Third made it when he was twelve."

Craig didn't just "get." He "gave" too. He worked slowly, deliberately, preferring to score big but as if by accident. I called it "tipitoes" humor. (It's no secret that I like my jokes to come in an army tank.)

The Shuberts were in the middle of a slump in the thirties. Shows opened and closed in the middle of the first act. One Friday, Craig left a note for me with the club receptionist: "Went to tour with a Shubert show. Will be ten minutes late for lunch!"

I did a little bombing too that year. In a Shubert show in 1934. *Saluta* lasted thirty-nine agonizing performances. The day after the opening, a large crowd was at the Round Table, as there was any time one of us bombed. What better time to get in a few stabs in the heart!

Attendance was way up after each opening in hopes that there'd be a bloodshed. Sometimes, however, the best-laid plans of critics… well…the Round Table met in '32 the day after Jack Benny made his debut on the original Ed Sullivan radio show. Benny was a smash. Jesse Block, of Block and Sully, a team much like Burns and Allen, brought up the show. Lou Holtz said that he hadn't heard it. Jack Waldron, one of the first one-liner comedians, hadn't heard it either. Benny said, "I told you fellows I was doing the show. I told you a thousand times. How could you not listen?"

Fred Allen explained, "There was a rare electrical condition last night. No radio belonging to anybody who does a single received the show!"

To make me sit around and sweat out my beating for *Saluta,* it was decided to give me the silent treatment. Not one word was to be said about the show. It would never be brought up. I think it was the equivalent of what happens in a home when mother says, "Wait till your *father* gets home!" The impending doom is worse than the actual. Ruth is good at delayed punishment. Her favorite weapon is, "We'll talk *later!*"

It was all quiet on the Berle flop front that afternoon at the club. But suddenly, at a remote table, a waiter spilled a drink on a lunchee. The lunchee jumped up and yelled, "Oh, shit!"

Craig jumped up too and yelled as much as he could yell, "We will not talk about Berle's show!"

The ice broken, the show became fair game. Craig hadn't seen it. He explained that he'd wanted to, but "at the last minute I had tickets to the doctor, who told me I had polio!"

Naturally I filled Craig in. *Saluta* was about American gang-sters putting on an opera in Italy. Bushwhacking my comic pal, I started at the top and briefed him on every gruesome detail. When I got to a mention of Pompey, Craig cut in, "Milton, get me to the lava!"

Running neck and neck with Richy Craig, Jr., as *my* personal comedian was Jack Osterman. Round-faced, ready to explode, Oster-man thought much faster than he could speak, causing him to spit and spray. Bob Hope told him one afternoon, "Jack, I can get you a job as a rainmaker!"

Not to be left out, Harry Hershfield, the Friars storyteller lau-reate, said, "When Osterman does three minutes he can water all of New Jersey!"

Osterman more than held his own. After Bobby Clark, the vaude-ville and stage comedy actor, took a shot at him once, Osterman said, "Bobby Clark never wanted to be a star and he made it!"

Osterman was very fond of what today comedians call "stockies"— "I never liked you and I always will!" "This guy's such a cheap bastard he goes into a restaurant for a cup of coffee and an over-coat!" "He needs only one thing to make a fool of himself—a chance!"

Osterman could be as topical as a headline. He had a gag for ev-ery item in the newspaper. One headline let the world in on the fact that there was going to be a government investigation of the Navy for buying and storing fifty million pounds of hamburger meat. Osterman said, "They'll never get any admirals to testify. They're too busy toast-ing rolls!"

A hit tune of the day was "Walkin' My Baby Back Home." Hear-ing it, Osterman said, "A typical Ben Bernie date."

Bernie snickered, "I spend more on a date than you ever did."

Osterman said, "But when I bring them home they're washed!"

As if Osterman had planned it, an aging John Philip Sousa came back from the Midwest with a valise full of medicine. In Kansas a Dr. Brinkley, whose degree came most probably from the Masons, had cures for rejuvenation starting at ten dollars. For seven hun-dred and fifty dollars, Brinkley offered the Compound Operation. The surgery involved the implantation of goat testes. Oddly, the surgery hadn't worked on the band leader–composer. Osterman said, "They must have given you my old goat!"

Osterman and I often took each other on. Osterman always insisted that this next line was his. I feel that I was its parent. Anyway, one of us said, "Do you want to throw lines with me? Let's start even, I'll check my brains!" Since this is my book, I know I said the line first. Also, Ruth points out, use is ninety percent of ownership, and I win hands down.

Frank Fay was another natural ballplayer. From vaudeville and clubs, he grew up to play "Harvey" in the hit Broadway play. I didn't like Frank Fay. I wasn't alone. Fay's friends could be counted on the missing arm of a one-armed man. Ed Wynn once said, "The second nicest thing Frank Fay ever did was—marry Barbara Stanwyck. The nicest thing Frank Fay ever did was—divorce Barbara Stanwyck!"

Much as I didn't adore Fay, I conceded his funny bone. And confidence? Fay went to court to testify on a business matter. His attorney coached him. Answer only what's asked. Don't volunteer anything. Just say "yes" or "no."

Fay was put on the stand. The other attorney asked, "What is your name?"

"Frank Fay."

"What is your profession, Mr. Fay?"

"I'm the greatest comedian in the world!"

Much later, the statement having caused havoc with the case, Fay's attorney said, "Frank, I told you to answer simply. The other lawyer asked you—'What is your profession?' How could you answer—'The greatest comedian in the world'?"

Fay said, "I was under oath, wasn't I?"

In the fifties and sixties, bred by radio and early television, another class of comedians was graduated. Life at the Round Table became faster and more furious. It became a little tougher to break into the conversation with a comment or a topper. I had to pull out my Class A material. What was left on the floor after an ordinary lunch would have serviced a Broadway show.

Exhibit A would have to be Jack E. Leonard. Looking like a Hebrew toby mug, Leonard was a machine gun with words. To an emerging Don Rickles, Leonard said, "Don, you've got a great act—mine!" After asking Sinatra his weight, Leonard said, "I had more than that for breakfast!" Another, looking at a frail John Garfield, Leonard offered, "John, I've seen your work in the movies and I'm sorry!" Leonard was feeling good one day because he had survived a direct confrontation with Ed Sullivan before Sullivan's show, *The Toast of the Town*, the previous Sunday. The dress rehearsal was long. Sullivan wanted Leonard to cut his spot way down. "Jack, what can you do in three minutes?" Sullivan asked the rotund comedian. Leonard answered, "Boil two eggs!"

The line earned him a seven-minute segment. Flushed with victory, Leonard was on a high all week. One midday, an hour after Sullivan had left for the *Daily News* to find out if the leprechaun he had on his payroll had finished the daily Sullivan column, Adlai Stevenson, the presidential candidate, came to the club. Leonard said, "Stevenson, I'm going to keep voting for you until you win!" Stevenson had a sense of humor too. Leonard left to knock some other people and William B. Williams, an important disc jockey, a hardworking Friar, and a dear friend until he died in 1986, said matter-of-factly, "Doesn't Fat Jack ever agree with anybody?"

Stevenson said, "Not if Jack finds out about it!"

At a luncheon, Leonard said about Danny Thomas, "Danny is very religious. He worships himself!" (Danny Thomas was fair game for everybody: "Danny Thomas wears stained-glass contacts!" "Danny is in the Sistine Chapel, posing for a wall!")

Not overly remembered is Danny's brilliance on a nightclub floor. He could carry an audience in his hand for ten minutes without a joke. But when he came up with a punch line, the roar was there! Fred Travalena, the mimic who does a better Mohammed Ali than the fighter, asked Thomas if he was really so pure in heart. "You played Vegas all those years. Weren't you ever tempted by those gorgeous chorus girls?"

Thomas answered, "Not in thirty-six years of marriage! However, the first woman who helps me cheat gets a hundred dollars!"

On another afternoon, Thomas admitted human frailty: "Once in a while I used to consider cheating. Then I would think of my Sicilian wife and a Sicilian funeral!"

As fast as Leonard but with a different slant, Jack Carter joined the Round Table and stayed for a few years. Carter has a reputation for being an angry man. He's on guard and nervous because sneak attacks are on the way. Jack Albertson, "the Man" in the TV show *Chico and the Man*, watched Carter fidgeting nervously one day. Albertson said, "Calm down, Jack, somebody'll be around soon to hurt your feelings!"

Another child of the fifties, with some roots reaching back a few years is Jan Murray. Jan can pick on the first inch of a loose thread and have you naked in ten jokes. He would have had a picnic with *Saluta* if he'd been around. He more than made up for it some years ago when I did a Broadway play that didn't fare too well. It closed between giving out the program and "Please be seated." Taking off from my having played a ninety-year-old man, Murray jabbed away, "How could such a play fail? The whole world wanted to see Milton Berle play a ninety-year-old man spitting and coughing, coughing and spitting. Theater parties from every state wanted to come in and watch Milton Berle spitting and coughing, coughing and spitting. Prince Charles offered Lady Di a fifty-carat diamond. She said, 'I don't want a diamond! I want to go see spitting and coughing, coughing and spitting with Milton Berle!' Eighth Avenue pimps wanted to give their hookers time off to see Milton Berle spitting and coughing, hacking and throwing up and wheezing!"

He left me for dead. A chilling thought, but part of the comedic process. The language of comedy is the language of death. Comedians say, "I killed them!"…"I laid them in the aisles!"…"I slaughtered them!"…"They laughed their guts out!"…Not a pretty sight, but a desired result.

Recently I wrote a short story for *Redbook* magazine in which a comic, sick of being abused for years, gets to an audience and doesn't stop until everybody in the room is dead. He then calls his wife and reports, "I killed them."

The half-pun at the end motivated my writing the story. It seemed kind of funny to me. After rereading the finished story, it was scary. An independent producer contacted me after the story was published. Would I sell the rights for a small movie? I told him my price. He said, "Are you trying to kill me?" I wondered if the language of money is also the language of death—"A wad big enough to choke a horse?" It makes me wonder.

In the fifties at the Friars we sheltered many gentle types from the wind and the rain. Dour-faced Joey Bishop passed lines around as if they were canapés. If you wanted one, you had only to reach out for it. If you didn't want any and passed, Bishop didn't pout. To Henny Youngman, he said, sounding as if he were giving the right time, "Henny, you have beautiful children. Thank God your wife cheats!"

After serving a term as one of the soldiers in Frank Sinatra's rat pack, a talk-show host, and some feature roles in movies that didn't win any Oscars, Bishop went into semiretirement. After a short stint as a Beverly Hills squire, he decided that he wanted the life of the open sea. He moved to Newport Beach. There he sat around waiting for friends to show up. When he ran into people he'd suggest a short cruise with him at the helm. How could friends dream of turning him down? He got a few turndowns. He ran into Harry Crane, the writer. He said, "Harry, I keep asking you to come for a spin and you keep telling me how busy you are. Every time you have something else to do."

Crane said, "All right, Joey, I'll tell you the truth. I don't go out on a ship unless the skipper's name is Lars! Or Sven!" Bishop is no longer in the boat business.

To represent the intuitive comedian, the kind who can say "Hello" and get a laugh, along came Buddy Hackett.

Hackett told us about being invited to join the members of his congregation in Englewood, New Jersey, in a funeral plot. He reported how he had declined, saying, "To tell you the truth, fellas, I'm not too thrilled spending time with you when we're alive!"

Hackett did an early sitcom, *Here's Stanley*. Its lack of success, the Round Table concluded, was because of the lady who played his wife. A no-talent broad! Her name was Carol Burnett. Hackett was alone in her defense. "The network was wrong. To play opposite a nice Wasp girl from Texas they should have gotten somebody more romantic—like Gabby Hayes!"

Somewhere between Hackett and the moon in the comedy spectrum today at the Round Table was Dick Shawn. When he played the Palace with Judy Garland she wanted to know where he kept his UFO. Dick explained that he had nothing to do with flying saucers. However, he had an uncle in Buffalo who made cups for them!

One day Shawn started to tell us about a one-man show he was planning. He went into detail for a half hour. He was interrupted by the arrival of Nick Uricchio, the Executive Director of the Friars in Beverly Hills. Uricchio had news of a terrible plane crash in Texas. We started to talk about planes and crashes. After a minute, a hurt Shawn asked, "Don't you want to hear about the first-act ending?"

Shawn was a chain cigarette smoker, most of them borrowed. The day after Yul Brynner died, Shawn wandered into the club, and when the Brynner death was mentioned, he said, "What some guys'll do to get me to stop smoking!"

Norm Crosby has a way of waiting patiently for a spot to drop in a masterpiece. He can wait an hour, then come up with "You think that's a miracle of science. I'll tell you a miracle. Last week at Cedars-Sinai, in the Cardiology Department, after eight hours of surgery and amnesia, they put the heart of a turtle into a human being. Last Monday that patient walked out the hospital. And Thursday he got to the parking lot!"

Crosby got off a second winner too, earning him a free trip to Disneyland. The line became a standard. We started to talk about the Viking who was to travel five hundred million miles to see if there was life on Mars. Crosby said, "We have no luck in space. They sent a Viking up last year to find out if there were living creatures on Mars. There was one living creature. Just one. The damn spaceship landed on him!"

Jackie Vernon is a more restrained killer. John Forsythe was describing an exquisite new restaurant. The china was Meissen, the silver from the fingers of Paul Revere, the chef a graduate of everything, and on the menu—*boeuf à la reine de Paris avec champignons en papier*. He went on to describe dishes the Queen of England has never tasted. Vernon listened and said, "Gee. Do they have burritos?"

Vernon's place at the Round Table would be secure in the club anyway because he's a great target. He's a rather unemotional young man. We've all hit him with "dull" lines—"Jackie once went out with the tide and the tide wouldn't come back!" "He could be the poster boy for Yawning!" Jackie is far from a style picture and somehow comes across as being sloppy—"He looks like the kind of guy who would come over to your house and crap in your pool!" "Just this week Jackie Vernon's underwear was chosen as the new logo for Kaopectate!" "He didn't go to Colgate or Princeton, but his underwear is Brown!" "I wouldn't say Vernon's house isn't neat, but his wife has to clean it with a shovel!"

John Francis, an erstwhile actor, boy soprano, and the head of the entertainment committee in the West, defends Vernon. Francis says, "These are only rumors started by people who have watched Vernon eat!"

As is obvious from the previous, nobody and nothing is safe or sacred at the Round Table. At a time when Marvin Davis, the oilman, bought 20th Century-Fox, most of Hollywood went around making nice-nice. A nod or smile from Davis could mean a job. At the Round Table, irreverence continued to rear its pretty head. Jan Murray said, "He spent a billion on 20th. Now what will I buy him for Christmas?"

Davis is a rather large man. I mentioned that I'd had dinner with him a few days before. Asked what he'd eaten, I said, "A Buick!"

Another day, Merv Griffin announced his retirement. Since his show was an important vehicle for promoting movies, books, and appearances, most performers made nice-nice. But at the Round Table Rich Little said, "It's a shame he's giving up his show. He used to sit so nice!"

Age is served at the Round Table and so is youth. From veterans like Dave Barry, who spent years with Wayne Newton, and a new Comedy Store winner like Bill Kalmenson, the goodies keep on coming.

Because I pick up my mail in California, I don't get too much of a chance to visit with the men at the Friars in New York. I come in for an occasional roast, do twenty minutes, and head back to the West before the audience comes after me. Only rarely do I stick around the Big Apple, and then only to visit Henny Youngman and jokes I don't use anymore. I miss out on the good stuff from the likes of Dick Capri and Freddie Roman. Do you know how tough it is not to be near Joey Adams?

On the West Coast I have to be satisfied with the likes of Richard Pryor, Billy Crystal, Jay Leno, and Robin Williams. Or a Marty Brill. Less known than the Lenos and the Pryors, Brill is one strong performer.

Brill is a deputy sheriff in real life. He's famous in the department for having had a famous murderer, "the Serial Killer," in his car on a traffic violation. Naturally, "the Killer" paid bail and walked out of the slammer.

Brill thinks like a policeman. When he reads of a gangland killing in which a body perforated with twenty bullet holes is found in the trunk of a car, Brill says, "Anybody found sleeping in the trunk of a car deserves to be shot!"

At the Round Table, as on stage generally, Brill is a screamer. His comedy anger bellows at stupidity. He shook his head when Chernobyl happened and yelled, for the whole dining room to hear, "We're not long for this world. We have a President without a colon and they have an idiot who can't change a fuse!"

Bill Kalmenson, one of the younger comedians, sat with us some time back. After doing his act, as most newcomers do, he sat back and relaxed. On the giant TV monitor in the corner of the dining room, a special newscast announced the arrival of a tornado in southern New Jersey. I said, "And it did five million dollars worth of improvements!"

Kalmenson said, not trying to be mean, "Funny, but somebody did that joke at the Improv six months ago." Suddenly I was reminded of a youngster telling the likes of George M. Cohan and Fred Allen about the origin of a joke. I was back in 1920. Lighting a cigar and having nothing else to do, I decided to hang around the old days for a while. Funny was funny then too.

Acting Is Easy (Just Don't Get Caught Doing It.)

Arness, you've got me worried. The last time you kissed your horse, it looked like you meant it!

Don Rickles

Mickey Rooney is something. A great actor. Sharp. Smart. Give him an inch and he'll be four foot one!

Wallace Beery

Nobody has more respect for Anthony Quinn than I do. That'll show you how far he's sunk!

Kirk Douglas

I don't like to brag that I have class, but without me Arpège is nothing!

George Sanders

John Barrymore makes his characters breathe and what strong breath it is!

Fred Allen

Now Jimmy Stewart will rattle off his name or as much of it as he can get out in ten minutes!

Ronald Reagan

Shortly before he died in 1966, I ran into Clifton Webb. Webb was a big star who surprised none of his brother Friars when he exploded on the Hollywood scene in *Sitting Pretty*, the first of the

49

"Belvedere" movies. From Broadway shows he'd done and Friars Frolics in which he'd always been a showstopper, we knew that he was major material.

The afternoon we met in Beverly Hills I asked Webb if he'd join me for lunch at the club. "I'd love to, Milton," he answered, "but I'm not dressed seriously enough." He looked in both directions down Wilshire Boulevard, glad that he'd avoided detection so far, and went on his "serious" way.

I was reminded of Gable in *The Hucksters* when he spends his case money on a "sincere" tie. I was also reminded that Clifton Webb was one of the shapers of my wardrobe. (Ruth can challenge many of my habits, but she concedes that I am a "serious" dresser. I lead her in pants, shirts, and golf socks. She wins in furs. I think she can beat the state of Alaska in furs. Her mother leads the world in bedroom slippers and housecoats with Kleenex in the pockets.)

The Clifton Webbs of show business believe that performing— prancing up and down onstage or on screen—is a serious way of making a living. Success comes from hard training, hard work, and dedication. Torn leotards and frayed leg warmers belittle the art. Offstage, as well as on, the actor must represent his or her profession with dignity.

Poodles Hanneford, a great clown who did a hysterical equestrian act for years, refused to carry his bride across the threshold, telling her, "I am an actor, not a porter." Having heard this story and believing it to be only apocryphal, I asked Hanneford at the club years later if there was any truth to it. "Master Berle," he said, "those were my exact words. My bride's words have never been recorded."

John Barrymore was always dressed neatly when he threw up on himself. Toward the end of his life, while doing a play in Galveston, Texas, the Great Profile felt an urge to evacuate a kidney. He walked to the curtain and relieved himself. After the curtain came down at the end of the usual ovation, the theater manager ran over and said to Barrymore, "How in hell could you take a leak against that curtain?"

Barrymore said, "I always pee away from my dressing room!"

Actors who pee'd away from their dressing rooms tended to join another theatrical fraternity, the Lambs Club. The pious aura around the place was reflected one evening when we were sitting

at the Round Table playing small talk while over at the Lambs Club
the annual membership meeting was being held. Will Rogers shuf-
fled up to the Round Table and said, "I passed by the Lambs fifteen minutes ago. The meeting must be over. I saw white smoke
coming from the chimney!"

My jabs at the Lambs are not impartial, being based on a bitter
brew squeezed out of some sour grapes. I tried to get into the Lambs
a dozen times. If I'd been blackballed one more time I would have
gotten permanent custody of the back way out. (Berles join everything. My brother Frank joined the Auto Club for the dances! My
brother Phil was turned down by the Auto Club. He was such a bad
driver the Highway Patrol gave him a season ticket!)

Performers who knew how lucky they were joined the Friars
Club. Anybody who thinks the bottom line is talent and hard work
should have been with us one afternoon when John Garfield, a new
kid in show business and four years away from a star on his dressing room, asked Moss Hart who was the best acting teacher around.
Hart said, "Luck! It can teach you the works in two hours!"

Marlon Brando wasn't fooled by the mystique of the profession.
Sitting with us in the late afternoon while waiting to put on torn
underwear as the lead in *Streetcar Named Desire,* he explained
acting technique to Ed Sullivan, "Acting is—honesty, truthfulness,
believability, and realism. As soon as you can learn to fake those,
you've got it made!"

Brando won every award but the America's Cup for his performance in *Streetcar,* but Tennessee Williams told us one day, in some
comments he never made again in writing or interviews, "Marlon
Brando made a new play of the one I'd written. He made something
beautiful, but he destroyed what I'd intended. Stanley Kowalski was
supposed to be a villain, a reflection of a worthless man who showed
how really empty life was along the Desire route. Brando turned him
into a Don Juan. I hated Marlon Brando for six months!"

Alfred Bloomingdale, the department-store-heir-sometimes-
producer, said, "The next time you write a play to hate Brando by,
please let me buy into it!"

The Round Table sense of humor about success was so thick,
it could almost be seen. Having made it big in Hollywood, plump
but urbane Walter Slezak came back to Broadway to appear in *Fanny,* a musical based on a magnificent French trilogy. Slezak told

us, after several days of rehearsal, "I don't belong in this play. I have no right to be in this play. I will probably win a Tony for it."

Slezak won the Tony. In accepting it, he told the gathered celebrities that he fell in love with the play the first time he read it.

In real life Slezak was the total continental. Slezak wouldn't even drink house wine. He told us at lunch, "My cat wouldn't drink house wine!"

Steve Lawrence asked, "Not even on Passover?"

The same day Slezak tried the goulash. After one bite, Slezak said, "Your cook will never know the extent of the crime he has perpetrated on the Hungarian people!"

We've always prided ourselves on the Friars kitchen, but Slezak made us waver. Looking from me to Jerry Lewis, then to Ed Wynn, Slezak, a master chef, said, "I would invite you gentlemen to dinner, but I might ruin you for life!"

Slezak laughed and, relenting, went on, "The goulash was fine."

Lewis said, "It's too late. The waiter blabbed and the chef hung himself!"

When *Fanny* was made into a film, Chevalier got the Slezak part. Slezak told us, "Chevalier plays a Frenchman, but you would never know!" (Slezak's remark is a first cousin of the question Billy Wilder, another continental, asked of a lunching Sheldon Leonard, who owned *I Spy* with Robert Culp and Bill Cosby: "How did you come up with the idea of Culp playing the white guy?" Leonard came up with a pretty fair topper: "The network wanted it that way!")

Much as we at the Round Table appreciate the incisive humor of the mildly accented, let me assure you that we also specialize in the home-grown actor. One of the home-grownest came to us via Elsa Maxwell. Now as forgotten as jujubes and Lucky Strike green, Elsa Maxwell was a short dumpy lady from Iowa who came to New York and made good by giving parties. Using the cash flow of those who had open money taps, Maxwell arranged some of the best parties in Big Apple history.

Among Maxwell's gimmicks was a guest list salted with famous names. A phone call from Maxwell got the old tux or gown out of the closet and on went the fancy shoes. Reading of a swank party to be held on Seventy-eighth Street in Manhattan, Gene Baylos, the Friars house comedian from the low-rent district, said to those of us at the Round Table, who hadn't asked him, "I turned down the Maxwell party on Seventy-eighth Street. It's six blocks from a bus!"

Baylos was a specialist in rich-poor jokes. Coming up to the club late one Saturday after working a high-class affair, and still in his rented tux, Baylos asked, "Anybody know any fancy parties tonight? I have this outfit till Monday!"

Buddy Hackett said, "We're all going to the movies tonight."

Eager to show off his finery, Baylos said, "Great, but can we sit downstairs!"

Had Elsa Maxwell known about Gene Baylos, she would have rolled out the red carpet for him. (Baylos would no doubt have spilled something on it right away.) Unaware of Baylos, this one week Maxwell had to settle for Clark Gable.

Maxwell wasn't one to leave anything on the plate, so she tried to get her money's worth out of Gable. Miraculously, Gable escaped on the second afternoon and hid out at the Friars, steered there by Walter Winchell after a short visit to the ailing Damon Runyon.

The manicurist in our barber shop got wind of Gable's presence. His biggest fan, she would have achieved multiple orgasms by being allowed to cater to his cuticles. An autograph would have to do.

A few moments later, one of the older busboys approached the Round Table. Pen and paper in hand, in a voice right out of the Gullah country of the Carolinas, the busboy said, "Is be one of you Mr. Gable?"

Gable admitted he be one and signed happily. His modesty was real. He explained, "Mr. Mayer doesn't let you outgrow your head. He has an actor in the bull pen waiting to take your place if you act up. Makes you think modest!"

When I started to think about Gable's words, I realized Louis B. Mayer was a genius for his side. Aware that stars could wreak havoc with the big studio system if they acted up, he had a backup for every star on the lot. The minute Gable got too big for his ears, James Craig was ready to get the high makeup chair. Gable did act up once. Craig was rushed into a big picture with Margaret O'Brien, the freckled box-office queen at the time. The move slowed Gable down. To keep Craig on an even keel, Mr. Mayer had another bull pen in which George Montgomery was warming up.

Of course after Gable made *It Happened One Night* he became too big to scare easily. However, he never did get the gumption to call the studio head "Louie," or "Lou," or "L. B.," or "Mayer."

At the club one morning, before heading for Hollywood Park, Mervyn LeRoy, the producer, commented, "Mayer has this town so cowed, they even call his horses 'Mister'!"

Gable's parole from Elsa Maxwell, the day of the Runyon visit, lasted about three hours. Midafternoon, Maxwell called Gable at the club with instructions for the evening's gala at the Waldorf-Astoria. The phone call over, Gable asked, "How did she track me down here?"

George Burns said, "I didn't tell her. I threw away her phone number when she took my cousin Goldie off her A list!"

I swore that I didn't tell Maxwell.

Winchell swore that he hadn't blabbed, but his utter sincerity was almost proof that he was the culprit. Winchell often exchanged items with Maxwell.

This not being a Raymond Chandler whodunit, the actual culprit need not be exposed. More important to the thesis is a final reminder from Gable that stardom is transparent and fame fleeting. (Andy Warhol once said that everybody in the world is or will be famous for fifteen minutes. I can't wait for my mother-in-law's turn. Maybe she'll strike it rich and get a place of her own.)

Calling to say good-bye, Gable filled us in: "When I left the Friars I grabbed a cab. All the way to the hotel the cabdriver kept telling me that he'd driven Groucho Marx around all day. He couldn't wait to tell his wife!"

Jerry Lewis's story in the same ballpark tops Gable's anecdote by a few inches. Martin and Lewis had just hit it big. The act was the hottest in the business. The price tag for Martin and Lewis was quintupled. At the moment, the boys were turning away tons of people at the Copacabana. The night before, at a giant benefit at Madison Square Garden, twenty thousand people in the audience had refused to let Martin and Lewis off the stage. Coming into the Friars, Lewis ran into Sammy Birch, a comedian who played some of the smaller neighborhood clubs in New York. After a brief greeting, Lewis asked, "What's been going on with you, Sammy?"

Birch said, "I played the Red Mill in the Bronx last weekend. It was big. This weekend I'm going into the South Shore Terrace. What about you, Jerry?"

Lewis told us the story while waiting for his seafood salad. Buddy Hackett asked, "Why didn't you tell him about Madison Square Garden? The Copacabana?"

Lewis said, "I didn't want to break his heart."

I said, "At least you could have told him you're doing a double!"

When actors arrived for a meal at the Round Table, the discussion wasn't always about the philosophy of the craft and the psychology of success. Once in a while, we took on more personal matters. Humphrey Bogart showed up one afternoon to debate an issue he'd put on the agenda on both coasts and in every restaurant from Lindy's to the fabulous Romanoff's in Beverly Hills. (Mike Romanoff, the owner of the restaurant, claimed to be of royal blood and a direct descendant of the great czars of Russia. Born and raised in Brooklyn, Romanoff never explained when and how one of the czars managed to impregnate Mrs. Romanoff, Mike's mother.)

Bogart's problem this day was important to him and received our undivided attention. Being forty-five, Bogart was concerned about marrying a twenty-year-young model named Lauren Bacall. Naturally, the Round Table borrowed all the young-old jokes. Echoing one of the oldest, I said, "Such a marriage could be fatal."

Jesse Block played along: "So if she dies, he'll get married again!"

Bogart wasn't canvasing the group. He'd made his mind up anyway. "Betty makes me feel like a kid again. I have to take an afternoon nap!" he told us, using his Jessel impression.

A gifted mimic, Bogart did a great filthy Bette Davis, a clean Eleanor Roosevelt, and half of Hollywood talking about Jack Warner. It was Bogart's Sydney Greenstreet that told the world, "Jack Warner would rather make a bad picture than tell a good joke!"

Bogart went back with the Friars to 1936 when he starred in *The Petrified Forest*. He played Duke Mantee, a vicious inhuman brute. Talking about the play at the club, Jackie Gleason said, "Bogart played a real creep. He must have studied Frank Fay for weeks!"

Fay, as reported earlier, wasn't always adorable. One afternoon, as we talked about a new play, Fay managed to knock every performance. Bogart said, "Frank, the way you find fault, you'd think there was a reward for it!"

The all-time anti-Fay line came from Bogart a few years later at a big dinner. As usual, Fay was being bitter. Bogart said, "Frank, if you were doing a one-man show, I bet you'd quit because you couldn't stand the cast!"

Maybe Bogart knew by this time that an ugly disease was trying to take over his body and resented those who looked at glorious sunsets without seeing them. He was bugged by people who rained on somebody's parade. When the Friars roasted him, he laughed longer and louder than anybody in the room. He told me afterward, "I didn't have the faintest idea of who they were talking about!" Mrs. Bogart taped a short message that was played at the affair. Liberally sprinkled with spicy language, it seemed to amaze Bogart. Having a nightcap afterward, Bogart told us, "I had no idea she knew that kind of language. I think I'll go home and jump on her!"

The steady march of actors' names is a reminder that the Round Table has hosted more than a lion's share of them. Ronald Reagan was head of the Friars and often hosted the Round Table. Reagan came up to the club one afternoon after appearing before a congressional committee. The congressmen were interviewing Hollywood figures on the status of the movies business. Reagan answered questions on things that would help the screen actor. He explained to us, "One of those congressmen, I think he was from Wisconsin, said I made a great presentation. He thought I should go into politics." He laughed. "That's all I need to complicate my life!"

Reagan was a Democrat in those days. When he divorced Jane Wyman, Gene Barry asked, "Did he find out she was a Republican?"

One day Reagan plopped himself down in the booth. He was tired, having come from three fund-raisers, each in a different part of town. He breathed out and asked, "How did I get to be a Democrat?"

When Reagan switched parties, some of us debated the change. When Sammy Lewis, the hotel booker, asked, "How could a man become a Republican like that?" Jessel said, "Maybe one night he sat next to Adolphe Menjou!"

Menjou was one of Hollywood's conservatives. He thought that Herbert Hoover was a Communist. Always dapper, Menjou once turned down a role because it required his wearing a scraggly beard. He said, "Turkish *women* have scraggly beards!"

On vacation in London, Menjou was roused from sleep in his hotel room by the fear that a small kitchen fire might grow into a holocaust. Indignantly, Menjou told the bell captain who was going from room to room, "I brought nothing for a fire!"

When Reagan was first asked to go into televison as a moderator, he was all set to say thanks-no thanks. Lew Wasserman, his agent, insisted that he take the job. Lew Wasserman believed that television was here to stay. He believed that the little tube would fill everybody's pocket. Most actors and directors felt that TV would go away if they pretended it wasn't there. John Garfield, on a real bad streak, was asked if he'd take the lead in a TV series. We bandied it about at the Round Table. Ed Wynn told Garfield, "What are you going to do on television? You can't sing and you don't wrestle!"

I'd been having some good luck with Tuesday night so I said, "Television's not going to go away."

Wynn said, "But you're working toward that end, aren't you, Milton?"

Jesse Block, straight man and stockbroker to his own millions, said, "John, if you want to work on television, work on it. If you don't, don't!"

Naturally, that succinct advice, along with ours, led nowhere. The statement itself ranks with what I feel is the greatest nonremark ever made. Alan Handley, the producer of Dinah Shore's early shows and later the recipient of an Emmy for his work with Julie Andrews, was with us to discuss a Jimmy Durante special. With Durante was the head of the advertising agency for the potential sponsor. Handley outlined the show. The agency breathed it in slowly, then said, "In part, this is not totally without merit!"

Durante's gone now, Handley has retired, the agency man is with the giant Nielson rating in the sky, and I still have no idea of what was meant.

My faith in television remains total. I fell in love with the medium when I was about twenty. As part of a small audience, I watched, my eyes as big as platters, while Jack Pearl and his partner tested the camera and its potential in 1929. My mother said, "Someday there'll be a television on every block in America!"

John Garfield had little chance to weigh all the advice. Sadly, the blacklist came along loud and clear. It shrieked Garfield out of television and movies both.

Edward G. Robinson was another caught up in the screaming. A brilliant actor and lover of art, Robinson was a fighter for his country. Unable to get into the armed forces, he went to entertain the troops. As he made his plans, he came to the club for some help. Burns, Benny, and I, assisted slightly by our writers, did a

long monologue for Robinson. In an officer's uniform, carrying a
music case, Robinson came out and said, "Pipe down, you mugs,
or I'll let you have it! Whaddaya hear—from the mob? I suppose
you guys think I am—Jascha Heifetz? Or Mischa Elman?

"That's what the USO committee thought when they sent me
over. I had to promise them I was going to play a little long-haired
music, like maybe the Unfinished Symphony! [OPENS CASE TO RE-
VEAL MACHINE GUN] But how can you play Beethoven on a Chicago
typewriter!"

That was the beginning. It went on to greatness—"General Marshall stays on the North Side and I stay on the South Side and
everything is jake until I get to thinking about all the shooting that's
going on all over the world and Little Caesar ain't in on it, and I
get real lonely, and my heart is sick. So I goes back to the draft
board, sticks my gat in the doc's ribs, and say, 'Doc, if you say I'm
4-F, I'll drill you so full of holes you couldn't hold rain.' So what do
you think he says? '5-F.'"

Robinson swore that his comedy routine shortened the war.
When the troops heard it, they became determined to end the war
quickly so they wouldn't have to hear routines like it again.

I volunteered to stage Robinson for his army appearances.
Robinson said, "Billy Wilder is willing to help me."

Indignantly, I said, "What does Billy Wilder know about comedy?"

Actually, Jack Benny helped Robinson rehearse. Benny swore
him to secrecy. "Why?" Robinson asked. "It's no big deal."

"Milton could get insulted," Benny said, "and if he gets insulted
enough, he'll want to stage me!"

A similar threat came from a Friar in the sixties. He manufac-
tured slacks and loved to give them to us for free. However, his
slacks were slightly less than well-made. One leg was longer than
the others, seams came apart, pockets fell off. One day Ed Sullivan
said, "I'm gonna tell him how crappy his slacks are."

Joey Bishop said, "Don't do that. If you say one word, he'll make
you a jacket!"

Where my reputation for taking over the reins comes from I'll
never know. I only tried to help Flo Ziegfeld, and Earl Carroll, and
George Abbott, and D. W. Griffith! And Cecil B. DeMille!

By the time I was nineteen I wasn't above giving advice to the needy. The Round Table itself was a well of brilliant thought from which the neophyte could drink wisdom.

In 1925, Damon Runyon brought a young hoofer to the Friars oracle. An ex-swimmer, he was in a show called *Outside Looking In* and felt that he wanted to be on the inside looking over his name in lights. George Burns told him, "Go back to swimming. We don't need another hoofer!"

W. C. Fields came over and was introduced to the dancer, who was very short. "This," I said, "is Runyon's friend, Jimmy Cagney."

Fields sized him up and said, "A jockey, eh? Which race do you plan to throw tomorrow?"

Young Mr. Cagney went into vaudeville, worked with a lady named Joan Blondell, did a few things in the movies, and ended up, in a way related to Fields's conclusion, as a breeder and trainer of magnificent Morgan horses in upstate New York.

Cagney called me once at the club to ask if it would be all right to name a horse "Uncle Miltie." I told him there was already a horse with the name and it would be unkind to damn another one with the epithet.

Doc Shurr, an agent of epic greatness, brought a young client to New York to try to get him into the Actors Studio. A Californian, Jimmy Dean was twenty-one. His goal in life was to play Billy the Kid and Hamlet, maybe even at the same time. Dean didn't talk much, although he was a good laugher. You had to allow the laugh extra time to flow out of the curl of his lip. Dean enjoyed especially the way we went at Doc Shurr. He roared at our Doc Shurr stories.

Two feet tall, Shurr was a splendid dresser and imagined himself to be the dream of any woman. When Hope plays the "greatest lover" character, the one who can't understand why he's resistible, he's playing Shurr. The propinquity is there. Shurr was Hope's agent.

In a scheme aided and abetted by Hope, Shurr was sent to MCA to interview prospective female leads for a Hope picture. Ladies were sent into the office he had taken over for the chore. An opulent office, it impressed all those who entered.

We sent four hookers up to read for him. Each was to pounce upon him and sap his libido. The first came in, read, had a drink, and then offered, "I'll do anything to get this part! Anything!"

Considering himself lucky for having struck gold so early in the audition, Shurr allowed himself to be seduced. The young lady left with a promise that she would hear from the studio soon. So far she was leading.

The second contestant came in. As beautiful as the first, she soon insisted that the agent play Attila the Attacker with her. Through the power of prayer, the agent succeeded in fulfilling his obligation.

The third young lady appeared. She was obviously also smitten. Again, Doc Shurr had to rise to the occasion. Since he was well into his forties at the time, rising to any occasion demanded a ladder.

Attempting a fourth conquest, Shurr must have fallen back in a faint. Or so we thought.

The next day Shurr came to the club with Jimmy Dean. Shurr was as chipper as ever and bore no signs of battle fatigue. We had a pleasant lunch. Finally, Robert Alda, still an Italian singer then, couldn't hold back. "How did your readings go?"

Doc Shurr said, "Fellows, I knew they were hookers. I recognized them."

I said, "You mean, you didn't let them jump on your bones?"

Shurr said, "Of course I did. They were paid for!"

"That's why I'm going to be a star," Jimmy Dean said.

Doc Shurr was an agent who worked for his clients twenty-four hours a day. Like Irving "Swifty" Lazar, the most famous agent today, Shurr drove on ten thousand cylinders.

Lazar has refined agentry to its essence. Art Buchwald, a client, came to California on a potential deal. Buchwald told Lazar about a dinner meeting with a certain personality. Lazar said, "He's not dinner, he's lunch!"

I ad-libbed a line one day at lunch that endeared me to my agents. I said, "I took my kid to Disneyland yesterday. I asked him what he wanted. He said he wanted a Mickey Mouse outfit. So I bought him the William Morris office!" The William Morris Agency, mine for years, is famous for having agents who aren't too tall. One agent is reputed to have had a baby. Looking at the child, the agent kvelled, "Look at my son. Only fours days old and he's already short!"

Jackie Vernon showed up one day with a new agent. Paul Schreibman, my attorney, asked him about the agent's background. Shreibman had a writer he wanted to connect with a good agency. Jackie said, "He can't be a bad agent. I saw his picture on a milk carton!"

It must have been a progressive agent who got the great Victor

Moore to do a walk-on as a plumber in a Marilyn Monroe movie. Moore, a Friar for years, was tiny but delivered a line like a heavyweight. The star of *Of Thee I Sing, Louisiana Hayride,* and a dozen movie adaptations of his hits, he played meek better than anybody else in the world. He made you laugh with the simplest straight lines. At the Round Table he'd asked the waiter, "Is the bread fresh?" and break us up. Moore asked the question as if it were painful to even bring up the matter.

One day at the club the elevator was out of order. Two men dressed in laborer's clothes, both obviously helping hands and not the boss type, were picking up pieces of plaster from a crack in the wall. Moore asked, "Is it all right if I walk up?" Halfway up the steps, he stopped. "So far," he reported, "no problems."

Meek as he was in battling laborers and waiters and cabdrivers—who he always greeted with "Are you going my way?"—Moore was an animal with the ladies. One lady friend, a raven-haired lovely, with a figure that had put her into the Casino de Paree, had eyes for no other man. Moreover, she was wealthy and needed none of his support. At lunch we asked him what his secret was. Moore said, "I'm an animal."

"You, an animal?" said Jack Waldron.

William Gaxton, Moore's co-star in many musicals, said, "If he doesn't act like an animal, she hits him!"

Friar Errol Flynn should have met up with the young lady, if only for her bank account. Errol and Orson Welles could have co-captained an Olympic poverty team.

In '52, a step ahead of every grocer, haberdasher, and liquor supplier in the Western world, Flynn headed for Europe. He stopped off at the club to borrow a few. He explained that he needed money to get him to London. Robert Merrill, the opera star, said, "Errol, I'll get you as far as the ship!"

Flynn insisted that his poverty was an error. While making heaps of money in California, he'd sent a decent amount to his bank in Italy. Each week he'd send money to the bank. Recently, after ten years, he decided to cash a check. It came back marked "insufficient funds." Angrily he'd called the bank and the international manager had told him, "When a check of yours is returned for 'insufficient funds,' it does not necessarily mean that you have no money. It could also mean that *we* have no money!"

The garment-center crowd chipped in and lent Flynn the needed funds. He swore to repay them as soon as he got to London. One of them, Morris Uchetal, a manufacturer of white-on-white shirts, did receive a picture postcard some months later. It was a request for a statement as to whom and how much Flynn owed in the matter. The cartel called its debtor only to learn that the Flynn group had left for Spain with no forwarding address. The manager of the hotel asked Joe Kipness, speaking for the cartel, to please send an address for Flynn as soon as one was discovered. There was a small bill that had been overlooked. Hanging up, Kipness told the others, "We may get dunned for this postcard!"

Marlon Brando was a Friar before he became a Tahitian, or whatever he is today in Dorothy Lamour's sarong. In '51, when he did *Streetcar Named Desire,* he promised to meet me at the club at one-thirty in the afternoon. He wasn't there at three. Alan King said to me, "Maybe he didn't have a torn shirt to wear!"

The player's parade is endless. A fine second-in-command at the Friars in California, Tom Bosley came up to the club for the first time with a Chicago buddy. At the table he was introduced to me and I said that it was a pleasure to meet him. He said, "Milton, we've met before."

I said, "I never did your show."

Bosley said, "It was a long time ago. Long before I did *Fiorello* even."

"At the Friars?"

"We met at Lindy's. I was the hat-check guy. You were the first star to stiff me!"

Bosley came out here in 1967 for three weeks. He never went back. There must have been a thousand customers at Lindy's waiting for their coats! Reminiscing about his days at Lindy's, Bosley told us about how small his tips were. At times, actors gave him a nickel. "An actor," Bosley told us, "gave me a dollar once. I got so excited, I gave him a good coat!"

Bosley's deep resonant voice reminds me of Wilton Lackeye's. A brilliant dramatic actor, Lackeye had a dignity that belied his being one of the fellows. He also had a special fondness for the ladies. Very liberal in his offerings, he shared himself with both famous actresses and unknown shopgirls. We were discussing his career one afternoon. Somebody asked, "What was the first thing Wilton Lackeye was in?"

Fred Astaire said, "The manicurist at the Astor!"

Flynn, Welles, Niven—almost all of the actors—have to be forgiven their trespasses. Most people think of comedians as children playing grown-up games. You have to be a child to play Robin Williams. Bert Lahr was a lot of child, as was Eddie Cantor. Yet, on average, I've found that serious actors are the true kids. Just as a baby wants to be suckled forever, the actor wants to be fed glory and all the perks. I remember sitting with George Sanders at the club one afternoon. I asked him why he didn't stop casting around for the big-fish parts. He said, "You don't understand. I don't have my rich woman yet!"

Sanders was in touch at least. Some of the Broadway actors were off on distant planets. They didn't always have both oars in the water. The Queen of England came to see *The Pajama Game*. Her mother had recommended it highly. Eddie Foy thought it would be nice if an autographed cast album was sent to her. Mulling it over on an afternoon, he decided to do it. He asked me, "Do you know her address?"

The actor's world is as wide as his fingertips. It's no wonder that this story made a round at the Round Table: An actor comes home to find another actor making passionate love to his wife. The actor looks at his libidinous friend and says, "What the hell are you doing? What the hell are you doing?"

From the bed, the other actor says, "Well, next week I'm doing *Dallas*. Then I'm doing *Murder, She Wrote* and an *L.A. Law*!"

That the actor is at least unusual is reflected in a story told variously about Clyde Fitch, Raimu, the French actor, of Laurence Olivier, John Barrymore, and, in the version told to me by Paul Muni, of the great Yiddish actor Boris Thomashefsky.

Thomashefsky, another libidinous lion, seduced this young lady in his dressing room. The encounter over, the maiden said, "This has been wonderful, but I'm a little hungry."

Thomashefsky said, "There'll be two tickets for tonight's performance waiting for you."

The lass said, "I'm hungry. I'd like a piece of bread."

The actor drew himself up to his full height and said, "I'm an actor. I give tickets. You want bread, f—— a baker!"

When I hear tales about actors or reports of actual happenings in which an actor is at one or both ends of a punch line, I find that my feelings are mixed. Part of me laughs at the peccadilloes, realizing that there are certain events that can involve only performers. Another part resents the slightest hint of slur or stain on the craft.

The pie-in-the-face Berle knows few limits. I don't wander off, I hope, into ugliness or into seaminess for the sake of being ugly or seamy. Yet, in writing the preceding pages, I found myself wanting to edit out funny anecdotes that might possibly detract from a Bogart or Eddie Robinson. I concluded, however, that the actor who was often the source of the joke would have laughed at it, and was aware that life comes with warts.

More is involved. I suspect that I'm conducting a private internal debate as to the gravity of acting. Is it a science? Or is it fun and games? Are actors special people blessed with a talent they must offer? Are actors merely children of all ages trapped in nursery games? Do I have to justify seventy-nine years of funny walks and one-liners? Should I have sold all the laughter for more tears from the sixth row? A tiny part of me, emerging only when I meet a "serious" actor, makes me wonder. The occasion presented, I have a great deal of fun doing "spook" and "fright" jokes about Vincent Price. And I wonder who remembers when he was Prince Albert to Helen Hayes's Victoria.

On the other hand...

Somehow, I'm reminded of an old Youngman joke (a new Youngman joke doesn't exist). Youngman says, "My wife wanted a mink coat. I wanted a car. We compromised. We bought a mink coat, but we keep it in the garage."

I settled for "serious" about my craft, but I keep it at the Friars, where the laughter is.

A Spot You Wouldn't
Give to a Leopard

The next guy who gets Milton started on one of his lists will be exiled to the sauna in August.

Phil Foster

If I could remember what came after "abra" I'd make this whole group disappear.

Harry Houdini

They must make lists in Heaven. If you don't like harps, there's nothing else to do.

Arnold Schwarzenegger

I could listen to you guys forever, and that's what an hour feels like.

Edward R. Murrow

This has been a unique lunch. Normally I would sue.

Melvin Belli

Toward the end of a testimonial or roast, before the honoree gets the plaque, one of the performers does a brief spot in which he or she destroys all of those who have dared to speak unkindly of the honoree. The spot is called "the wrap-up."

The wrap-up is reserved for the heaviest hitter. To follow many pages about the funniest performers ever to rub elbows at the Round Table, a special wrap-up is called for. In this case, it happens to be a "list."

Our first formal Round Table list was born in 1932. I was at the club resting from rehearsals for Earl Carroll's *Vanities*. Carroll was a tough taskmaster. I was wiped out from being under his magnifying glass all morning. Carroll saw everything—"Milton, your socks have clocks on them. No good." "Milton, please turn your head another eighth of an inch to the right...No, no, that's a quarter of an inch!" Much as I deplored his fastidious ways, I conceded privately to myself that I was a worse nitpicker than he was. When I was eight I was already doing everything in a theater but knitting the fire curtain.

Bushed from the Carroll treatment at the rehearsal, I said to Jack Benny and Frank Tinney, a vaudevillian who became a bigger star in the *Follies,* "I've really been through the wringer today."

Benny said, "Who are the ten worst people in the business to work for?"

Tinney said, "Everybody."

Benny said, "Really. The ten worst?"

So it was Benny who was responsible for the lists. I can be blamed only for picking up the standard and becoming a pain in the neck with it.

I can't offer the names on the list we came up with because I hadn't learned to record them yet. I do remember one of Tinney's. He hated a theater owner in Washington, D.C. "Mr. Kurtz," Tinney said, "actually charged for dressing rooms. One community dressing room was free. Privacy came if you paid a dollar a week as a deposit on a key for the lock on the door of one of two small cubbyholes near the exit. Kurtz explained that the dollar was a deposit for the key. The catch was that nobody could get his deposit back right away. Kurtz insisted on waiting six months to make certain that an act hadn't made copies of the key and sold them to newly arrived performers. At the end of six months, an inquiry was always greeted with the information that other keys had showed up. The deposit was forfeited."

Benny and I agreed that Kurtz was a lowlife. Tinney went on, "I thought I had a way of getting even with him. I went to Sears and had fifty copies of the key made. They cost eight cents apiece. I spent four dollars. I was going to give them to every act who would ever play Washington. I would give them to any act passing through Washington. All they had to do was stop off and take a leak in the sink, half of which was in each cubbyhole. The son-of-a-gun went and changed the lock on me!"

I said, "You went into the hole for four dollars?"

Tinney said, "No. The next time I played there, Kurtz bought the keys from me for a penny each and put the old lock back!"

It's now a long time after Jack Benny's initial query that fathered the first list. John Forsythe recently prompted another list of which Benny would have been proud. It's a fitting wrap-up for a parade of comedians and actors. Forsythe had come by after a few hours of agony as Blake Carrington on *Dynasty*. To welcome him, I did my world-famous impression of a man who has bet on a Forsythe horse. In the bit, as if looking through glasses, my eyes remained fixed on the starting gate. The other horses run like mad. I keep exhorting my Forsythe horse to get out of the gate alive. The other horses run. My horse is still glued to one spot. John Francis, the entertainment director of the Beverly Hills Friars, said, "That's the funniest chunk I ever saw."

I said, "Sensational it was, but not the funniest."

Francis said, "It was hysterical."

I said, "Maybe you're right. Maybe it *was* the funniest spot ever done."

Buddy Arnold, the songwriter and my bosom companion, said, "Milton also comes in second, third, and fourth."

Forsythe asked, "What was the funniest bit any of you ever saw?"

I said, "The meeting will come to order. The ten funniest chunks."

Red Buttons asked, "You mean in a show? On the stage? Television?"

Forsythe said, "Yes."

I said, "Of all time?"

Forsythe said, "Why not?"

Bob Culp said, "That's cutting it down."

I said, "What do you know? You think *I Spy* was funny!"

Buttons said, "The man asks a legitimate question, he deserves a legitimate answer. You really want to know, John, don't you?"

Forsythe said, "Not anymore!"

I said, "Great, then we'll tell you!"

Jan Murray stopped picked at his cottage cheese and said, "I nominate Milton in anything. He's paying for my lunch!"

George Burns said, "If they weren't painting the card room at Hillcrest, I wouldn't be here. But I'm here and I'll tell you what was truly funny. Frank Van Hoven's act."

"Who?" Culp asked.

Buttons asked, "Ho. Ho. Not who. Hoven."

Jan Murray said, "I don't think Forsythe's question will be answered in our lifetime!"

"Frank Van Hoven," I said, "was a comedian and magician who asked for volunteers to join him onstage. He'd give one a block of ice to hold and the other an unevenly stacked pile of eggs. Volunteers would hold the stuff during his act, the ice melting, eggs dropping. That was it. Screams from the audience."

Murray said, "If Milton wasn't here I'd nominate 'Makeup.' Where every time the word 'Makeup' is said, somebody gets a faceful of powder. Berle's 'Royal Quartet' wasn't too shabby either. The teeth blacked out. A classic! Now Milton has to buy me food to take home," Murray said.

I said, "Jan, why should I argue with you?"

Burns said, "I have a couple, maybe three. Eddie Cantor and Sam Hearn did the tailor sketch. The way Eddie measured the poor customer was hysterical."

Forsythe said, "I saw that show. I must have been two years old!"

Culp said, "When you were two years old, Washington and Martha were a dance team!"

Buttons said, "Attention! I have a nomination."

Burns said, "Wait, I didn't finish."

"Let Burns finish," I said. "He may be gone when we come around again!"

Burns ignored my remark. "Ignored" isn't the exact word. He made a face that wiped the remark off the face of the earth. "Smith and Dale in 'Firehouse,' when they're playing cards. Nah, 'Dr. Kronkheit' was funnier. Then, Willie Howard on the deserted island."

Culp said, "I never saw Willie Howard."

"A genius," Burns said. "Never a wasted move, not an eyebrow that didn't get a laugh. In 'Shipwrecked' he's on this tiny island with a radio. He hasn't eaten in a month and a guy comes on the radio and describes a fancy meal. Such laughs!"

Red said, "Finished?"

"Soon. Jack Benny's hillbilly sketch, a classic. Bert Lahr in 'Flying High.' When he takes the physical for the Flying Corps."

Murray said, "If we include shows, how about the election returns in *Of Thee I Sing*? Poor Wintergreen losing to a monkey."

I said, "There's the red tie sketch with W. C. Fields."

Buttons said, "I don't know that one."

I said, "Fields is on his honeymoon. As his wife gets undressed and makes herself ready for the whoomboom, he just keeps unpacking. But all he keeps unpacking are red ties. One red tie after another. The poor girl is bursting, he keeps unpacking red ties and rambling on."

Jan asked, "How many do we have so far?"

Culp said, "Ninety-six."

Murray said, "Good, because I want to add the Marx Brothers' stateroom scene."

We all nodded. We couldn't leave out that one.

Buttons said, "Sid Caesar's spy sketch."

I said, "The Robin Williams concert at the Met in New York! It was on cable."

Burns said, "Williams is a true comedian. The black kid, I like him too."

Murray said, "Eddie Murphy?"

Burns said, "If that's his name."

Forsythe said, "Of everything, which was the single funniest piece?"

Picking up my imaginary binoculars, I started to do my Forsythe horse routine again.

Buttons said, "And my wife thinks I'm having a good time when I'm here!"

How to Cook
Somebody

In 1975 I was roasted for the fifty-eighth time. I had watched, in the last twelve months alone, six thousand people eat rubber chicken and cherries jubilee. (Norm Crosby, who was roasted only twelve times until that year, pleaded, "I'm beginning to fart zucchini!")

Since 1975 another fourteen roasts have been added to my total. During each one I sit back and hear guest speaker after guest speaker voice the same jokes I and others had done the night before at another dinner. I love it still. I'm glad I'm being roasted. It is, I honestly feel, the best way a large group of friends and peers can let a roastee know the depth of their affections. (Cash would do it too. I don't need any more watches. Red Buttons made his preference clear at the end of a Man of the Year dinner. He was given a watch, looked at it with less than total appreciation, and said, "I didn't need a watch. I wanted a bedroom set!")

Yet with all its faults, I do love it still. I'm also glad that I can claim for the Friars the perfecting of the roast.

Until the Friars came along, with its huge pool of talented wits and writers, celebrity dinners were dull. (Jack Benny hated to go to "straight" celebrity affairs. One time I picked him up and we drove to the Ambassador Hotel for an award dinner. As soon as we walked into the ballroom, Benny said to me, "All right, anytime you're ready.")

The roast had to be made funny, fast, and furious. The Friars did it, coming up with fifty pounds of funny comments on any condition enjoyed or suffered by an honoree. Diminutive Abe Beame, then mayor of New York, was a happy hunting ground for "short" jokes. I said, "I think he's taken off height!"

At one affair we offered Beame a metal milk box on which he could stand so he could be seen by the audience beyond the lectern. Beame said, "I can't help being short."

Alan King said, "Yes, but you could stay in your drawer more!"

There were a lot more where those came from. I had a whole night of La Guardia jokes available when the first of the tiny mayors graced us with his presence. I spared him after Robert Merrill said to him, "Mayor, when you sit you have no lap! You are a lap!"

Another past mayor, also honored, was John Lindsay. A lover boy with the profile of a Grecian god, he earned my saying, "John Lindsay once took a look at himself in a mirror and knocked himself up!"

Other public figures haven't been spared—bankers, stars, athletes—anybody of note with a few soft spots has been probed and, the weak areas found, mangled with words. My modest talent for put-downs must certainly come from my mother. She could cut an antagonist to shreds with four words. She found out that I'd been taking private boxing lessons from Sugar Ray Robinson. Accosting the champ, she ordered him to cease and desist. He ceased and desisted fast. I said, "Sugar, how come your knees wobbled when my mother came at you?"

Robinson said, "Milton, your mother's mouth has the best left hook in town!"

When we have a roast, many times, spurred on by the excitement of the affair, non-pros can raise themselves to great verbal heights. Adlai Stevenson, the Democratic candidate for President at the time of our Jack Benny dinner, made a giant score. Fred Allen had preceded him and was beyond brilliance. His pauses got screams. Came Stevenson's turn, the gentleman from Illinois stood up and explained that he had gone to the bathroom shortly before. There he met Mr. Allen who was in a panic for fear that his material wasn't funny. Being a nice guy, Stevenson had given the comedian the speech he had written for himself. Thus, Allen had delivered Stevenson's words. Stevenson sat down to a huge laugh and a hundred tons of applause.

I'm not certain as to why I indicated that Stevenson was a non-pro. Many of the politicians could make a handsome buck doing an act. Senators Goldwater and Humphrey, with whom I shared more than one dais, had fantastic timing. At a testimonial to Dean Martin at which both appeared, I ran into Senator Goldwater backstage after the show. I congratulated him on his joke-telling. "Senator, you have incredible timing."

"Not in 1964 I didn't," he answered.

At times the roast goes off in a direction not intended by the founding fathers of the affair. At a roast for Muhammad Ali, the honoree stood up when it was his turn to roast the roasters. Material had been prepared for the champ. After reading three lines, he decided that "prepared" material wasn't his forte. He started a diatribe about "Hollywood" jokes and "Jewish" jokes. The prepared material was not him, nor was it of the people, by the people, for the people. As an example of "people" jokes, Ali gave, "Why do Jews have long noses?" Nobody answered his question so he responded himself: "Because the air is free!" He turned to Don Rickles nearby and asked, "Don, are you Jewish?"

Like little Jack answering the giant at the top of the beanstalk, Don said, "Whatever you want, Muhammad!"

Whatever the diversions taken by a specific roast, the form owes a debt to the Friars. The debt has been acknowledged by the constant pairing of "Friars" and "roast." Even if the tossers and the tossee live in Buell, Idaho, the affair is a Friars' roast.

The media have chomped on the roast notion. For years a major part of Dean Martin's show were his roasts of famous people, evenings in which the biggest stars took on personalities as divergent as Hugh Hefner and Joan Collins, stopping off to tell a guest like Bob Newhart, "Bob, you're dull. Last night a Peeping Tom watched you make love to your wife. Fell asleep!"

Dick Van Patten, of *Eight Is Enough*, was told, "Dick, you're six months from a mayonnaise jar!"

On a roast for Wilt Chamberlin, Willie Shoemaker was admonished, "How can you pick on Wilt? When you were first starting and didn't have a place to live, Wilt let you sleep in his pants!" (Personally, I would never pick on Wilt Chamberlin. Or Kareem Jabbar. They're good guys to know if there's a fire and you live on the second floor.)

In the last year or two, television seems to have put the roast notion on hiatus. Live roasts have more than taken up the slack. As honcho of the club, I continue to volunteer my services for our own roasts. As honcho, I generally accept my offer. (I've accepted my kind offer over two hundred times. Twice I declined, but I overruled myself.) Of course I swear that appearance will be my last. "Next year, I mutter, let Billy Crystal or Richard Pryor host the show." Let the paying customers suffer—get Robin Williams!

The desire to quit has a half-life of two seconds. A coffee refill, and the Round Table, Berle at his usual seat, goes to work on the next show. (The fact is that people keep telling me to retire. I ask only, "To what?" My son Bill can't understand my desire to keep going. He's never had a job and he's ready to retire. His attitude may be my punishment for having done a certain joke about my brother Frank forty years ago—"I keep telling my brother Frank to learn a trade, so he'll know what kind of work he's out of." He never took me up on it.)

That I like to perform is not the best-kept secret since the recipe for Mrs. Fields's chocolate chip cookies. If roasts and dinners had never existed, Frank Sinatra once told an audience, Milton Berle would have invented them.

I have the strange feeling that I did eighteen minutes at my recent bypass surgery. I was operated on at a great hospital—Our Lady of Malpractice! Five years ago they spent three million dollars on a new recovery room. It hasn't been used yet!

I don't recall much of the surgery, although I recall some big laughs. I hope they didn't come from the surgeon, although Dr. Jack Matlof is a funny guy. He told me, "Your sex life will be terrific. Especially the one in the winter!"

Dr. Matlof's bill is funnier than his jokes. It's a good thing I'm covered by Black and Blue Cross! Matlof's bottom line has more zeros than a three-hour tennis match between Stevie Wonder and Ray Charles!

The one thing I do recall about my surgery is that I worked the lights in the operating room. I used a Leco and a Funell and made them pink and amber. Pink and amber aren't my colors, but made the anesthesiologist look dashing. (Anybody who wants to hear the next fifteen minutes of my medical routine can come over to my house.)

Yes, I do like to perform. I relish working a roast. It feels good to be able to knock giants down with a few well-directed words. It feels especially good to realize that the laughter evoked, for one moment, erases uncomfortable differences and puts envy to rest.

Funny People

Jessel—The Toastmaster General

George Jessel is one of the best producers on the 20th lot. That'll show you the trouble we're in!

> Spyros Skouras

I married George because he bought me clothes and candy.

> Lois Andrews, age fourteen

I had to divorce Jessel. He wanted me all to himself.

> Norma Talmadge

This was the best eulogy he's done so far today.

> Harry Groman, mortician

It's often been said that George Jessel is a great American, and here's the man who said it— George Jessel.

> Governor Al Smith

Gus Edwards was the master of "kid" shows in the years before World War One. I was invited to a rehearsal of one of his revues. In the show, another kid, a teenager from my block, George Jessel, did a brief turn as an impressionist. He did Bert Williams and Eddie Foy among others. Since I was about six and knew it all, I didn't think much of Jessel's work. After the rehearsal, my disdain turned to jealousy. Jessel had changed from rehearsal clothes into tan trousers, a blue blazer, and carried a cigar that must have cost at least a quarter. I would have killed to look so sharp and successful. Cantor was a "name" and didn't dress that spiffily.

To crush me even more, Jessel spoke the language of the stage. Another performer in the Gus Edwards show was a "fish"—he did a bad act. One kid was going into a show in Philadelphia, but it promised to be a "Brodie"—a flop. Jessel bragged about being able to "do a Houdini"—get out of a very tough spot. For about two weeks afterward, I limited my speech to show-business language. I tired of explaining what I meant and went back to English as she was "spoke" in Manhattan.

I learned to appreciate Jessel in time. The move was wise on my part, because he had much more to offer than sartorial splendor. Over the years he proved himself in a dozen ways. He became the Toastmaster General of the United States and served six Presidents. President Eisenhower was the only Commander in Chief he wasn't crazy about.

At the Friars one afternoon, Jessel explained his dislike. "Eisenhower doesn't understand a joke unless it has 'darky' in it! And he doesn't like cats." Why a feeling for or against cats should have concerned Jessel will never be known. The fact, however, was that Ike hated the felines. At Camp David he ordered them shot on sight.

Jessel's anti-Eisenhower stance was balanced by Walter Winchell's total adoration of the Chief. Winchell wore an "I Like Ike" button for three years after the election.

Jessel, overseas, in time of war, entertained hundreds of GI's, which is not bad considering the fact that he appeared before *millions* of GI's! He wasn't handsome, yet he married everybody. He divorced everybody.

Generally he preferred young women. Young! He was late for a lunch meeting once and we wondered where he was. The writer of "High Hopes" and "All the Way," Sammy Cahn, said, "He's out buying his new wife a wedding gift—Pampers!" (Jessel's fondness for Lolitas served as a good proving ground for "young" jokes later used at our dinners and roasts to poke fun at Frank Sinatra after marrying Mia Farrow, Dean Martin, and Dr. Jerry Buss, the owner of the Los Angeles Lakers, for their dating and mating habits, and all the other dirty old men in our circle. ("Dean Martin was supposed to be here tonight, but his wife isn't feeling well. She's teething!" "Jerry Buss was supposed to bring his fiancée but she has a spelling test in the morning!")

On one occasion where death didn't concern him, Jessel thought he could charm his way back into the heart of Norma Talmadge, a big star when they were married, but now his former wife and retired to a mansion in Florida. Jessel borrowed ten thousand dollars from Eddie Cantor, bought a fair-sized piece of jewelry, and headed for Florida. Arriving at the mansion, unable to wait, Jessel handed the gift to his ex-wife as she opened the door. Miss Talmadge, ever graceful, accepted the gift and started to shut the door. Jessel said, "At least you could let me use the pool!"

Why he wanted a replay of the marriage was a tough question to answer. The marriage was tempestuous. Jessel was thrown out of the house regularly. One time, returning to New York for some engagements, he told us, "The bitch actually locked me out of the bedroom!"

Ted Lewis said, "It's happened before, hasn't it?"

Jessel said, "This time I got back in. I used the gardener's key!"

"Why would the gardener have a key to your bedroom?" I asked.

"For the same reason I have a key to the maid's room!"

Jessel was always trying to be helpful. When Miss Talmadge's dog died, she contacted her ex-husband, received his okay, and sent out invitations to the funeral with the engraved promise that Jessel would do the eulogy. After Jessel returned to New York, Ed Wynn kidded him, "George, are you now reduced to making speeches about a mutt?"

Jessel drew himself up to his full height, which wasn't much, and said, "That wasn't a mere dog. That dog contributed a million dollars to Israel!"

Jessel was a brilliant excuse-maker. As he was downing a third double at the bar one evening, I must have looked at him strangely because he felt compelled to come up with an excuse. He looked me straight in the eye and said, the saddest man on earth, "Norma Talmadge left me!" Of course the drinking was taking place forty years after Norma Talmadge left him!

The master eulogist, for humans as well as poodles, Jessel came back from a morning burial all shaken. He explained, "As I was saying the words that would speed the departed to Valhalla, I happened to glance at the open coffin. I actually *knew* that man!"

At the Round Table, Jessel threw away great lines. Hearing about a marriage newly enacted, he said,"I hope that they will be as happy as I might have been on several occasions!"

Jessel arrived at an affair in the company of a beautiful and well-endowed young lady. He was greeted with an ovation, having just risen from a sickbed, where he'd been kept by one of his "conditions." Jessel invented wonderful names for some of his more esoteric conditions. Several socially acquired diseases were called "Cupid's Eczema." Another condition was an early Valentine's Day gift from his latest fiancée—a heart-shaped rash! A budding entertainer, this young lady was introduced as "Miss Lark, she sings like a mink!" At the dinner itself, Jessel paid her a mighty compliment. He said, his face reverent, "As many of you know, I have been quite ill. It is only due to the diligence and attention on the part of Miss Lark, my nurse, that I am able to get out of bed and come here in ten days. Of course, if she hadn't been around, I could have been here in *four* days!"

What made Jessel's humor work was his duality, especially as he aged. Outwardly he was serious and self-impressed. Inside, he laughed at the world. He knew that he was a short, shriveling man with no hair and actually little fame outside of the Friars and New York. From the beginning, Jessel was never a hit in Iowa or Kansas. In Brooklyn he was the best and the biggest.

Jessel never married for love. He married because the institution and the notion of coupling with a gorgeous woman made him laugh. He told jokes for the same reason. He was amused to see a thousand people in the audience laughing at a joke they'd heard before being told by a man who spoke English badly and who used words and phrasing that didn't come from his background.

That he knew what he was all about was made evident one evening as some of us waited in a small room off to the side of the grand ballroom at the Century Plaza Hotel. The idea was to gather the members of the dais and then march them into the ballroom impressively. As it was for about twenty years of his later life, his hairpiece was askew. It made no pretense at being real hair. Mr.

Get-It-Right even at dinners, I said, "George, you ought to take a look at your hair."

He smiled and said, "We'll see who gets bigger laughs." I finally realized that he was his own biggest prop.

Less than a week later, we worked a stag roast together and I saw how he used every element to further his performance. It looked to many in the audience that the old guy was one step from senility. He walked slowly. His look was remote. His words seemed to be a little more slurred than they'd been before. It would be a good deed to laugh at every word he said.

Midway in his opening monologue, which was unbelievably clean for a stag affair, Jessel started to tell a stock joke about an "Italian lady who comes to the fruit man in her neighborhood in downtown New York. She asks for broccoli. The fruit man says, 'We have no broccoli.'

"The woman says, 'I want some broccoli.'

"'This isn't the season for broccoli. There's no broccoli!'

"'That's nice. I'd like some broccoli.'

"Angry now, the fruit man says, 'Lady, do me a favor. Tell me— how do you spell "dog" in dogmatic?'

"The lady says, 'D-o-g.'

"'And how do you spell "cat" in catastrophe?'

"'C-a-t.'

"'Now tell me how you spell "fuck" in broccoli?'

"The woman says, 'There isn't any "fuck" in *broccoli*.'

"The fruit man says, 'That's what I've been trying to tell you— there's no fuckin' broccoli.'"

Jessel didn't quite make it to the end of the story. He waltzed through the first part but went blank at the name of the vegetable in the lady's last response. He stood there, waiting for a miracle to help him out. Jan Murray came to his rescue. Leaning over, Murray whispered, "Broccoli."

Jessel looked at Murray incredulously and asked, "Who the fuck eats broccoli?"

The laugh went through the roof. I'd settle for half of it on my epitaph.

Jessel sat down. His lips were puckered as if he were forcing back a smile. The joke had come off exactly as planned. Murray looked at me and said, "Milton, you and I still have a lot to learn."

To camouflage his skill, Jessel managed to make himself the brunt of the litter of most of his tales. The story that follows, Exhibit A, has never been told before. Only the ladies of the chorus know it and they're not talking. (The one on the couch is now married to the owner of several hundred theaters in South Africa.)

As was his hobby, Jessel had a lady friend in Hollywood for whom he was paying the bills—rent, phone, food, car rental—the necessities. To reward his generosity, Jessel asked only that the apartment on Melrose Avenue in West Hollywood be a stopping point that would break Jessel's long trek to his home in the Valley from the airport when he'd return from a fund-raising dinner out of town. Since he was away at least half of each month, making speeches for Israel, attending functions where he could get more medals, and visiting lady friends in other parts of the country, his young mistress took in a boarder, another young lady. The newcomer paid half the bills, thus Jessel's girl made a slight profit on the apartment. On the rare days that Jessel was expected, the new girl had to find a place to sleep. This wasn't difficult as she often slept at hotels and other apartments one hour at a time.

Unexpectedly one night, Jessel came home from Toronto, Canada, let himself into the apartment, saw in silhouette a feminine form asleep on the couch, undressed, and started to have his way with her. The young lady stirred and opened her eyes. They widened in surprise. Jessel whispered, "Don't stop. You're dreaming."

The young lady said, "I'm not dreaming!"

Jessel said, "All right, I'm dreaming. Don't stop!"

Jessel set the tone for the Round Table. Cruelty and viciousness were out. One night, he came into the club after learning he'd been stabbed in the career. Everybody knew he was responsible for the success of *The Jazz Singer* on Broadway. He worked with the writer, shaped the scenes, and often created the dialogue. He even hired the cantor in the show, an actor named Warner Oland, who grew up to become Charlie Chan. It was Jessel's baby all the way. When Jack Warner bought it, Jessel had a great deal to do with the sale. Jessel thought that he came with the package. He didn't. Firmly believing that author, Samson Raphaelson, sold him out, he came to the club fuming. He wished the author the deadliest death, part of which consisted of flames, pointed stakes, and acid. "I hate this man with all of my heart!" he roared. Bob Ripley, of "Believe It or Not" fame, tried to cool him down. "George, you're the fellow who preaches love and happiness."

"F——-g I preach! This man I detest. I'm going to pray for his death tonight!"

"We're not supposed to leave here hating."

"Tonight I'll kill. Tomorrow when I do his eulogy he'll be a saint!"

Jessel's prayers weren't answered. The author lived. Jolson played the part in the movie. Again, Jessel fumed. He hated Jack Warner. He swore that he would break Jack Warner if it cost him every penny he had. "I will destroy that hawk-faced peddler if I have to give up my last bite of bread!"

Time went by. The picture came out. Jack Warner rolled in money. Jessel showed up at the Friars. Laughing, he said, "Warner doesn't know he's almost finished. I'm down to my last two hundred dollars!"

Jessel built this story into another ten-minute smash at dinners.

Jessel took Lena Horne to the Stork Club, a posh poshery in Manhattan. The owner, Sherman Billingsley, didn't like "colored" people, especially when they came in with a white escort. Because it was Jessel, the couple got one of the preferred tables. Seeing it, Billingsley came over and asked, with more charm than he felt, "Who made your reservation?"

Jessel said, "Abraham Lincoln!"

"Say Goodnight, Gracie"

George Burns is so old his birth certificate is on a rock.

> Jack Benny

George Burns is so old he was circumcised with a stone knife.

> George Jessel

George Burns is at that age where he can go to a topless bar and look at the menu.

> Danny Thomas

George Burns has occasional streaks of silence that make him a brilliant conversationalist.

> Walter Matthau

George Burns never seems to look older. It's not possible.

> Cary Grant

George Burns is a real optimist. He once bought work clothes for Gracie's brother.

> Al Jolson

According to George Burns, stardom, for talking acts, is measured by the amount of time a performer is allowed. In vaudeville thirteen minutes was the border line. Thirteen and under put an act near the start of the bill, talking and telling jokes while the audience was still getting comfortable. A fourteen-minute act demanded respect and got it.

George Burns is a seventeen-minute act and then some. Even when he was part of a dance act, his name changing daily, he was a headliner in his heart. Today he is one of the ten biggest stars in show business, in demand for movies, television shows, and the few remaining hotel rooms and nightclubs where legends can perform. It's close to being a miracle because Burns has never pushed and, to this day, never tried to be funny. He never tells a joke. He reads lines like the straight man he was trained to be. Audiences howl when he opens his mouth.

Burns can't explain his gift. For years, when he and Gracie Allen were a top team, he swore that he did nothing. He simply asked a question and stepped back while Gracie answered. Today he just stands, talks, and sings a few bars of ditties nobody has ever heard of. Some years ago he sang a Sam E. Lewis song Lewis didn't remember having written. Here too Burns doesn't sing to get laughs. He sings his inane songs because he likes to sing them. If the audience is amused, the plus is incidental.

That's really the secret of George Burns. He works to enjoy himself. The audience's pleasure is its own affair. Relieved of the audience as burden, Burns can go off in any direction and say what pleases him. Because he's a nice man, he makes his audience feel good. He makes himself the brunt of the humor. Even when working with Gracie Allen, he never for one second allowed the audience to think that the routine demonstrated Allen's stupidity. Burns was the "dummy" for not understanding her logic. Audiences like a chivalrous man.

Working alone today, Burns still kids himself. At one of the many tiny birthday parties thrown for me by the Round Table, a cake was brought in. Loaded down with lit candles, it honored me for reaching seventy-seven. It also was an acceptable excuse for allowing all the dieters, a permanent state with most of us, to pounce on a huge piece of cake. I made a wish and, with the help of a dozen pairs of lungs, blew out the candles. Red Buttons felt at the air above the table and said, "Call the janitor. The heat is off again!" Buttons referred, of course, to the days of our youth when many of us froze in unheated apartments and managed to keep warm only by banging on radiators and pipes to alert the janitor. My mother called the racket "Jewish tomtoms."

Amused by Buttons's line, I repeated it later in the day to George Burns. Burns said, "I had a cake like that a few years ago. It was for my birthdays in 1977 and 1978."

I played straight, "Two years?"

Burns said, "Well, I started to blow out the candles in 1977!"

Burns laughs at his age. God bless him! Since he played the Lord in some movies, Burns may have carried the role too far. When he sneezes and somebody says, "God bless you," Burns responds, "I will, I will."

The ability to kid his years has given Burns a new lease on great jokes. He tells the world that he goes to airports just to be frisked! He doesn't go out with women his own age because there are no women his age! At lunch at the Friars one afternoon, I asked him if he still had sex. Burns answered, "No, but when I see a beautiful woman my eyeballs get hard!"

At roasts and dinners I like to throw a salute in his direction. I say, "George Burns wanted to be here tonight, but something came up! And he's very proud! And he's waiting till the Krazy Glue hardens!" One time I added, "And he's waiting to see if it's real so he can have it bronzed!"

Jack Benny's line about Burns and sex was a big winner too— "George Burns having sex is like shooting pool with a rope!"

That Burns keeps charging ahead is an inspiration to us younger folks. His response to a question at the Round Table was a two-word sermon. Asked by one of the Friars why he didn't retire, Burns said, "To what?"

When nobody's looking I make believe that Burns is the basis of the story coming up: George Burns came back from Las Vegas last week. When I saw him at the club he looked very unhappy. I said, "George, what's wrong?"

George said, "The night before I closed at Caesar's Palace I met this gorgeous twenty-year-old girl. Just gorgeous, lovely. She wanted to come back to Beverly Hills with me. I brought her. She's a great cook. She cleans the house. The sex is terrific."

I said, "What's so bad about that?"

George said, "I forgot where I live!"

If I'm allowed to be slightly off-color, I offer one more George

Burns story: George meets this beautiful young woman who is more than willing to go up to his suite with him for some private pleasure. They go upstairs, both get undressed, both lie down in bed, and George says, "All right, spread the legs."

The girl starts to separate her limbs when George notices and says, "Not yours! Mine!"

Although his walk has slowed down some and it may take him a millisecond longer to get into a story, Burns is in remarkably good shape. Some of his peers find his condition a problem. Harry Tobias, the only songwriter around who can match Irving Berlin for longevity, listened as Burns talked about his physical condition. "I feel fantastic," Burns said, "I don't have an ache, a pain, a twinge, nothing."

Feeling concerned for him, Tobias asked, "What does the doctor say?"

Burns topped him, "I don't know. He died in April."

My affection for George Burns is obvious, but I must paint in one wart. Until recently Burns had no taste in cigars. His weakness didn't come from novelty. Burns started to smoke cigars when he was eight. At the club he recounted, "I smoked my first cigar when I was a kid. I wanted to look important. For an eight-year-old, that's important."

Time didn't heal his palate. Burns smoked quarter cigars when he was earning ten thousand dollars a week. Never a spendthrift to start with, Burns felt that upgrading his taste from his ten-cent specials was more than enough.

One afternoon, as Jackie Osterman and I were walking to the club, we happened to inhale some smoke from a tar heater down the block. Osterman said, "I thought George Burns was out of town."

To overcome this deficiency in the Burns character, I tried to show him the way. One evening, before a Friars celebrity dinner, I offered him a decent cigar. Taking it, he studied the texture and asked how much it cost. I said, "That's only a three-dollar job."

Burns said, "Three dollars! For three dollars I'd have to hump it first!"

That nicotinic naïveté is the sole weakness in the Burns armor indicates a fairly staunch individual. Vaudeville is gone. The seventeen-minute act remains. He keeps getting better. Even his cigars are getting good. (Not that good yet. One Christmas Ruth saw an attractive silk smoking jacket that she wanted to buy for Burns. Unfortunately, we went to his house for dinner before she could make her purchase. On the way home, Ruth mentioned that she didn't think the smoking jacket would be the right gift. She said, "With one puff, George went from a silk jacket to polyester!")

Banjo Eyes—Eddie Cantor

After Cantor's fifth daughter was born: Cantor couldn't get a boy if he sent for Western Union!

Lou Holtz

In two minutes Eddie Cantor gets more laughs than he gets in ten minutes.

Joe E. Brown

I never miss Eddie Cantor's radio show. I never listen to it so I never miss it!

Ed Wynn

Eddie Cantor must get very tired of having himself around.

Frank Fay

Eddie has a golden tongue. He can convince Ida she looks bad in mink.

Sophie Tucker

Cantor's made the top of the heap and that about covers it.

Jack Osterman

Eddie Cantor had to fight for his laughs. Unlike some comedians who are ready to garner laughter a minute after birth, Cantor wasn't born a funny man. George S. Kaufman summed him up once: "Cantor's humor is painted on like his blackface."

Cantor had the desire to be funny, the urge to evoke laughter. The equipment was missing. There's an analogy in many respects between Cantor's search for the comedy muse and my son Bill's deftness at flying gliders.

Bill is a natural in the sky, a half brother to the clouds. He was a natural from the first moment he touched the controls. Another student, a Cantor type, matched Bill in schooling, but the skill came slowly. The Cantor type had none of the soul that makes fliers. He couldn't hear the silent music to which gliders sail. He had to sweat to succeed. He became a fine glider pilot. He worked, practiced, practiced more, and wished himself into a measure of skill. Of course if you could get me into a glider, I'd prefer Bill at the stick.

Eddie Cantor wished himself into comedy. His energy was limitless. He was willing to spend it on any tools that would bring him laughter. It was hard for him. It would be nice to draw Cantor as a magnificent natural comedian. He was, after all, a good friend, part mentor, and he did introduce me to the Friars. Grateful I've always been. When it comes to comedy, I also become *serious*.

Cantor needed writers. Many comedians need writers. But Cantor NEEDED writers. One afternoon at the Round Table, Cantor became angry with Bert Gordon, a comedian who played a character called "The Mad Russian" on Cantor's very successful radio show. Gordon had refused to let Cantor eat the cole slaw that came with Gordon's lunch. As lord of the manor, Cantor demanded it, saying, "If you don't give me the cole slaw, your career will be hanging by a thread."

Gordon said, "You can have my wife, but never my cole slaw."

Cantor leaned back to a writer behind him and whispered, with more truth than poetry, "You got a fifty-dollar bonus if you come up with a line so I can fire Gordon funny!"

Cantor's writers gave him pounds of punch lines for the Round Table. Once in a while we'd throw him a mercy laugh. Yet he had gumption. He kept punching.

To feed his bottomless hunger for laughs, Cantor hired almost anybody who claimed to be a writer. A cab driver named Eddie Davis used to hunt Cantor down daily to tell him new lines. Cantor hired Davis. Davis became a cornerstone of Cantor's staff.

Cantor's second cousin was going with an NYU student who, upon learning that she had access to the star, hinted that he was a funny writer and would like to write for him. Arrangements were made. Cantor and Davis met with the young man, who introduced himself, "I'm Thurston Goldfarb."

Davis said, "Thurston Goldfarb? If your mother named you, she could get the job."

Later in the day, Cantor told us the story at the club. Naturally, he claimed the punch line.

The patron saint of writers on one hand, Cantor also managed to alienate those who worked for him. It seemed that he was bent on bending goodwill until it broke.

A group of show people got together one evening at the Friars in Beverly Hills to start a B'nai B'rith lodge to be named after Cantor. In addition to actors, one writer after another rose to tell about how wonderful Cantor had been. One told how Cantor wouldn't let him go home to visit a sick parent. Another related an experience in which Cantor kept the horny young man from an assignation with two stewardesses.

The story of Eddie Davis's illness was the topper. One week the writers had come up with a sketch without a finish. It came unglued a minute before the end. Davis was in the hospital with broken legs.

Cantor suggested that the staff go up to the hospital and get Davis to help.

"The guy has two broken legs!" one writer said, pleading for a little sanity."

Cantor said, "It's his legs. We don't want him to dance. We need a joke. We do that with our heads!"

Cantor, the staff, and a typewriter arrived in the patient's room two hours later. The typewriter was plunked on Davis's healthy chest and a writing session ensued. A nurse walked in, saw the industry, became upset, and started to usher everybody out, saying, "Have you no pity? This man has two broken legs!"

Cantor said, "You have no pity! The sketch has no finish!"

The nurse went on, "Mr. Davis, as soon as they're out of here, it's time for your nap."

At the door, Cantor half-whispered to Davis, "Don't nap! Think!"

As the Cantor anecdotes went by, each one had a disclaimer on it. "What a great guy he was!" "He was so much fun; he was so good to people." Milt Rosen, taking time off from his twelfth rewrite of a Doris Day picture, said, "I got a great idea. Let's go down to the Red Cross and withdraw blood in Cantor's name!"

Cantor wasn't all basket case and the contents of Pandora's box. He had a nose that could sniff out great talent when he saw it. Dinah Shore, Deanne Durbin, Bobby Breen, Eddie Fisher—all were Cantor "finds."

Cantor had more than a sniffer, energy, and the desire to please. He had respect for the poor guy who reached deep in his pocket to come up with the money for a ticket. A dollar was a lot of sweat in Cantor's day. Knowing this, he was among the first Broadway stars to play past the critics to the audience. The critics may have grimaced when Cantor rolled his banjo eyes. The audiences roared with laughter. Cantor defied the dictum of the first three decades of this century that a show could be a hit only if it pleased the critics.

On stage and later in the movies, Cantor wore a public rump. He knew what would make an audience start to squirm and when. In *The Last Tycoon,* Fitzgerald's hero also had a public rump. He knew the picture was getting long or boring when his ass started to hurt.

When Cantor went on radio, he brought along audiences. The laughter had to be real. The jokes had to be funny to effect that laughter.

At the risk of being called a braggart for the first time in my life, I "ponder" on my television shows of the late forties and the fifties. The sketches had to be funny or we were dead. We went live and couldn't add laughs later. My kind of humor was tempered by that consideration. Fred Allen was cerebral and off the air. During an interview throughout which I shook with reverence, Carl Sandburg told me, "Poets and comedians shouldn't dictate. They serve."

Cantor served. He helped to teach me my role.

Sterling Silvers

They say, "It's not whether you win or lose."
Sounds right, but I wouldn't know. I never won!

Phil Silvers

My mother thought of little Phil Silvers as an adorable young lad. More than anything, my mother admired his sweet soprano voice. He was the only show-business kid my mother allowed me to associate with. When we went off to enjoy ourselves in the candy store, my mother gave me extra spending money. The first time we went out together, Silvers rewarded my mother's trust and benevolence by taking me to a whorehouse in Newark, New Jersey. He cautioned me to act experienced. He had a reputation to uphold. He didn't know that I was the veteran of many wars.

Silvers finished his stint with the young lady of his choice quickly. Being young, after a few minutes, he asked for a free second helping. Not one to give samples, the girl turned Silvers down. Silvers snarled at her, "No wonder you have the back room!"

Silvers always had the right word. We went to see an old Chaplin silent picture once. After sitting two minutes, Silvers yelled out, "Louder!"

Then he grew up and became a dedicated, driven, two-fisted betting unfortunate. So extensive was his poverty of willpower, losers from the rocky coast of Maine to the craggy shores of California felt sorry for him. Tony Martin, no mean loser himself, said once, between card games, "Silvers is a cripple. I'm a limper, but Silvers is a cripple!"

Silvers worked overtime to achieve monumental losses in the

card room. Sitting with us after another Waterloo at gin rummy, Silvers summed up the day's activities: "I lost a few."

Jack Lemmon asked, "Phil, how much do you imagine you've lost in your life?"

Silvers said, "In what? Horses? Cards? Football? In *polo* I'm way ahead!"

Having escaped a day's work on *Some Like It Hot* with Lemmon, Billy Wilder said, "In your whole life, what's the figure?"

Silvers said, "If Howard Hughes dies and leaves me a billion and a half, I'll be even for last month!"

Wilder pressed, "We have a card game. High stakes. But we're not insane. Phil, don't you think therapy might help you?"

Silvers said, "I go to a psychiatrist. Yesterday we cut high card for what I owe him!"

His coffee downed, Silvers got up to leave. I asked him where he was going. Silvers said, "I'm going to get my hair trimmed unless I lose my next!" At that time Silvers was down to four hairs on each side of his head. He went to the barbershop because his barber was good on picking football winners. Silvers once said to me, more than a touch of sincerity in his voice, "I wish I had a barber for the track!"

Once Silvers locked horns with someone in the card room, only death could part the tangle of antlers. In one of his many matches with Ted Briskin, Betty Hutton's ex-husband, Silvers found himself behind. The contest was bitter. A break was effected. Briskin returned from washing up and said, "Phil, you won't understand, but—"

Silvers said, "You're right, I won't understand."

Briskin said, "I called home. It's a good thing, too, because we have to go to the Music Center tonight and I forgot."

The figures for the day were added up as Silvers stood by disgruntled, mumbling about Briskin's tin ear and how bad the orchestra was. As Briskin started away, Silvers was a step behind him. Never one to give up hope, Silvers thought a last-minute reprieve might be given.

At the Round Table, Briskin stopped for a few words. Silvers caught up with him. Briskin said, "Can you believe this man? He won't leave me alone."

Silvers said, "My luck was changing, that's why you're leaving."

Briskin said, "I have to go home and get dressed. I'm a sponsor at the Music Center. I have to be there for the party."

Silvers adjusted his glasses and said venomously, "Beethoven would forgive you. Me—never!"

Silvers craved action. After one of our Sunday-morning brunches, Shecky Greene, another benevolent soul who believed in the improvement of the breed through betting, talked Silvers into a trip south to the track at Caliente in Tiajuana, Mexico. I went along as chaperone. I'd also heard that travel broadens. Vince Edwards, Ben Casey himself, met us at the track. Ours was a fearsome foursome.

Caliente had advantages over many other tracks. Its foreign book enabled players to bet six other tracks and several future races like the Kentucky Derby. A player in track shoes could bet sixty-five races in one afternoon at Caliente. Silvers did. He bet horses he'd never heard of ridden by jockeys nobody ever heard of at tracks that possibly didn't exist. Edwards was just about as carefree. Greene only bet races in which there was one jockey with a name he could pronounce. As the sanest of the insane, I bet the New York and Florida tracks. I lost money on sixteen races. I was the big winner with the foreign book.

The four of us teamed up to buy a ticket on the five-ten. As at most tracks years later, the idea was to pick the winners of six designated races—the fifth to the tenth. Because each of us had opinions, the basic two-dollar ticket ended up a thirty-two-hundred-dollar ticket. We won five out of six races and split eleven dollars and eighty cents—less than three dollars for an investment of eight hundred. I wasn't thrilled. Silvers said, "Why are you complaining? We got back money, didn't we?"

Because all horseplayers in pain are capable of great humor. Edwards topped the day with "Are you guys going to be here next week? I want to know if I should kill myself!"

At the Round Table the next day, Silvers was biding his time until another Briskin showed up. The real one would have been all right too. The Briskin-Silvers games deserved a *National Geographic* documentary. One afternoon, as the two losers went at one another, Sammy Lewis, the former Las Vegas booker, standing behind Briskin, offered to take a bet on either one to win. He had no takers. Puzzled, Lewis said, "I don't care which side I take. One of them has to win."

Standing behind Silvers, Jonie Taps said, "Not necessarily. It could rain!"

The pickings slim after another Caliente trip, Silvers tarried as

I worked him over. Nat Hiken, the creator of *Bilko*, listened to me describe our safari to Caliente. Since no horseplayer can confess his own illness, I'd just finished twenty minutes on Phil Silvers and his weakness. Hiken proceeded to tell us a Phil Silvers story so good, Silvers applauded.

One bright and sunny New York day, Phil Silvers was sitting crunched into the Round Table, trying not to be seen by people he owed. Which was everybody! This was when Sergeant Bilko was the world's favorite soldier. (He'd knocked me off the tube.) Money poured in. Silvers managed to help it pour out faster than it poured in. At all times, Silvers owed every bookmaker in town.

Jan Murray had a great run on him: "There's an old lady in Latvia. She books numbers—two cents, three cents, the biggest bet she ever handles is nine cents. Silvers owes her seventeen hundred dollars! On a mountaintop in Peru there's a bookie you can only bet with in cash. He holds the money. You have to take four planes to get to the train in Bolivia that takes you to the bus in Colombia that gets you to a stable where you rent a horse that takes you to a certain valley in which there are snakes and flies four feet long and after you traverse this valley without food for nine days and you get to the edge of the mountain where you climb and you climb and you climb and your hands will be red with blood and blisters on every toe, skin ripped off, and you get to the top of the mountain where there's a bus stop with a bus that runs once a month at four-thirty in the morning. You ride over a bumpy road for six hours. If Silvers can't get anybody to take a two-dollar bet on the Dodgers, tomorrow he leaves for this bookie, who will turn him down. Your credit's no good! Who told you that? The bookie on the next mountain!"

As Silvers sat, musing about poverty, Joe Kipness walked in with a fair tip on a fight. A natty dresser, tall, Kipness was a manufacturer with stage lights in his blood. He was one of the backers of *Guys and Dolls* and the producer of *High Button Shoes*, the musical that had made Phil Silvers famous. Kipness was close to the brotherhood of the bulging jackets. Among Kipness's very close friends was Frankie Carbo, the czar of boxing. Nobody won or lost at the Garden without Carbo's permission. This week is special— the black trunks win in four!

Kipness slid in next to Silvers. Kipness said, his accent just the slightest touch European, "There's a good fight tomorrow. Bet the kid in the black trunks. Beg, borrow, steal, kill for some money, and bet the black trunks. You'll be even with everybody you owe!"

"A shoo-in, huh?"

"Phil, please, just bet the black trunks. Here—I'll lend you five grand. But beg, borrow, steal!"

The next afternoon, a delighted Kipness rushed in to look for Phil Silvers, the solvent TV star. Silvers sat there glumly. Kipness asked, "Couldn't you borrow any money to bet?"

Silvers said, "I borrowed forty G's."

"Couldn't you get it down?"

"I got it down."

"So now you're wealthy!"

Silvers shrugged, "I liked the kid in the white trunks!"

Joe E. Lewis—The Day He Died, Bookmakers, Pit Bosses, Loan Sharks, Hookers, and the Night Shift at Cutty Sark Died

Joe E. Lewis could dive into a barrel of tits and come up with a thumb!

Johnny Carson

Joe E. Lewis smokes three packs of cigarettes a day because it gives his hands something to do— shake!

Joey Bishop

Many Friars were immortals in the Valhalla of the lost souls.

Joe E. Lewis, sadly for those who love the art of show business, didn't stick around long enough to become an eternal household word. Yet, just as Sinatra was and is the epitome of saloon singers, Joe E. Lewis was the quintessential saloon comic. (Lewis loved the word "quintessential." The first time Lewis heard the word tossed off effortlessly at the Round Table by Goodman Ace, the saloon comic fell in love. Lewis smiled sheepishly and said, "I want to live long enough to use that word in a regular sentence!")

Lewis also liked "magnanimous." "It's the kind of word," he told us, "that could get you a raise in Cincinnati!"

On another occasion Lewis told us about a third word of wonderment. Tallulah Bankhead was in Hot Springs when Lewis was appearing in a gambling joint. Bankhead came backstage to see him. As they talked Bankhead allowed some of her natural gases to erupt. Being a true southern belle, Bankhead apologized for the flatulence. Lewis had the most innocent look on his face as he explained to us, "When Tallulah said 'flatulence,' I felt like I was being knighted!"

Joe E. Lewis was not stunning of face and feature. Often, Lewis complained, "I got my looks when I was too young to refuse them!" Lewis also saw the sunny side of things: "I'm the best-looking one in the family. My father looked like his hobby was stepping on rakes!" Still, when Lewis was onstage, drink in hand, his accompanist, Auston Mack, at the piano, a warm lovable pixie metamorphosed. (I never used that word at the Round Table. I would have been whipped with day-old breadsticks.)

In a deep raw voice that sounded like Brillo in heat, on the floor Lewis sang parodies and interjected jokes between the flat notes. The material was adult and about the subjects dear to the comedian's heart—booze, horses, women, and a dice table. In his life Joe E. Lewis never did one joke about the causes of the Industrial Revolution. Nevertheless, sitting at lunch one afternoon, Lenny Bruce told us, "If I'm brave, it was Joe E. Lewis who made me brave. The real difference between us is that he makes jokes. I give opinions with a joke inside."

Lewis was visited at the club one dinnertime by a struggling young writer named Paddy Chayefsky. From the Bronx, Chayefsky, not yet named the writer of *Marty* and *Network,* was living off an option the Shuberts had taken on a play he had written after the war. Option money runs out quickly, so Chayefsky tried some one-liners. A mutual friend, a local comic, brought the young man to Lewis's attention. An inveterate buyer of material, Lewis gave all submissions an honest reading. Chayefsky's jokes were about wine, women, and song, but they had too much literary quality. The jokes would have looked good in print. Lewis told the young writer, "You have fun in you, kid, but I need jokes you write on cocktail napkins!" Chayefsky went out to Hollywood and tried to sell there. A job acting in a Ronald Colman picture, *A Double Life,* helped Chayefsky to a hamburger and coffee for a few weeks.

The networks were wary of Joe E. Lewis appearing on any of the variety shows that shared the tube with cowboys and inane fathers, heads of inane families. When Walter Winchell booked Lewis for a guest shot on his popular variety show, NBC came close to panic. The network contact man was ready to jump off his ratings. In order to ease the pain, a phony monologue was put into the first draft of the script. The monologue was as filthy as anything B. S. Pully could have come up with. (Pully, a legend in the annals of raw filth, once appeared onstage holding a cigar box in front of him. When he raised the lid of the cigar box, a prominent part of the comic's anatomy was revealed. With that for openers, Pully went into a long list of the grossest four-letter words. After thirty seconds of four-letter words, Pully said, "Oh, excuse me. I thought the mike was on!")

Not quite perfect Pully, the monologue in the Winchell script was enough to shatter the network contact man. Raising himself to his full two foot three, the network man said, "I'd burn the studio down before I'd let this show go on the air!"

In a spirit of conciliation, the show's producer replaced the monologue with the words Lewis intended to say. The network was thrilled with the exchange. Not one of the new jokes was excised.

After the show, before leaving to appear in Las Vegas, Lewis came up to the club. He happened to be carrying the first draft of the script. Buddy Hackett asked if he could glance at it. Lewis said, "Sure. Look at my monologue, you'll see what the networks get away with!"

Joe E. Lewis would have turned down most if not all of the offers to appear on television. Actually a shy man, Lewis didn't really relish performing. The business was worth the effort because it brought him lots of money. Lewis needed the money so he could indulge in gambling, one of his truest loves.

Joe E. Lewis's gambling habit made mine look like abstinence. The card room didn't excite him. Lewis felt that card games required no skill. To pick one horse out of eight that could die in the stretch or back up from a photo finish because he didn't like his picture taken demanded skills beyond those of a surgeon or a Raphael. (To help Lewis decorate a place he moved into, several of the "boys" from Chicago sent him some extremely good paintings. After the third painting arrived, Lewis said to his writer, Eli Basse, "They must think I'm made of nails!")

Lewis would have traded a dozen Michelangelos and the ceiling of the Sistine Chapel for one good tip on a horse. Lewis had more bookmakers than Random House. Joey Bishop told us one afternoon, "Dial any seven numbers. I bet you get a Joe E. Lewis bookmaker!" And if it's not a bookmaker, the guy'll give you a number for one!"

Touts sniffed Lewis out with a vengeance. One tout interrupted a pleasant evening of cocktails by showing up with a written introduction from another tout in Saratoga. Lewis invited the tout to join us for a drink and then asked, "You got something for tomorrow?"

The tout said, "I just got in. I haven't established anybody in the paddock area."

Lewis handed him a menu, saying, "Pick me out a good sandwich."

When the tout left later to find a nice hotel lobby to sleep in, Lewis turned to Lou Costello and me and said, "A good tout would have given me something to tide me over till he connected."

Costello said, "Hey, the poor guy's been in town a minute and a half."

Lewis said, "No matter how far a tipster is from the barns, he always *hears* something!"

Lewis lost money that hadn't been printed yet! His will was made out to the fifty-dollar window! In a movie he made, there was a scene of Lewis collecting a bet. They had to use a stunt man!

Early one evening Lewis was sitting around the Friars waiting for the Copacabana to open. He'd lent his suite in the hotel above the Copa to a friend in from Hot Springs, Arkansas, who was attempting to become friendly with a chorus girl. Into the club walked Bert Frohman, a singer. Never a star or moneymaker, Frohman also had bookmakers in all directions waiting for whatever he did earn. When he knew that he'd be out of town and away from the means to call in his bets, Frohman often bet future races by the numbers—the number four horse in the sixth on Thursday. On Tuesday, the number two horse in the eighth.

This one day, Frohman was unhappy to the verge of tears. He told us at the table, "I have a club date tonight and I lost my music!"

Lewis said, "Bad handicapping!"

When playing in Las Vegas or any of the gambling towns, Lewis was able to squeeze in a few hours at the crap tables. This was a courtesy extended by those who ran the casino because they knew that in a matter of forty-five minutes Lewis could lose enough to wipe out the salary he was supposed to get. (Mickey Rooney was good at that too. Before his first show when the New Frontier was reopened, Rooney lost the works. Backstage, as they waited to go on, Rooney consoled Joey Forman, his gifted straight man who was to be paid out of Rooney's pocket. Rooney said, "Joey, I want you to know one thing. I realize I lost all your money. I realize that we'll be here three weeks working for absolutely nothing. I want you to know one thing— if you're going to be upset I'll understand!")

The rumor, false but enjoyable, was that Joe E. Lewis, being a toy for the mob, no longer worked by contract. Each week he received a decent sum so he could look affluent, but what he played with at the table was Monopoly money. The markers didn't count. Neither did the winnings, an issue that seldom came up. It's nice to think that Vegas has a heart. Vegas could afford to have a heart with Joe E. Lewis because he was the poster boy for "unlucky."

Lewis himself admitted his lack of good fortune with "I was never lucky. Even when I was a kid, when I went on the merry-go-round, I got the only horse that limped!"

Gambling didn't own Joe E. Lewis. Gambling had a partner that came in bottles. Lewis had a black belt in scotch. Lewis drank only scotch. A diabetic, he had to limit his sugar intake. Scotch had no added sugar. Once a day Lewis took insulin for his disease. Never less than thrifty, Lewis opened a new vial for each injection. The vial contained a week's shots but Lewis passed on the other six days' worth. His logic couldn't be disputed—"If it comes in a bottle, you're not supposed to leave it over!"

Starting to drink before dusk teased the city, Lewis kept going as long as there was scotch in the house. Not a drunk by Toots Shor's definition, Lewis was merely a determined drinker. (Toots Shor, the restaurateur, was also the Emily Post of the imbibers.) Shor made the rules—A man wasn't drunk if he could count to zero! A man wasn't drunk if he could fall down under his own power! Rule 4b indicated that a man wasn't drunk if he could go to work the next day. Applying 4b elevated Lewis's status. Lewis could empty Scotland while sipping away the hours, but the next day he was ready to work. He did two shows even though he didn't know that he'd done two shows. Rarely, ever so rarely, Lewis managed to show the effects of a ripsnorter. On one such occasion, J. C. Flippen, the actor, said, "Joe, I've never seen your eyes so blood-shot before."

Lewis said, "You should see them from the inside."

What made Lewis even more remarkable than most of our other lovers of the grape was his ability to absorb 120 proof with so little food. Others, like Jackie Gleason, could down a few too, but Gleason had to have food along the way. Since the boozer's world is almost always indoors, Gleason, among the many, had no idea of time— A.M. and P.M. were concepts from some alien planet. Gleason could sit down at six in the morning and eat twelve ears of corn and most of a roast beef.

One night, after having spent hours trying to beat a ringer in pool, Gleason got the urge for corn flakes. Passing the Round Table on the way to a corner where he could slurp away to his heart's content, Gleason looked at the slices of pie and pieces of cake upon which we were desserting. He made a face and said, in disgust, "After cereal?" (Frank Tinney, a great comedian and boozer, also needed food. He explained one day, "I eat a lot of food, because when I throw up I hate to think it's whiskey!")

Shortly before a dinner in which the Friars Club was to honor Joe E. Lewis, some of us sat around nursing a martini or screwdriver. Robert Merrill happened to bring up the subject of drunk jokes. "What," Merrill asked, "are the ten funniest drunk jokes?" We were off and running.

Jolson the Great

Every time Jolson looks in the mirror he takes a bow.

Oscar Hammerstein, Sr.

Jolson takes a look at a girl and knows what kind of past she's going to have.

Jack Durant

Jolson couldn't have more women eating out of his hand if he was a waiter.

Harry Hershfield

If Jolson had his life to live over he would still fall in love with himself.

Ed Wynn

Jolson and I are the two greatest entertainers in the world.

Sir Harry Lauder

Why do the rest of us bother putting on makeup?

Sophie Tucker

In 1929, Al Jolson suggested that the Friars honor him. He was willing to give *two* nights to the affair if an ordinary three-hour dinner wouldn't suffice. From another star the request would have reeked of vanity. In this case it was just Jolson being Jolson.

Jolson had been honored by the Friars twice before but the events hadn't impressed him. At one affair, George Gershwin, still taking bows for his recent "Rhapsody in Blue," played a medley of Jolson's big songs. Jolson wasn't overwhelmed. Without him, he felt, the songs lost something. Hearing this, Gershwin said, "On Mother's Day, Al must send himself flowers."

The fact was that Jolson had rescued "Swanee" from a fate worse than Carmen Lombardo. Without Jolson singing it at the Winter Garden one night, Gershwin might have been spared his biggest popular hit. Great songs poured out of Gershwin for years, but none went as high on the charts.

Actually, Gershwin, in his early twenties at the time, wasn't bothered by the seeming dependence on Jolson. Gershwin was more concerned with the fact that Jolson was a Lothario bent on leaving no ladies for the taking by others. Obviously deprived in Brooklyn during his teens, or held back by a mother like mine, Gershwin also wanted to set world records with the ladies. The week of my seventeenth birthday, I ran into him as he strolled down Seventh Avenue with two young ladies. I asked for an intro. He declined. At the club, explaining his reluctance to my brother Phil, older than I and a true man of the world, Jolson said, laughing, "I live in dread that someday I'll run out of new women."

Phil said, "There's a hundred million of them."

Fred Allen said, "There won't be by tomorrow. Jolson's show is dark tonight and he has the evening free."

Because Jolson was so certain of his magnetism, he sometimes traveled dangerous paths of love. With a dozen stunners to pick from, he decided one time on a beautiful dark-haired lady who happened to be the girlfriend of a mobster named Johnny (Irish) Costello. Costello happened to be the jealous sort and volatile. Jolson wasn't deterred. Persisting, Jolson won the round and the fair damsel named Ruby Keeler. Texas Guinan, for whom Ruby worked as a dancer, told me a few years later, "Your friend Jolson came close to being alley meat. Irish was going to put some holes in him, but Owney called him off."

Owney Madden was Guinan's husband, the owner of the club, and a power in Manhattan. "Owney liked Mom songs," Guinan explained. "When Jolson sang 'Mammy,' it made Owney cry." Owney Madden didn't live to enjoy many more Mom songs. Disgruntled because he was forced to take a pay cut when business slowed down, the club's doorman shot his employer. At the club, Groucho Marx told us, "Instead of airing their differences, the doorman aired Owney."

Jolson's cockiness radiated in all directions. He had no doubts as to who was the greatest performer in the world. So certain was he of his ability to seduce an audience, he once stopped a play in the first act, told the audience that sets and story weren't needed, and ordered the curtain closed. He proceeded to sit down, tell the audience the story of the play, and hold everyone in the room breathless as he sang all the songs. Never for one moment did he doubt the coming ovation. (My mother went to "school" on Jolson. When I was tentative about a joke or unsure about a sketch, my mother would say, "Learn from Jolson. The audience is only sure when you are." When I wavered, I took from my mother. She sure was sure.)

On the air with millions of ears listening, Jolson insulted a hotel he'd stayed at. The hotel sued. At the end of the trial, before going to the theater where he was in *Hold On to Your Hats,* Jolson came to the club and told us the result. "The guy wanted a couple of million bucks. I ended up giving him four tickets to the show!"

George Burns said, "You certainly know how to hurt a guy!"

In what is still the unsolved mystery of 1933, Judge Crater pulled his famous disappearing act and was never heard of again. Jolson said, "Offer him my house seats for Saturday; he'll be there!"

A Stone Age Sinatra, Jolson came around after beating up Walter Winchell. Told that he should have considered the power of the press, he said, "A newspaper doesn't get down on one knee like I do!"

In one of his shows Jolson did a number in Russian. He asked the great Russian star at the Met, Feodor Chaliapin, to come see how well he did it. At the end of the show, Chaliapin asked, "Which one was the Russian song?"

Unscathed, Jolson answered, "You sing slang!"

Jolson was doubtless spoiled by his worshipers. He had "groupies" with stature of their own. Tommy Hamlin, a shirt manufacturer, followed him everywhere. He was willing to sleep in the lobby of the hotel in which Jolson was a guest.

Jolson called Sam Lubalin, his dentist, from California. His tooth hurt. Sam closed his office for good, came to California, and never left. He filled two bicuspids and ended up with a piece of Jolson's end of the pictures.

One eulogy wasn't enough to send Jolson off after he died. It took two packed houses, one in New York led by Eddie Cantor and the other, a stirring ceremony, in California conducted by Jessel.

Jessel looked at the big crowd and said, "Jolson turned them away again!"

In 1986 a television commercial appeared in which the background music was a Jolson impressionist singing "About a Quarter to Nine," a Harry Warren–Al Dubin song he introduced in a movie in 1935. It was on the tube recently when I was in a department store trying to get instructions on how to use my VCR. (Ruth insists that she'd like to record one show before we both die. Ruth doesn't think much of my ability to work with things mechanical or electronic. Ruth believes that Berle and a screwdriver could destroy civilization as we know it.)

The salesman in the store was demonstrating the ease with which he could record the whole twentieth century. Nearby, three teenage girls had glanced at the row of sets on display and started to hum along with the Jolson sound. One girl, a blond with a row of freckles across her boxer nose, said, "That's a cute song."

One of the other girls, also a blond with a Camp Beverly Hills T-shirt on, said, "Who's singing?"

The salesman, twenty-two at most, turned from me and said proudly, "That's Al Jolson!"

The girls nodded and walked away. The salesman turned back to me. I said, "How do you know Jolson?"

He said, "I saw the movie."

Because I liked him, I was sorry that he had never seen the real Jolson at the Winter Garden.

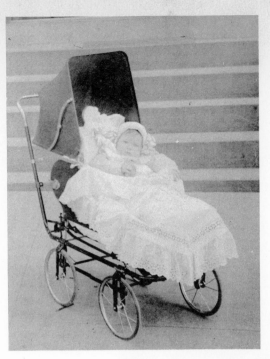

My first limo in 1909, at ten months.

A vision at eighteen months—this could explain my later love of dresses.

A trio of fathers: Jack Pearl's, Jack Benny's, and mine, 1934.

My mother at Lake Arrowhead in 1949. Sometimes her act was funnier than mine.

TOP LEFT: In 1912 I could have been another Heifetz, but a cow stepped on my hand.

TOP RIGHT: Modeling paid well in 1914—two dollars a day, but no meals.

ABOVE: "Floradora," 1920. I was the one on the right—not the girl! The dresses came later.

RIGHT: In the "Tidbits of 1919," I learned how to be shy . . . for twelve minutes.

ABOVE LEFT: Jack Holt was everybody's favorite star in 1922. Taken at Paramount Studios in Hollywood.

ABOVE RIGHT: In 1922 I went to California and met Hoot Gibson, the cowboy star, so I'd have something to report to the Round Table.

LEFT: The best report card I ever got.

Professional Children's School

Record of *Milton Berlinger*

Year 192*2-3*   Grade *8*

Subjects	Sept.	Oct.	Nov.	Dec.	Jan.	Feb.	Mar.	Apr.	May
Arithmetic	B-zon	B-	B-	B+	A	C	A	P	
Spelling + Composition	B-	B-	B-	B-	B-	B-	B-	B-	P
Reading	B	B/C	B	B+a	C+	B	P		
History		B	C-	C+	B-	C+	C+	B-	P
Geography		C+	C	C+	D	D	B-	C-	P
Science			B-	B-	B-	D		B-	B	P
French			C	C		C	C		P
Thorndyke	Reading test								

Average	C+
Days Late	
Days Absent	
Deportment	

ABOVE: Proof of who had the long pants. This is me on my 21st birthday. Honest!

RIGHT: By 1927 the word for me was—dashing!

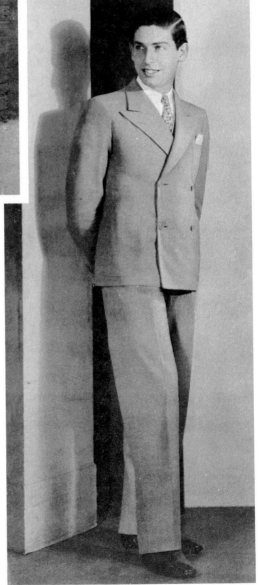

ABOVE: 1931. *(Richardson Studio)*

RIGHT: Chicago in the 1930s. There were crowds—lots of them trying to get *out* of the theatre!

BELOW: In 1930, Charles Renthrup, a Memphis promoter, gave the world an exhibition between me and Joe Gluck.

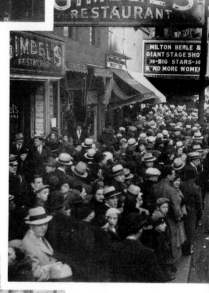

ABOVE: By 1936, my motto was "Anything for a laugh on stage."

RIGHT: In 1937, returning from Hollywood, I played Garbo.

BELOW: Things I just happened to mention at the Round Table . . . in all modesty, 1943.

ABOVE: My humble arrival in California, 1950. (*Metropolitan Photo Service*)

BELOW: Jonie Taps in the double-breasted overcoat and the music placard welcome me to California. Obviously it was a spontaneous demonstration my mother knew nothing about.

I could have been
Irving Berlin.

Back to my old tricks.

Friars Club logo.

ABOVE: The original Friars Club in New York, 1923.

LEFT: The Friars Club in New York today. (*Sam Siegel*)

BELOW: The Friars Club in L.A. (*Irv Antler*)

George M. Cohan

Geo. M. Cohan | *March 1920* | XI Irving Berlin
Jimmy Walker | V Daniel Frohman | VIII Sam Harris | XII Bugs Baer
Willie Collier | VI David Belasco | IX Raymond Hitchcock | XIII Ben Bernie
Will Hayes | VII Tom Wise | X Eddie Cantor | XIV Joe Laurie, Jr.

Some of the early Friars.

SOME of The FRIARS in The FRIAR'S FROLIC, MAY, 1916

Standing Left to Right—1 Andrew Mack 2 Neil O'Brien 3 Jas. J. Corbett 4 Harry Kelly 5 Felix Adler
6 Harlan Dixon 7 Geo. Daugherty 8 Vaughn Comfort 9 Johnny King 10 Tom Dingle 11 Eddie Garvey
12 Julius Tannen 13 Geo. Sidney 14 Tommy Gray 15 Bert Leoy

Seated Left to Right— 1 Max Figman 2 Laddie Cliff 3 Will Rogers 4 Sam Harris 5 Jerry J. Cohan
6 Louis Mann 7 Fred Niblo 8 Geo. M. Cohan 9 Lew Dockstader 10 Frank Tinney

ABOVE AND RIGHT: Will Rogers

George Jessel

George and Gracie, 1923

Jack Benny, 1922

Carl Erbe, a top PR man, paid the price for bringing Jess Willard, the giant on the left, to the attention of Jack Dempsey. I met all three the second time I came to Friars. (*A.G. Wight*)

Roscoe "Fatty" Arbuckle on the night before his famous trial.

My mother thought he was such a nice boy—Bing Crosby.

ABOVE: Two out-of-work Friars—
Jolson and Jessel in the '20s.

RIGHT: Tony Canzoneri loved
movies, right hooks, and the Round
Table.

Franklin Roosevelt and Herbert Lehman (seated in the middle) gave us class
in 1924. A closer look will also show Sidney Howard, the playwright, Victor
Moore, Pat Rooney, Jimmy Lord, and Eddie Dowling.

Sophie Tucker handing me a check. She must have thought I was her husband Al.

ABOVE: In 1936, a crooked card game with Tommy Mack at left and Bert Gordon, the mad Russian, in the middle. This is the reason I can no longer get into a card game.

LEFT: Ed Wynn—the Perfect Fool.

A Friar by dint of having broken the club in the '50s.

Caruso

Two people understand Enrico Caruso's English.
Only one of them wants to!

John Barrymore

At the 1916 Friars Frolic in honor of Caruso:
Those of you who care to speak Italian on this
occasion, please feel free to do so. There are many
non-English-speaking people with us tonight.
Among them—the Italian Consul General, the
head of the Italian Trade Commission, and the
Mayor of Ithaca, New York!

George M. Cohan

I never worry about insulting Enrico Caruso at
the Friars Round Table. He doesn't hear a word
we're saying because he's too busy looking down
and eating everything in sight...including place
settings!

Irving Berlin

I'd heard of Enrico Caruso, of course. In the house we had all his records. Everybody did. You couldn't make it across East Harlem without Caruso music coming out of every apartment window. Caruso made $150,000 a year from record royalties in those days. That would push him way past platinum today. Also, a buck in the early part of the twentieth century had no taxes chewing at it.

111

Classical music and its musicians weren't my cup of tea in 1920. (I don't think I liked *tea* at that time. I liked egg creams, chocolate sundaes, and any sodas made at the soda fountain except green ones. I don't like green to this day.) Although great opera stars like Risë Stevens, Robert Merrill, and Lauritz Melchior, the Wagnerian tenor, guested on my radio and television shows over the years, to this day I don't rush to start the car when the opera comes to town. Ruth manages to get me to a ballet by booking my bets on which swan wins. Or to *Rigoletto* by giving me five points and an aria on the tenor most likely to get stabbed by the chubby guy with the goatee. At times she has also brought up the words "divorce" and "community property." I've countered with a fierce glance, a look of defiance, and "Yes, dear." One time I reared up and said, "If you think you're going to get me to that opera, you've got another 'think' coming!" She had another "think" coming, so I went!

All I knew in 1920 was that I'd played on several bills with amply endowed divas and starched baritones. I wasn't in love with the "screamers." When they sang they got an ovation and wiped out the act that followed. Theater owners and bookers liked them. They worked cheap. In Pennsylvania there were Italian singers who'd sing everything Giuseppe Verdi wrote for two dollars. Unless opera singers were big stars, they made few demands. The owner had all those other Italians hanging around the Sons of Italy hall near the railroad station. In six seconds they could be in show business and have the complaining act at the railroad station waiting for the next milk train out of town.

More than anything, my background taught me that opera singers kept other acts from sleeping between shows because they vocalized all the time. The only thing worse than vocalizing Italian singers were ventriloquists. Vents hung around backstage talking to their dummies. It was spooky.

Not all Italians who sang opera in vaudeville were really Italian. Sharing the bill with me for a week at the Duchess Theater in Poughkeepsie was a Benjamino Verducci, a son of Pisa and a product of the Leaning Tower Opera Company, who, by popular demand, was making his first appearance on this side of the Atlantic. His real name was Harry Rubenstein and the Pisa his folks came from was around the corner from Warsaw, Poland. Verducci/Rubenstein didn't make the route with us to Pennsylvania. The Italians down there *knew*. (I ran into Verducci/Rubenstein at the Rajah Theater in Reading, Pennsylvania, the next year. A name job had turned him into Luxor Bergeron, the toast of Marseilles, France.)

One minute after I met Caruso I knew he was a real Italian. I suspect that his accent was laid on a little thick in self-defense so he wouldn't have to match lines with everybody else at the Friars Round Table. What did come out was covered with marinara sauce.

My suspicions didn't surface until the third or fourth time I saw him. On that occasion, while taking a pen from his shirt pocket to sign a picture for a Friar whose sister in Chicago was going to die if she didn't get an autograph, Caruso saw a big blot of ink on his shirtfront where the pen had leaked. He let out a stream of good old Anglo-Saxon epithets, unadulterated by passage through Italian ancestry. He cursed the manufacturer of the pen, the maker of the ink, the mothers and grandmothers of both, and his own wife, who had gifted him with the "f———g" contraption. She was a dumb broad! Et cetera! Each word came out loud, clear, and American. I said, "Mr. Caruso, you curse pretty good in English."

He said, "Emergency!"

A beat later, Caruso, the accented, rejoined us.

At the first lunch, Caruso laughed at everything twice—once at the original punch line and again after he'd translate the joke in his head. Then he'd repeat the English punch line. The dial telephone had just gone into use that week and the subject came up after a brief discussion of the fortune Caruso had just been paid for a concert in Mexico. Commenting on the new phone system, Corbett said, "Now we can get a wrong number without an operator!"

Caruso laughed, did his translation bit, laughed again, and said, coming up with *his* subtitles, "Now we gonna operate the number!" Or words to that effect.

Cohan said, "Caruso, you've been coming to America since 1903. When are you going to learn the language?"

Caruso answered, "I spik." Starting to count on his fingers, he went on, "A hunert thousand, a hunert ten thousand, a hunert twenty..."

(I liked Corbett's joke. I asked him if I could use it. Billy Van said, prophetically, "Go ahead, you may never ask again!" Van had the right to assign Corbett's joke to me. He'd written it earlier. A few, very few, performers prepared material for the daily lunch gathering. Not the funniest man since Attila the Hun, Corbett needed mucho help. Much of it was provided by Van.)

For a Round Table lunch in 1922, after Will Rogers's return from several years in Hollywood, Corbett had a line, "Will Rogers couldn't have been in Hollywood. He still has the same wife!" Forewarned, the Round Table for the day with Joe Laurie, Jr., the storyteller, and the pride of New York, Jimmy Walker, as centerpieces, managed to stall any attempt to bring up the Oklahoma Cowboy's return. Finally, Rogers walked in. Corbett readied himself. In on the gag, Rogers asked, "Isn't one of you bastards going to congratulate me? *Before* I left Hollywood I got a divorce!"

Laurie said, "Couldn't you have waited till Corbett told his joke?"

For an opera star, in spite of the many jokes made about his appetite, at least during the time I knew him, Caruso wasn't a heavy eater. Frank Tinney said that Caruso could make sparks come from a knife and fork! I never saw Caruso in an advanced state of gluttony.

I had an inkling that opera stars knew their way about a menu. It's a belief I still have. In the 1950s, when my wife, Ruth, and I went to Hollywood, we were invited to a party at Lauritz Melchior's house on Mulholland Drive atop Los Angeles. Sitting in the Friars that afternoon, I mentioned the party. Kirk Douglas asked what time the party would get started. I said, "It starts at seven."

Douglas said, "The way Melchior eats, you better get there at six-thirty or the food'll be gone!"

The Berles arrived at eight. Oddly, the appetizer tables were a little bare. Never one to let an open wound go by without tossing a little salt at it, Ruth told Mrs. Melchior, "Why don't you open a few of your gifts? Maybe some of the people bought you food!" (The Berles get a lot of first invitations to parties and dinners. It's the *second* invite that's tough.)

Caruso didn't shy away from a big steak, but he didn't charge into it as if the Russians were coming around the corner. He did like his bread. So did I. At that age I could undo a whole bakery in fifteen minutes. (On Sunday mornings, one Berle son was sent to buy a dozen fresh kaiser rolls and a dozen Danish. It was never me. One time my three brothers all had pneumonia. I wasn't given the chore. I think my folks sent a neighbor's dog. It ate two Danish. My folks figured they'd come out ahead anyway.)

Caruso had a special relationship to his vino. He didn't drink it neat and down the gullet. He sipped, chewed, and talked to it. After each mouthful he'd laugh as if the wine had told him a private joke. At lunch he was a two-liter man and not a hair out of place. He was also a one-man oven, smoking five cigars and ten cigarettes during a long meal. He averaged, he told me, twenty-five cigars a day and five packs of cigarettes. I asked him if all that tobacco didn't bother his throat. He said, and this is close, "Come tonight to hear me cough *Don Giovanni!*"

The last time I saw him was at the Friars in July of 1921. He offered me free tickets to a charity concert he was giving in Brooklyn. I passed on them. I didn't know he was dying and the concert would be his last.

After Caruso passed away, I told Eddie Cantor that I'd turned down tickets to the concert. Cantor said, "Milton, I feel sorry for you. That theater holds twelve hundred. Twenty years from now you could have been one of the two million people who say that they were part of the twelve hundred at Caruso's last concert. But *you* wouldn't be lying!"

Will Rogers on Opera Stars

Will Rogers is a country boy. And he owns most of it!

Frank Tinney

A good composer has nothing to fear from a man with a lariat.

Victor Herbert

For what Will Rogers is costing me a week, it would be nice if he talked faster!

Flo Ziegfeld

At the Friars in 1923, Will Rogers reminisced about an endless week in Seattle, a city with an inclination toward rain and in which "there's not much to do if you aren't a pair of galoshes!" Without the Oklahoma twang laid on too heavy:

"We had this here Italian tenor on the bill. He was fresh from his 'last' engagement at the Metropolitan in New York. Course, when he plays New York, he's fresh from the San Francisco Opera House. It's kind of hard for an opera singer to play St. Louis because there's no place far enough for him to have had his 'last' engagement in.

"The best thing is to book them in as coming direct from La Scala in Milan. Nobody'd be fool enough to check up on that. Although folks who like vaudeville are a suspicious breed. In Denver

117

some man asked if I really had Cherokee blood in me. For the sake of the Pantages circuit I was ready to bleed for the man!"

After a brief pause to carry out the laughing wounded, Rogers going on, the twang sneaking in:

"Mr. Vitoro came out. He nodded at the applause, then stood around for ten minutes tucking at his shirt cuffs and adjusting his fine coat. He finally nodded to the audience, which got him some more applause. He nodded again and again. He nodded some more. Each nod meant applause. When the audience was about nodded out, Mr. Vitoro's accompanist, Mr. Garvelli, came out. He stood around and nodded to the audience and to his boss and then back the other way. He nodded to the stagehands, to the pit, and to the darn piano.

"Mr. Garvelli sat himself down, stretched his fingers, had a change of heart, and nodded to Mr. Vitoro. They both nodded for a while. About two hours into that heap of nodding, Mr. Garvelli managed to find a reason to play and he did so. Mr. Vitoro joined up with him soon afterwards.

"The first number over, here comes the nodding again. And the worst thing is—the two of them rehearsed four encores and were planning to do every bedarned one of them! And they did!"

Rogers might have been slightly jealous. He didn't believe his voice matched those of the Vitoros of the world. At the Round Table, but not that same day, Rogers said, "I have the kind of singing voice that could make a starving locust give up new wheat!"

During his second stint in the Ziegfeld Follies, Rogers worked his rope and told the audience, "I got into playing with this here rope and talking kinda odd. There was talk of me singing some in this show. I figured if I was ordered to sing, it'd be better if it was *me* that had the rope!"

A final Rogers comment on opera: Reading in early 1928 that the Met was doing an opera in English, Rogers said, "That stuff's more dangerous than I thought!"

Coogan—The Kid

*Never let a kid actor live longer than is
necessary.*

W. C. Fields

*Little Coogan didn't steal many scenes, but he
did borrow a few.*

Charles Chaplin

A wistful lunch in the early fifties. Jackie Coogan was in New York to play the last few local theaters that were still showing variety and vaudeville. He'd called me to see if I knew a writer who could help him with his act. He was tired of doing "drunk" material that wasn't even his in the first place. He'd borrowed it from the "Mad Dog" routine James Barton did for years. Coogan wanted his own material.

I invited Coogan up to the Friars for lunch. I also called a writer who might help. (I won't mention his name because he never showed up. If he came begging today, I wouldn't even give him an intro to Henny Youngman. On second thought, it might be better to give an intro to Youngman! It would serve him right!)

Movie buffs know that Jackie Coogan was the kid in Chaplin's *The Kid*. Adult actors today can still learn from his performance. Most movie buffs don't remember that Coogan was a superstar. Louis B. Mayer offered him a million dollars to come over to Metro. Today that would be the equivalent of fifty million. Just for signing a contract. (And the kid didn't even have a good curve ball!)

119

Arthur Knight, one of Hollywood's favorite film historians, insists that there is no time on earth when a Jackie Coogan picture isn't being screened somewhere. It could be in Burma, Tonga, Mali, a small town in Mexico—somewhere a Coogan picture is playing.

Coogan also owned a giant slice of downtown Los Angeles for several years. Much of it was traded for desert property in a little town called Palm Springs. The timing was bad. Palm Springs wasn't yet *the* Palm Springs.

The money went. Coogan grew up and the hair went. Still he had enough going to enable him to woo and marry a pretty starlet named Betty Grable. I had nice hair, yet *I* never came close to marrying Betty Grable. I did dance with her once. In 1944 she and Harry James, her husband by then, were in New York as part of a tour to get people to buy war bonds. After their show the three of us went to a nightclub where I asked if I could have the next dance. She nodded but said, "No dipping. I've heard about how you dip!"

I happened to mention our dance to the Round Table the next day. Humphrey Bogart asked, "Is she a good dancer?"

I said, "She's okay, except she keeps trying to lead."

Bogart said, "Follow her! Wherever she wants to go!"

Television fans who like to scrounge around the old shows can still see Coogan as Uncle Fester in *The Addams Family*, a series based on *The New Yorker* cartoons of Chas Addams.

So Coogan came to lunch and we waited for the writer to appear. A little less than thrilled at being stood up and not overly joyous about his future, Coogan said to me, "Milton, I'm here waiting for a writer. I'm going to pay a thousand, two thousand for an act that I'll do in the Loew's Boulevard in the Bronx. Or the RKO in Syracuse. Why am I doing this, Milton?"

"Because you blew your loot!" I answered.

(I once asked George Sanders why he'd signed to perform on a dreadful variety show. He was supposed to dress up like a British cowboy and wear a monocle. He'd have to do jokes he hated. "Why on earth abuse yourself like this?" I asked.

Sanders said, "That's the price I have to pay because I blew all my loot when I was young!"

Sanders found another solution later in life. He married bank accounts. When the bank statements came back finally marked zero, he took the pipe.

What I really remember about George Sanders is his being dressed in a tux, spiffy with a Nöel Coward cigarette holder somewhere in the vicinity of his curled lips, and his accompanying himself on the piano as he sang chichi English songs. Bad Cole Porter, but he gave it class.

Coogan and I ordered some food. He mused on, "Tonight I'm taking a subway to Brooklyn and I don't even close the show."

I said, "You'll kill them."

Coogan said, "When I was three years old I sat in the lap of the Queen of England. Where the f—— do I go from there!"

I didn't even try to make a joke.

The next afternoon Coogan came by to tell me to destroy all the tapes of the day before. He hated to feel sorry for himself and it wasn't the way he wanted to be remembered in anybody's book of memories. Then he went on to tell me about his safari to Brooklyn. Not self-pitying, just reporting what he thought was funny. "We got to Canarsie early. Next to the theater there's a little cafeteria. We went in for coffee. A lady comes over to me. She's bashful, as if she's afraid to ask whatever it is she wants to ask. I smiled at her. A fan is a fan. Finally, she said, 'have a bet with my husband. Are you Jackie Coogan's father?'"

Two wistful lunches.

By George, He Had It

*George S. Kaufman looks as if he has his hair cut
by a Con Edison power surge.*

Groucho Marx

*Kaufman doesn't believe he's Shakespeare's equal.
He does feel that Shakespeare comes close!*

Alexander Woollcott

Kaufman has no bigger fan while he lives!

Josh Logan

*Kaufman believes that he was put on Earth to
satisfy all women. He's already finished the
Western Hemisphere!*

Fredric March

*Nobody named Kaufman should make that much
money.*

Adolf Zukor

*I didn't come to the Round Table to praise
Kaufman. That's why Kaufman is here.*

Victor Moore

*He was a different man to every woman. The
name he signed on the hotel register proved that!*

Oscar Levant

George S. Kaufman looked like Woody Allen when Allen had hair.
Not as handsome as Allen, Kaufman managed to overwhelm women
with his wit, charm, and an inner electricity that charged the air.

Kaufman also overwhelmed me with the best set of verbal fangs on or around Broadway. A charter member of the Algonquin Round Table, Kaufman was seldom topped. Dorothy Parker, another member, ribbed him once for having failed to conquer a young actress newly arrived in New York. Kaufman answered, "Dorothy, some women don't get laid a lot by choice!"

Another afternoon Alexander Woollcott raved about the first act of a Kaufman play he'd just read. He believed, with Kaufman, that it was the best thing the playwright had written. Franklin P. Adams, the newspaper columnist said, "Let's go on to something else."

Kaufman said, "Frank, please respect the man's right to agree with me!"

Finding the challenges at the Algonquin less than adequate and the pickings on Broadway slim one afternoon, Kaufman stayed home with his wife. He worked on his new play as Mrs. Kaufman played decorator, a pastime Kaufman allowed her so that he'd be allowed his. Mrs. Kaufman decided that she needed new living-room drapes. Bothered by momentary writer's block, Kaufman decided to accompany his wife to Bloomingdale's department store.

At the drapery department of Bloomingdale's, Mr. and Mrs. Kaufman were greeted by a salesman. The salesman fawned over them and failed to sell them on any material presented. Mrs. Kaufman said that she'd wait with the drapes. The salesman asked, "Is there anything else I can do for you?"

Kaufman said, "Do you have a curtain for a second act?"

The next day Kaufman, still in search of a curtain, soothed his racing mind and came to the Friars. The phone rang as if on cue. The phone call came from one of his conquests who had decided to use our lunch at the club at a time to let him know that she was rather pregnant. Into the phone, Kaufman said, "Oh, you must want the other George S. Kaufman, the one who wasn't shot up during the war!"

On three different occasions Kaufman was at the Friars when he heard from young ladies who had helped a rabbit to an untimely death. After the third he said to me, "Just once I'd appreciate it if the rabbit was only in a coma!"

Kaufman enjoyed writing my kind of one-liners. "Writing lines for you," he told me, "doesn't tire my hair!"

In breaking from trouble he was having with another play, Kaufman tried to think of something that could get his mind as far away from the play as possible. He decided that one-liners for Berle might do the job. He sent them over to me with a suggestion that, if I liked them, I should give a check to an unwed mother, as he was probably the father.

The lines intended for my use were as good as his second act. I so informed Kaufman by telephone from the club. Concluding, I told him, "How come you don't send that crap to Groucho Marx?"

Kaufman said, "Friendship!"

Kaufman was being gentle because he might have felt that I was still wounded by his remark to me years before when I was twenty-three. Having heard about his new musical, *Of Thee I Sing,* I asked him if I could play the part that later went to William Gaxton. (At twenty-three I volunteered for every part that came. I came within an inch of playing De Lawd in *Green Pastures.* I turned down Maxwell Anderson's *Elizabeth the Queen* because the money wasn't good and I couldn't show my legs. I already had the wardrobe. To this day, I go for "it." My mother taught me, "Go for anything big because they don't know either!" My mother also had utter faith in me. Toward the end of her life, my mother said once, "Milton is a triple-threat man. And two more!")

Kaufman wasn't impressed by credentials issued to me by my mother. He hemmed and hawed and explained there was a reason he and Morrie Ryskind couldn't give me the part.

"What's the reason? What's the reason?"

"I can't think of it right now."

Knowing when to press and when to let go, I backed off. We had a bite to eat and talked about the world. An hour later Kaufman said, "I got it. I remember the reason."

I'd forgotten our original discussion. I said, "The reason for what?"

"The reason why we can't give you the part."

I said, "Oh, what's the reason you won't give me the part?"

Kaufman said, "Because we don't want to!"

It was in our card room that Kaufman's star glistened brightest. A brilliant bridge player, he detested bad players. Fate, jealous perhaps of the Kaufman mythology, managed to partner him with cripples whenever possible. In one session he was teamed up with

a partner for whom hanging was too good. In bridge the bidding is
a crucial part of the game. Each bid is intended to inform the partner of the holdings in the hand. This partner had no idea of what
he was doing. The team reached contracts a cheating Culbertson
couldn't have made. On a contract of four spades, the partner put
down his cards to reveal the "dummy." Kaufman was stunned. His
partner, unaware of impending doom, said, "I'm the dummy. If
you don't mind, I'll go to the bathroom."

Kaufman said, "Good. For the first time tonight, you'll know
what you have in your hand!"

Later in the game the bad partner bid seven, which is the highest bid in the game. It declares that the bidder will take every trick.
Kaufman studied his cards and bid eight—eight hearts.

"What kind of a bid is that?" the partner asked.

Kaufman said, "It's a Morrison bid."

"But we can only take thirteen tricks."

"In the Morrison bid you concede defeat but you lose only half
the points." The other players went along and a hand of Morrison
was played.

Fate can be vicious, so a situation arose later where the bad
player felt defeat staring him in the face. He bid eight diamonds.
The contract was his. The hand was played out and the defeat cost
Kaufman's side many points. The bad player asked, "That was a
Morrison bid?"

Kaufman said, "A Morrison bid can only be used once a night!"

Understanding finally got through the bad player's thick skull.
At the end of the session he volunteered to pay Kaufman's losses.
"To whom should I make out the check?"

Kaufman said, "The Cunard Line and try to be on it."

Kaufman returned to the card room later in the week. Chico
Marx invited him to be part of a bridge foursome, pointing to the
empty chair, which happened to have been the one the bad player
had sat in earlier. Kaufman declined, saying, "That idiot loused
this seat up so badly no one can play in it!"

At the Round Table, George Burns drew the ultimate picture
of Kaufman. We were talking about difficult choices. Arthur Tracy,
an accordionist who called himself "The Street Singer" and par-
layed the idea into stardom, had just told us that he had opted for
a trip to London rather than a major engagement in Chicago. Dave

Chasen, later the restaurateur, said, "That's not such a tough decision. That's not an impossible choice."

Burns said, "An impossible choice is when George Kaufman is in the middle of a seven-spades game and there's a broad on the phone and she's just used her last nickel!"

All's Well That Ends Welles

The most dangerous sport in the world is lending Orson Welles money until next week.

Paul Stewart

(A memo)
Orson, if you find out what the picture is about before you finish shooting, send me a note.

Harry Cohn

Orson Welles loves to take things for gratis.

Sir Alexander Korda

One thing about Orson Welles. When he goes somewhere there he is.

Joseph Cotten

Orson Welles is a true heavy weight...No, what I meant was that he carries a lot of weight...No, I mean, he's a whale of a guy...No, no...They don't come any bigger. Forget it!

Mike Todd

Orson Welles has done everything. Fortunately the police weren't around at the time.

Tommy Chong

One line sums up Orson Welles. When he came into the club one afternoon, somebody said, "There but for the grace of God goes God."

129

A line used earlier to describe William Jennings Bryan, it was the essence of Orson Welles.

I met him in 1936. We happened to see *Modern Times* the same night. We both knew one another by sight so there was an immediate smile of recognition. I asked him how he had liked the movie. Welles answered, "It needed better editing."

Twenty-one at the time, Welles wasn't being the youthful renegade who likes nothing. Welles was already being Welles. Whatever it was, Welles believed, he could do it better. *Citizen Kane* proved that it wasn't empty vanity talking.

I saw him again at a political dinner months later. There was the same smile of recognition, but it was shallow. He honestly couldn't remember having talked earlier.

When we became friendly over the years, tied together by our mutual love of magic and card tricks, Welles still remained apart. He was an island. Around him was a circle of space that kept everybody out. When he laughed, always with at least two chins moving up and down, it was deep, guttural, and what George S. Kaufman called "Faustian."

At the club one afternoon, Everett Sloan, a mainstay of the Mercury Theater company, told me that Welles was the best phony laugher in the world. When Welles laughed, Sloan believed, he wanted something. Another giant with the company, Paul Stewart, said, "When Orson calls with a smile in his voice, he's already lying." Stewart knew. Welles got to him four times to play scenes in a film epic about a director. Welles gone, the movie will probably never be completed and never would have reached a final cut even if Welles had lived. Each time Welles called, Stewart asked, "Is the money there?" Each time Welles said, "I have the money. I even have for the union and the pension." Each time there was no money to pay the actors, unions, pension plans, or, for that matter, the lunches. On the third trip downtown for location shots, Stewart found Welles was serving Almaden wine, a gift from a company for which Welles had done commercials. Stewart ended up getting two bottles of wine. Welles bragged that none of the company players got free wine. Called a bastard for lying about the money, Welles said, "Some bastards became kings of England."

Welles made his own rules, was surprised that they were accepted, and laughed to himself at the fools who let him get away with murder. After the Friars Life Achievement Award dinner for Gene Kelly, Welles dropped into the Friars for the box of cigars I'd promised him if he showed up for a bow at the dinner. He didn't show up for the dinner or the bow, but having entertained the thought felt that the spirit of the deal was honored and thus payment was due. Welles, it must be pointed out, believed that after one of his checks bounced three times, the debt was paid.

Unnoticed by most of the Friars, Welles sat with me at a booth on the other side of the room. (It's a weird human quirk. We associate a person with a place or a look and the pose is set forever. Dress up a Denny's waitress in an Ungaro gown, present her at court, and who would dream that four hours before she was lost in butter patties. I have that problem with Ruth frequently. I'll come into the bedroom and she's not quite sure of how she knows me. When she finally remembers, she laughs and asks, "How come the bus dropped you off in this room?")

In the quiet of the booth, Welles asked me about the cigars. I said, "You didn't show up for the dinner."

Welles said, "I watched *Singing in the Rain* and that seemed to be enough."

I called my son to bring Orson's cigars over. We continued to talk about the big dinner. I wondered why President Reagan hadn't put in an appearance. He was a charter member of the California Friars and Kelly was an old acting pal. I said, "All he had to do was get into Air Force One and zip out here."

Welles said, "Maybe he couldn't remember the number of the flight."

A little later we were talking about Europe. Welles was dying to go to Europe, but he had no money. Now at the booth, Tom Bosley, the man from Glad Bags and *Murder, She Wrote*, was surprised that Welles wasn't able to pick up some television guest shots. Bosley mentioned *Love Boat*. Welles passed on *Love Boat*.

"But you want some loot quickly," Bosley said.

"Dear man," Welles said, "you don't seem to understand. Imagine this scenario—I'm dying of a vicious disease. I need an expensive operation. I'm also thrown out of my house for nonpayment of rent and have to spend the freezing winter nights in the snowy city. And I haven't had a glass of wine in two months, not even shit wine. And I haven't smoked a cigar in a month, not even one of Milton's semi-goodies, the cigars he tips with. And I'm forced out into the boulevard where I have to sell apples for a nickel each and I stand there for six, seven, eight, sometimes ten hours a day begging people to buy an apple. I have reached absolute bottom! Then I'd do *Love Boat*!"

Bosley said, laughing, "So you'd do one?"

"Yes," Welles hissed, "but the deal is off if I sell one apple!" Welles went on, "You may ask why if I have apples to sell, don't I eat one?"

Lou Edelberg, an attorney who'd heard the tirade from the next booth, leaned over: "Yeah, why don't you eat an apple?"

With as much disdain as he could muster, and he could muster a lot, Welles answered, "Because I didn't want a meal. I wanted a finish!"

The quintessential Welles is mirrored in an anecdote truer than apocryphal. A discussion of Welles brings out the five-dollar words in me. The big words also remind me of the day that I found out Welles was mortal. One of the guests on the Dean Martin roast for Muhammad Ali, Welles was sent a routine written by the show's writers. Welles called and asked if it would be all right if he reworded some of the material. He did so. The day of the show, Welles showed me his handwritten copy of the routine. A third of the bigger words were misspelled. It was as if Mt. St. Helens had erupted and Jell-O had tumbled out. Later I told Ruth about how the discovery had shattered me. Clutching me to her bosom, Ruth said, "If he likes to play for money, invite him over for Scrabble."

Welles, the anecdote starts, was getting ready to open a Broadway show. Naturally, it being a Welles production, he ran out of money. The company providing the sets wanted some money or there'd be no sets. The costumers said—no money, no shirtees. About a dozen unions were coming down on the head of the young genius. Louis Quinn was the writer of Welles's radio show and a close friend. Welles said to him, "How much money do you have, Louis?"

Quinn said, "A few hundred dollars."

"Will that be enough to get us to California?"

"I think so."

Soon Welles and Quinn were en route to Hollywood. Arriving, Welles asked, "How much do you have left?"

Quinn said, "Not much."

Welles said, "We don't need much."

Welles and Quinn took a cab to Beverly Hills, making a brief stop at a flower shop where Welles bought a beautiful red rose. The taxi then took both men to the Beverly Hills branch of the Bank of America.

Rita Hayworth, from whom Welles was separated at the time, banked there and had neglected to remove her husband's name from the various accounts. Welles signed in at the safety-deposit desk. A moment later he looked down at a mint of money, most of it given by Harry Cohn to Miss Hayworth whenever she acted up. Orson removed just enough to cover his bills in New York, placed in the rose, closed the box, and returned it to the wall holder.

Welles and Quinn returned to New York. The play opened as scheduled. Louis Quinn didn't get back his investment. Obviously, Miss Hayworth didn't either.

When she discovered the pilferage, Miss Hayworth demanded repayment. Through her attorney she promised to have Welles tossed in jail if the money wasn't wired to her bank by the following Monday.

Welles called the florist in Los Angeles and had a rose sent to the attorney.

In accepting an award for *Citizen Kane,* Welles declared, "I will be remembered because I was a parade."

He was a genius. He refused to be puny.

Funny Music

A Medley of My Hit

I think they bombed the wrong Berlin!

Harry Warren

*Mack Gordon sleeps music, he eats music, he
drinks music...now if he could only read music!*

Frank Loesser

*Once you've heard all of Buddy DeSylva's songs,
you've heard one of them.*

Ira Gershwin

*It's fitting tonight that we honor a musical giant.
A man whose songs shall live forever. A man
whose music brings happiness and a glow to our
hearts. A man who is the highest symbol of
music. But enough about Mozart. Let's talk about
Richard Rodgers!*

Jule Styne

The day after Churchill made his "blood, toil, tears, and sweat"
speech in 1940, I walked into the club with my brother Frank. The
club looked empty. The card room, usually going full blast by early
afternoon, was just about deserted. Puzzled, I asked around. One
of the garment-center guys said, "They're all home writing a war
song."

I realized suddenly that all the songwriters in the world were Friars and possibly all Friars were songwriters. Lou, the garment-center mogul, wasn't just reciting poetry. Inspired by British heroism, the songwriters *were* working on numbers. Tin Pan Alley was on a war footing long before the army. An event like the Churchill speech or the evacuation of Dunkirk made the lights burn late in Tin Pan Alley. It also seemed to empty out the Friars Club for the time it took to put down thirty-four bars of a catchy tune.

Walking into the dining room, I found that I wasn't surprised at the plethora of songwriters at the Friars. It was always thus.

Cohan, Berlin, Victor Herbert, Harry Warren, all of ASCAP and BMI showed up at the club at one time or another. Sigmund Romberg could be found off in a corner, generally with a guest whose Hungarian accent was as thick as his. (Romberg was once challenged to name all of the Broadway and Hollywood musicals he wrote. He came up with fifty-four. He actually wrote seventy-nine!)

Jack Norworth was a steady too. He wrote what's surely the most popular summer song ever written, a little thing called "Take Me Out to the Ball Game."

Nobody had to look too hard to find Louis Alter. His "Manhattan Serenade" is, as far as I'm concerned, the best song written about New York. Another song of his was Franklin Delano Roosevelt's favorite pop tune—"Twilight on the Trail." The Bing Crosby record of the number is in a special display case at the Roosevelt Museum in Hyde Park, New York. (Slightly Republican and ever-sentimental, Crosby told us at the Round Table, "It's not a big deal. I made a penny and a half!")

In the et cetera that follows the partial list of Friars songwriters and composers, I'd have to make room for—Jimmy McHugh, Harry Ruby, the Tobias brothers or, as most folks would know them—"I Can't Give You Anything But Love," "Three Little Words," and "Miss You." The et cetera to the et cetera would be ten feet long.

At an average rehearsal of a Friars Frolic it wasn't hard to find the likes of George Gershwin, Paul Frances Webster, the wordmaker for a whole slew of Oscar tunes, Harold Arlen, and, always an elder statesman, George M. Cohan.

Elderly and a little cranky toward the end of his career, the Yankee Doodle Dandy found it hard to like other people's material. He wasn't crazy about the book of *I'd Rather Be Right*. The musical by George S. Kaufman and Moss Hart was too jokey for him. The music and lyrics of Richard Rodgers and Lorenz Hart were ordinary. A spoof of FDR and the White House, the play was no good, Cohan felt, because it was about Roosevelt. Ten feet to the right of Attila the Hun, Cohan didn't adore Roosevelt. Along with Eugene O'Neill's *Ah Wilderness*, the play turned out to be one of Cohan's biggest successes.

(Isn't that the way it always happens? Not necessarily. I hated *Spring in Brazil*, but starred in it. It flopped. Cy Howard, a writer whose best lines seemed to surface after Broadway flops, couldn't wait to get to the Round Table to tell me, "I saw *Spring in Brazil* last night. Milton, you should have gone to Brazil in the spring!" To pinpoint Howard just a little more for the few people who may have forgotten him, he was the gentleman about whom I first said, "He has more talent in his little finger than he does in his whole head."

Cohan never forgave Kaufman, Moss, Larry Hart, and Rodgers for reviving his career and bringing him back from the dead. Cohan told Ira Gershwin at the club, "If the show were a fish, I would throw it back."

Gershwin looked up from his cheese plate and said, "I'd like to be waiting for it with a net!"

If being knee deep in musicmakers at the Round Table wasn't enough, those hungry for more had only to traipse off to brownstones, apartments, and offices where other Friars songwriters were gluing words and notes together to make songs for our Frolics that would be sung by Hildegarde, Helen Morgan, Sophie Tucker, Richard Tucker, Frank Sinatra, Bing Crosby, and incredible masters of melody like Errol Flynn, Lou Costello, and George Jessel. (George Burns told us, during a well-deserved break, "Jessel sings like each note spent a week in his sinuses!")

Errol Flynn, according to Frank Sinatra, "the only Irishman incapable of carrying a tune," was a sport as long as there was champagne and buttered white toast.

The hard stuff was for other occasions. The toast, he explained, was "to keep me from sloshing!"

In the club for a Round Table bash or in some room as stars rehearsed, wall-to-wall with music people, you had to feel as if you were in the Brill Building. A massive structure at 1619 Broadway in New York through which Tin Pan Alley flowed like a vertical river, the Brill Building teemed with song people. Of course the resemblance ended there. The Brill Building looked as if it had never been new. Marty Melcher, Doris Day's husband a wife later, said, "The Brill Building was built condemned."

Jimmy Monaco, the man who came up with "You Made Me Love You," and thus a lover's anthem, didn't quite agree about the condition of the building. "The Brill Building would have to be rebuilt before it could be torn down!"

Sammy Fain, the writer of "Love Is a Many Splendored Thing," said that the Brill Building was built by the man who built the Roman ruins. "But much earlier," Mitchell Parish added.

Parish was the magician lyricist of "Stardust." With music by Hoagy Carmichael, "Stardust" is the champ. "Stardust" has been recorded over eight hundred times. Its message has been delivered in a hundred and fifty languages. An Israeli tank brigade sang it riding out to take on the Arabs during the Six-Day War. Reading about this in a magazine, Jack Benny said, "Between their singing and the Arabs dancing, how could it have been such a short war?"

In spite of the grime and one elevator that is rumored to have been the first Mr. Otis worked on, most of the songs that lovers have danced, kissed, and fought to came out of the Brill Building. Writers, song pluggers, and publishers ground them out twenty-four hours a day. Once in a while the factory whistle sounded a recess to the grinding and many of the citizens of the U.S. of Brill would close up shop and head for the Friars.

A few emigrés turned out to be normal and blended in with the fixtures. Many became Round Table fables.

Harry Woods, the writer of "When the Red Red Robin Comes Bob-Bob-Bobbin' Along," was a *series* of fables. Woods, first of all, was by birth an exception to the rule. He didn't come from the Lower East Side or Brooklyn like everybody else in Tin Pan Alley. Born in New England, he was a Harvard man who sang in church choirs. Also, he was always in perfect physical shape except for a minor handicap. Born without fingers on his left hand, he took on anybody and everybody. Bobby Clark, the Broadway star and comedian, yelled at him one afternoon across the table, "You're so tough, if cannibals cooked you, they would just eat the vegetables!"

There were lines galore about Harry Woods. Another one about his toughness came at the table from Sid Gary, the singer: "That Harry Woods pretends being tough. He probably wouldn't hurt a lion!"

Some guest asked innocently about what had happened to Woods's fingers and Lou Holtz explained, "It was due to an accident. Harry had the right of way, but the other guy had the car!" Not true, of course, but funnier than a birth-defect joke!

Woods loved to fish. Often he'd disappear and head up to New England to troll for some big ones. After a week or two, he'd return, head for the club, have a few belts, eat a meal, and hang around, waiting to be greeted like a long-lost brother by everyone who came in.

Mort Dixon, with whom Woods collaborated on such giant songs as "I'm Looking Over a Four-Leaf Clover" and "River Stay Away from My Door," hated to be left in the dark when Woods took off. This one evening, Dixon ran into Woods as both reached the door together, Dixon leaving and Woods returning from a long trip. Without breaking stride, Dixon asked, "Going somewhere?"

Bla Bla, a real nickname, honest, belonged to a black car thief from Brooklyn who seemed to have a lock on the distribution of hot wheels in New York. His ring handled a hundred and fifty cars a week. He tried to sell one to Harry Woods one day. Woods said, "I only have to go to Sixtieth Street. Can you steal me a *cab*?" (Bla Bla was finally caught. Because justice works in strange ways, his final fate was only to be expected. Not able to get away from cars, he was sent to Sing Sing, where he ended up making license plates. Seeing the item in the newspaper, Sid Gould, Lucille Ball's cousin by marriage and Gary Morton's cousin by fate, said, "I like people who do government work!")

To help Harry Woods play bass on the piano he often wore a peg, much like the peg leg worn by pirates in every Maureen O'Hara picture before John Wayne. When Woods played the piano he drummed the chord with his stump and played melody with his good hand. One day an obnoxious drunk made fun of Woods's infirmity. Woods took it for a while, then, when the abuse kept coming, lifted his peg and whacked the drunk silly. Others at the bar had to pull the songwriter away. Calm returned. There was a round on the house. A customer asked the bartender who the mad pummeler was. The bartender answered, "Oh, that's Harry Woods. He wrote 'Try a Little Tenderness'!"

At the Round Table I suppose I was drawn to tunesmiths because I've been sensitive to the songwriter's craft since I was about twelve years old.

Early on my mother taught me that one song could make me a star. She hunted down every writer who could come up with the smash lyric that could shove me into the limelight and keep me there.

By the time I was fourteen my mother had invested a hundred and fifty dollars in song material. When songs didn't work, and none of them really did, she pled poverty and tried to divest at fifty cents on the dollar.

One song was about a youngster working in a Pennsylvania coal mine. He had a canary that sang "Tawit, tawit, tawit." As long as it sang, no noxious gases were in the mine. Along came a gas cloud, boy and bird bit the dust together. But Alex the coal boy will live in a happy eternity. From his seat on a soft cloud he'll hear "Tawit, tawit, tawit."

Arthur Fields and Walter Donaldson offered us a song when I was fifteen. Before we could make up our minds, a vaudeville star, Willie Solar, ran with it. He won the brass ring with his version of "The Aba Daba Honeymoon." Ruth Roye borrowed it, added "Waiting for the Robert E. Lee," and was held over at the Palace for fourteen weeks.

Neither Willie Solar nor I suspected that the Aba Dabas would go on a second honeymoon sponsored by Debbie Reynolds fifty years later and give Debbie a best-selling record.

When the Berles weren't sniffing in all directions for material, I was writing. I had a pad of music paper that I'd found at an audition. I wrote lyrics. Music and its notes have always baffled me. To this day I can pick out "April Showers" on the piano with one finger. It's my encore too. And my second encore.

Limited to the words in my search for a perfect Berle vehicle, I wrote the beginnings of hundreds of songs. I wrote the start of ballads, aware that the world would never be able to resist a gangly kid in knickers singing about unrequited love.

I started to write a song called "No." There had never been a song "No." There still isn't in the ASCAP catalog. I wrote, "No, I didn't need you, No, I didn't care. No, you didn't need me, No, lala la la lala." That's as far as I got with "No." When I was working with Marilyn Monroe in *Let's Make Love*, I offered to rewrite it for her and make it sexy. Marilyn said, "No."

"Yes" didn't get as far as eight bars. The word itself is hard to musicalize. "Maybe" had composers waiting in line.

I began "mother" songs. I put different "mothers" through all kinds of hell. In one song she went blind. In another she was driven from the house by drink and an irate daddy. One "mother" I sent to jail. In the news there were stories of bad floods in Ohio and Indiana. About a thousand people died. I killed off one "mother" in a flood.

My real mother saved my little scratches and pieces of papers for years. When I was about seventeen, the thought of becoming a full-time songwriter appealed to me briefly. To show me how she felt about it, Mother threw out pads, loose pieces of paper, all the sensational lyrics I'd written. There was no chance I wasn't going to become a stage star, not with the Iron Eagle of the Berle family sitting out front.

Whatever the reason, to this day I'd sell my soul for a catalog of monster hits. I almost made a pact with the Devil. I was to become Irving Berlin. In exchange I was to renounce all the jokes and sight bits, all the laughter and applause. I came within this much of signing. I didn't go for the deal because the Devil wanted me to give up a week in Allentown, Pennsylvania.

Buddy Arnold, the only man in the world who can keep me from roamin' through the gloamin' when I tell a story, is a brilliant musician and songwriter. He was responsible for the big production finales on *The Milton Berle Show*. For a few pennies more, he and Woody Kling, the son of the king of horse-racing tipsters through his column in hundreds of newspapers, wrote openings too.

Kling and Arnold penned the song of the Four Texaco Men. Everybody in the country knew and hummed it. Frank Sinatra suggested that we add some other lyrics and record it. But what did Sinatra know about music and recordings! He turned down "Tawit, tawit, tawit" at the club a few years ago. He thought I was kidding!

I refuse to let Buddy Arnold go home at the end of the day until I'm sure that I'm not about to come up with a sensational melody or lyric. His wife may need him. Shows he works on may need him. The UN, the Pope, and the FBI may need him desperately. I need him more. God forbid I should get an idea and he isn't around to get it down!

My handwriting is terrible. I could put down a fantastic lyric and never be able to read it back. I suspect "God Bless America" and the entire score of *The Sound of Music* got away from me that way. Buddy Arnold has great penmanship, spells well, and knows grammar.

I don't really come around empty-handed. I write a decent parody. Some years ago, using the melody of a lovely Victor Young song, "Lawd, You Made the Night Too Long," I came up with a version that is the only parody listed in the ASCAP dictionary.

Written as a wedding gift for a tailor, "Sam, You Made the Pants Too Long," became a standard. It seemed to blend perfectly with Joe E. Lewis's voice, which Al Jolson described at the Friars as "the only voice that sounds as if it was bought second-hand!"

Some of our other parodies have also rung the bell. When the Friars roasted Sophie Tucker, Buddy Arnold and I wrote a parody that kept them laughing. It was slightly risqué. No, that's not it. It was dirty. It certainly was. Had it been just a little more obscene, Tucker, the patron saint of off-color, would have used it for a Mother's Day card! You had to know Tucker to understand. Truck drivers took from her. Still, she was capable of singing a ballad that could make a listener cry a river.

To keep the record straight, I have to confess that Buddy Arnold wasn't my first choice for pen pal. Long before his sanity came into my life I searched out many potential partners. While I was working on a Friars Frolic I asked George Gershwin to write a number with me. I had the idea—a song about Jesse James's wife. The whole world thinks he's rotten. To her he's an angel. Gershwin liked the idea. "It's a good idea, Milton, but I don't want to hurt my brother, Ira." Ira was responsible for some of the outstanding lyrics that were glued seamlessly to George's music.

I said, "One little number with me will hurt Ira?"

Gershwin said, "He'll see me crying. What hurts me hurts Ira!"

I think Gershwin chickened out because our one collaboration would have led to another and another, and then an endless flow of "anothers." (Frankly, I would never have had the time for him!)

Gershwin picked on other people too. At a rehearsal, George Raft started to sing. Gershwin stopped him. "You're singing in the wrong key."

Raft said, "What's the right key?"

Gershwin said, "There is none!"

Others, asked nicely to share the warm sun of friendship at the

Round Table, have also given me the cold shoulder. Settling for someone who had worked with Gershwin instead of the master himself, I asked Irving Caesar to co-write my Jesse James number. By now I've probably asked everybody in ASCAP and BMI to work with me. The writer of "Tea for Two," Caesar knew something about "southern" music. He'd written "Swanee" with Gershwin. Actually, they even wrote it in one day in Gershwin's house while six men played poker in the next room.

"Swanee" wasn't a hit the first time around. Jolson tried it out at the Winter Garden, was well received, and put it into *Sinbad*.

No such luck with the ballad of Jesse James. Caesar passed because he didn't know much about Texas. I never did get a chance to explain where the James family lived.

At one of our luncheons we honored radio stars. The fearless defender of the people, the man who righted every wrong, Graser, the Lone Ranger, never got to the luncheon. A pickpocket relieved him of his wallet and the fare. My Lone Ranger song died on the vine.

Later in the day, at the Round Table, Graser was miserable. The thief had taken his identification, his driver's license, several honorary badges, and all the personal things men keep in their wallets. Lou Holtz, a master storyteller, who didn't shrink from a one-liner, tried to cheer him up: "They didn't get your mask!"

The ability to write good song material wasn't necessarily one of the criteria for getting into the Friars. More important seemed to be the eccentricity that could be generated by the applicant. From the beginning Friar songwriters had that special quality that separates them from the purely sane.

Rudolf Friml, a fine Friar, never played with a full deck. Interviewed on a local radio show in Los Angeles, he spent a half hour threatening to sue every other composer for stealing from him. Lerner and Lowe had taken the music of *My Fair Lady* from ten of his shows.

On another radio show Friml threatened also to go after Rodgers and Hammerstein for the musical theft. His threats could have been marked up to an advanced age, but they actually reiterated things he had told newspapermen fifty years before. Friml went after Victor Herbert in 1917. *Her Regiment* was, Friml contended, taken from a musical he had written in 1912. Herbert challenged him to pianos at forty paces. Each would get themes and have to write a song. Friml said, "That would only give him more to take from me!"

Victor Herbert didn't have his porch light on all the time either. During a full moon Herbert wrote four operettas at one time. Herbert went from one to the next only after guzzling vino from the area he was writing about. "Vino" for Italian music, "vin" for a French locale. One of the operettas was *Ameer,* a show about Afghanistan. Afghan booze isn't easy to come by even at the Friars. An Afghan bootlegger was discovered. He invented Afghan scotch. It looked and tasted a lot like brandy, and the young bootlegger, under close scrutiny, resembled a young actor in blackface. It did the job.

I didn't know Victor Herbert well. I met him briefly in 1922 at the club. Sam Harris, the producer who became fat and sassy working with George M. Cohan for years, introduced me as a young stage performer. Mr. Herbert was involved with a succulent slice of roast beef. He said, "Young man, I will look up soon!"

Other musical giants did look up often enough to make me happy. I continue to appreciate the songwriter.

A story I brought to the Round Table that more or less sums up the poor songwriter, battered by bad singers and awful musicians: Lenny Posely is a terrible singer. He can't carry a title. He changes keys in the middle of a note. He sings so flat he has to work *under* the piano. Show business has offered ten thousand dollars to the first person who kidnaps Posely's throat!

Posely is hired to work a club. He opens with "Everything's Coming Up Roses." The audience hisses.

Undaunted, Posely goes on to a medley from *Oklahoma* and four songs by George Gershwin. The audience, openly hostile, starts to stamp its feet.

Posely presses on and sings "Impossible Dream," "Till There Was You," and "Some Enchanted Evening." The audience starts to throw bread and food at him.

When he sings "Over the Rainbow" and "Let It Be," there's a shower of half-eaten sandwiches, desserts, and ponds of thrown coffee.

Posely motions to the band to stop playing and stares at the audience angrily. "What the hell do you want from me? I didn't write this shit!"

Crooning Glories

*Anthony Newley has a great voice. It's a shame
that it's in Mel Torme's throat.*

> Jack Carter

*Jerry Vale will not be with us. He's in Lourdes
for his voice.*

> Pat Henry

Here's Liz Taylor's latest release—Eddie Fisher!

> Earl Wilson

*Frank Sinatra had a terrible accident. He was
taking a walk and got hit by a passing
motorboat.*

> Dean Martin

*You're great, Como. I have every one of your
album!*

> Jack E. Leonard

I made my debut as a band singer in 1938.

It resulted from a lunch. Sharing the Round Table for an afternoon was a worried Meyer Davis. He'd provided the orchestra for a fancy affair in Forest Hills, New York, but he was short a boy singer. The alto sax man in this unit who generally doubled as a boy singer was ill. Distraught, Davis went off to the phone near the bar to see if he could get the drummer to do the vocals.

At eight-thirty that night, unbeknownst to Davis, a Lyle Taylor, boy singer, showed up. Taylor looked a little like Milton Berle in a dark wig and a pencil-thin mustache. Abe, the bandleader, accepted Taylor's explanation that the gala was important and Davis had gone for the expense of a singer who didn't play an instrument. In the back of the hall, awaiting my debut, were two of my brothers, Ted Healy, the owner of a brilliant comedy mind and the force behind the Three Stooges, and Harry Ritz of the Ritz Brothers, an act from whom every performer stole.

My moment came on the fourth number. I faced the mike and started to sing a Joe Burke song from the year before, "It Looks Like Rain in Cherry Blossom Lane." One bar in, the band suspected sabotage. Not knowing all the words of the song, I made up lines. I managed to work in "sprain" and "drain." "Drain" let Abe know he was in trouble. He signaled the shortest chorus of all time. In the back, my fan club was hysterical. Healy's stomach hurt from laughter. My brother Frank thought I sounded pretty good. He had the best ear in the Berle family.

I sat down to mild applause from the nondancers at the hors d'oeuvre table. Abe didn't call on me again. After the first set, the joke over, Lyle Taylor went into the kitchen, changed from his light-blue jacket, and was never seen again.

How strange are life's turnings. Today I could have been Julio Iglesias.

It would have been nice if some of the singing Friars had allowed a note or two to rub off on me. Bing Crosby could have spared a C flat.

Bing Crosby was an active Friar. With his soft manner Crosby brought along a gentle, subtle, and literate sense of humor. Crosby came up to the club one afternoon and stopped to watch Jackie Gleason destroy Ben Bernie in pool. After each hit ball rolled into the designated pocket, Gleason kept gloating and called Bernie a fish: "Where has this fish been all my life? No mercy on this poor fish!"

The game over, Bernie thought out loud, "I wonder if I should play him again."

Crosby said, "I'd suggest you go north to spawn!"

At the Round Table later, Crosby watched George Jessel down some agonizing drinks. The soused Jessel, celebrating the end of another romance, took one sip too many, passed the point of no return, and, bango, his head went onto the tabletop. Crosby nudged him: "George, tell us when you've had enough!"

During the football season, Crosby lived for the score of the Gonzaga game. Since his beloved college played most of the juggernauts of the West, the score was generally lopsided. At one time St. Mary's had an awesome team. It played powerhouses of the day like Fordham University to a standstill. Coming in, Bing asked if anyone knew the Gonzaga score. Joe Laurie, Jr., the storyteller, ever eager to rub salt on somebody's open wound, said, "Halftime it was St. Mary's 42, Gonzaga zip."

Bing asked, "You didn't happen to catch *which* Gonzaga that was?"

Because Crosby was easygoing and liked lighthearted diversion, he collected amusing followers. Joe Frisco was one of his plums.

Blessed with a stutter that belied the sharp comedy mind that had made him a star, Frisco decided early on that a laugh from the wings was all he needed. When I was about to open for the first time at the Loew's State in Manhattan, I ran into Ted Healey. I told him that I wasn't nearly as certain as I was pretending to be. Healey said, "They bought you so they must like you and what you do. I have just one suggestion, Milton—never play to the band!"

Frisco played to the band, to other people in show business, and, once the wedding was arranged, to Bing Crosby. Walking down Forty-eighth Street with Crosby one midmorning, both men saw a punched-out fighter leaning against the wall next to a closed bar. The fighter's face was flat, his nose pushed in and shapeless. His cauliflower ears could have served six vegetarians. Not one tooth issued from his constant grin. Frisco said, "You'd n-n-never known they l-l-laid a hand on h-h-him!"

The comment drew a chuckle from Crosby and somehow his deeply imbedded but rare sense of charity. Crosby peeled off two fifties and handed them to the lost soul. Crosby and Frisco moved on, but after a few steps Frisco turned and called back to the fighter, "I only owe y-y-you a h-hundred now."

An hour later, they saw the fighter on Forty-sixth Street, now leaning against the window of a barber shop. This time Crosby got the laugh. "Business must be good," Crosby said. "He opened a branch office!"

After a fair stab at a career in the East, Crosby was signed up to become God's gift to the movies. A farewell dinner was thrown for him at the club. It was an ugly rainy night. The usual jokes followed, jokes about his voice, his hairline, which had already receded halfway down his back, and his Catholic fanaticism. Fred Allen was in the middle of a hot diatribe about how good a Catholic Crosby was. Suddenly a bolt of lightning flashed against the window. A moment later, a clap of thunder rolled out of the sky. Allen stopped and said, "Bing, I think it's for you!"

Taking a cue from the Statue of Liberty, the Round Table often welcomed singers from out of town. In the fifties, Maurice Chevalier made the Friars a stop on any trip to the United States. The womanizer that George Jessel always wanted to be, Chevalier considered it a sin if he didn't bed down all of his leading ladies. When he played opposite Jeanette MacDonald, the lady Nelson Eddy sang to later in all those MGM musicals, Chevalier was furious that he couldn't score with the lady. In that special French accent of his, he told us one afternoon, "I tried. I tried. I could get nothing from that MacDonald bitch. It was the second saddest day in the history of France!"

Frank Sinatra asked him, "Which was the saddest day?"

Chevalier said, "The day I could not go to bed with Grace Moore!" (Miss Moore was a beautiful opera singer who went into pictures after a few seasons at the Met. Chevalier tried to get her starring parts opposite him in hopes that the path to romance would be smoothed.)

Chevalier had a good sense of humor and loved one-liners. Hearing a joke, he'd translate it into French immediately and store it in his mind for later use. Everybody knew it. Most of us didn't care. I wasn't too big in Rouen or Marseilles. One afternoon, however, Jack E. Leonard announced that he was going to Paris. Chevalier asked, "Do you know anybody there?"

Leonard said, "Only my act!"

Chevalier's greatest accomplishment was his ability to avoid paying checks. In his entire life, Chevalier never picked up a tab. Frank Fay said, "Chevalier doesn't have to worry about the clap. He never picked up anything!" (Close to Chevalier, but never quite able to beat him to the winning line, were some other glue-fingered individuals. The Round Table had them covered—"Charles Boyer threw a nickel around as if it was a manhole cover!" "Boyer had an impediment in his reach!" "Boyer used to practice sitting with his back to the check!"

Also high on any list of nonspenders was the indefatigable Rudy Vallee. At lunch one afternoon, Pat Buttram said of Vallee, "He's so tight, when he winks his kneecaps move!" Buttram added, "Vallee gives no quarter. He gives no dimes either!"

When Vallee lived in New York, he breakfasted daily at Kellogg's Cafeteria on Seventh Avenue. For ages his bill was twenty-three cents. After several years, the tab went up to twenty-eight cents. At the club to meet Groucho Marx, who was going to appear on his radio show, Vallee complained, "Kellogg's is trying to get rich quick!"

Lou Holtz, Fred MacMurray, Henny Youngman, Al Jolson, Benny Davis, the songwriter, and other titans of thriftiness were in at the finish of any check-avoidance contest, but as a group, the columnists led every parade. Danton Walker, Jack Lait, Lee Mortimer, and Nick Kenny, the radio columnist, had black belts in cheapness before black belts in anything became fashionable. Kenny, especially, has had oratorios written about his frugality.

One afternoon we were gathered for lunch. Eddie Cantor was coming up to the club after a round of appearances for his charity, the March of Dimes. Kiddingly, I said that we should all have given him a dime when he showed up. Kenny said, "I don't have a check with me."

Most singers are easy marks. Tony Orlando volunteers for every charity and contributes on his own. One Friday before he was leaving to work in Atlantic City, he was supposed to talk about our annual big dinner. Time went by and Orlando didn't show. I finally said, "He's at the studio making a recording of the Puerto Rican national anthem, the Rodgers-Hart tune 'I'll take Manhattan.'" I went on, half-singing, "We took Manhattan, the Bronx, and Staten Island too."

Orlando finally appeared, apologized because his plane was late, bought two tables for the dinner, and asked what he could do on the show. Buddy Howe, the Friars Dean in new York, was appreciative of Orlando's largesse and, looking right through a seated Lou Holtz, master cheapie, told the young singer that he was showing the true spirit of the Friars. Holtz, whose total purchase in forty years hadn't added up to a third of a table, said, "We each give in our own way."

Dick Shawn said, "Lou when you find yours, we won't need anybody else!"

Always democratic, the Round Table accepted even the handsome with open arms. Of course our resolution is tested when somebody like a Tom Jones shows up. (When Jones performs on stage in Las Vegas, women throw their panties to him, their bras, their room keys. The best I can attract are dentures, torn Supp-Hose, and, once in a while, an industrial-strength girdle.)

Jones came in one afternoon about a week before we honored him. He was probably getting ready for the jokes we would throw at him—"Tom Jones's pants are so tight you can tell his religion!" "Tom Jones crossed his legs the other day. He's in intensive care!"

This particular day, however, Jones was out of costume and wearing a pair of loose-fitting pants. Seeing him, Bill Murray, the *Saturday Night Live* star and movie headliner, said, "Tom Jones doesn't look comfortable. They'd better give him a tight booth!"

George Dorsey knows the Round Table. That was his name before he changed it to Engelbert Humperdinck. Honest. Humperdinck lives in Beverly Hills. His home, once Jayne Mansfield's, is palatial and has thirteen bathrooms. Asked at lunch one day why he needed so many bathrooms, Humperdinck explained, "When I was a kid we lived in a dumpy place. There was one bathroom to service a half dozen families. I hated that. When I started to grow up, I promised myself I'd work hard, make a lot of money, and get a big house. It would have a dozen bedrooms and for each bedroom there'd be a bathroom. I got lucky and I did it!"

Norm Crosby said, "Same thing with me. I swore I'd have a house with lots of bathrooms. Today I have a house with eleven bathrooms. Today I can't go!"

Harry Groman was the Friars friendly mortician. He was one of the first people I saw after my successful bypass surgery. Returning to the club after my recovery, as I passed his table I said, "Sorry, Harry!"

Groman sat with us and asked Humperdinck what his actual name was. Humperdinck said, "Why are you asking? Do you know something?"

A little later, Humperdinck, in response to a question, said that he'd picked his stage name because it sounded romantic. Jesse White said, "That name wouldn't even be romantic to the Maytag Man's sister and she's lonelier than he is!"

As a singing Friar, Francis Albert Sinatra belongs with the first run of soloists. I met him in 1940. Tommy Dorsey, the bandleader, was a good pal and I tried to sell him a song for his boy singer. Dorsey and the boy singer hated the number. I love it to this day. It helped me get to know Sinatra. In meeting Sinatra, I met the source of a quarter of my act and forty percent of any Friars' roast.

Pat Henry, the comedian who opened for Frank for years, could talk about Sinatra endlessly and often did. "Sinatra," he said more than once, "loves good behavior. That table over there represents about a hundred years off for good behavior!" "Sinatra thinks of the press as family. How often I've heard him say to Jilly, 'Get rid of these mothers!'"

For years Jilly Rizzo was Sinatra's confidant and bodyguard. At the club once, I hit at the relationship with "Sinatra's not here this afternoon because he's at a taping. He's taping Jilly's hands!" Henry told of the time Rizzo went to a funeral and was amazed. He'd never seen anybody before who'd died of natural causes!

Take your pick from some of my other Sinatra specials—"This is the man who personally built the Eisenhower Hospital…and helped fill it!" "What a crowd is here tonight. I'd say 'mob,' but I know how sensitive he is!"

I added one after the Kelley book on Sinatra came out. At a dinner I said, "Kitty Kelley wanted to be here tonight, but an hour ago she tried to start her car!"

One story wraps up my sortie into Sinatraland. Frank went to a hospital once to entertain the patients. In one room, he stood over an old man and sang a song. About to leave, he said to the old man, "I hope you get better." The old man said, "You too!"

Frank, incidentally, has a few hidden talents. He is a fine artist. Hint—I'd love to own a Sinatra painting! He's also self-educated, but as aware of current events and history as any Ph.D. He also has a wallet that opens whenever a tear is shed within a hundred miles. Quietly, he hands out more than the loud ones give. That he has a few weak spots isn't in contention. We could wait a lifetime for the saints among us to count off.

Sitting at the table one afternoon, Sinatra put his life in perspective. His father's name was Marty. In '44 we threw a party for Marty because he'd been named Fire Chief in his hometown, Hoboken, New Jersey. Frank said to us, "When I saw Marty in his uniform, I saw a proud man. I keep looking for my uniform."

One singing Friar, however, had no doubts about himself. The aura of Asa Yoelson has always been so overwhelming, it has never allowed him to share a chapter with others, no matter how great. Even Sinatra.

"A one and a two-a"

Dis band should dis-band!

> Jack E. Leonard

Poor Guy Lombardo, he just died of confetti poisoning.

> George Burns

Ben Bernie plays torch music, and that's what should be put to it!

> Walter Winchell

Every man in Eddie Elkins' band lives music, sleeps music, eats music. It's a shame they can't play music!

> Lou Holtz

Glenn Miller played "In the Mood" as if he wasn't.

> Ed Sullivan

Artie Shaw gets married so often his clarinet has rice marks!

> Jack Benny

Buddy Rich is like a pet...if you raise gorillas!

> Johnny Carson

Danny Shapiro, the song and comedy writer, had a theory. The ending of vaudeville, Shapiro offered, helped change the population percentages of Friars. Vaudevillians, thrown out of work, looked around for a new profession. Since they were unequipped to do any work of socially redeeming quality, most of them picked up batons and became bandleaders. It required no knowledge, talent, or training to stand in front of ten musicians and wave a stick.

The merit of this theory was discussed at the Round Table. Alan King offered some support for the pros. "Did anybody ever see or hear Cugat play anything? He stood up in front of twenty guys with frilly shirts and did a rhumba with a dog."

"Agreed," said Red Skelton. "How about Sammy Kaye? Which instrument did Phil Harris play?"

William B. Williams, the disc jockey, said, "He played the drums."

I said, "He *drank* from a drum!"

Although no resolution came from our discussion, the theory seemed to be an adequate explanation of the changed scene. Where once every inch of Friar territory was host to a songwriter, bandleaders now cavorted.

What's more, Friars bandleaders were a special breed.

On one side of a chord, when the world and the Friars were new, stood John Philip Sousa. Sousa was a modest man who called himself "the biggest fraud in music since Beethoven." Sousa could lead sixty-five drummers and one fifer in the complete score of *La Traviata*, pretending it was a piece of cake as long as the beat was there.

Sousa loved drums and tubas. Ba boom ba boom baboom. Oompah, oompah, oompah. Ba boom ba boom baboom. De Wolfe Hopper, the star of the last theatrical show Sousa worked on, came around to the club one day after watching Sousa rehearse the orchestra for one of the rare concerts the composer gave during the last years of his life. Hopper reported, "Sousa wrote two songs for the concert. One is a lovely ballad." Clearing his throat, Hopper started to sing the "ballad": "Boom. Boom Boom Boom!"

Remembered today mostly for some martial compositions like "American Patrol" and "The Stars and Stripes Forever," which isn't bad remembering, Sousa liked to conduct less sanguine music too. Describing another charity concert in which Sousa conducted the orchestra, Walter Woolfe, the star of my "deflowering" show, *Floradora*, said, "Sousa played every waltz as if it were a march."

George M. Cohan asked, "Did he play any marches?"

Woolfe answered, "Yes, as if they were wars!"

Sousa and his concertmaster came to the club after a rehearsal. Both wore their gaudy braided show coats. With his imposing physique, Sousa looked like the prince in a Viennese operetta. Damon Runyon leaned over from the bar and said, "John, the princess called. She's eloping with the peasant boy!"

A teenager at the time, I was amazed at the friendship between Sousa and Irving Berlin. Sousa was a Marine. He'd actually served in the Corps. Harry Hershfield, the wit and a founding father of the Round Table, said one afternoon, "Sousa is tough. Last week he went to a gypsy to have his fist read!"

Irving Berlin, on the other hand, was small and thin and, even in his thirties, looked as if he had twenty-four hours to live. Hershfield had a line for Berlin too. "Irving Berlin," Hershfield said, "looks as if he forgot the first doctor and went right to the *second* opinion!"

Berlin and Sousa met while both worked on a show at the Hippodrome. A stab in the dark would hint that both composers were brought together by their love of America. We're talking heavy patriots here; for real too! Throw in George M. Cohan, and the Friars had a lock on saluting the flag. Jolson belongs in there also. World War Two almost killed him.

Only one slight tear ever appeared in the bond of friendship between Sousa and Berlin. Berlin never really knew how bad his voice was. One afternoon at lunch, the coming Friars Frolic was being discussed. Berlin wanted to sing a Cohan song. Cohan suggested that Berlin do one of his own numbers. Cohan added, "Better still, sing a Gershwin number. That'll make George sorry he missed the meeting!"

Had he been around, Sousa would have offered an alternate motion: Let's keep Berlin from singing at all! (Sousa said once, as drinks were being served, "Irving sings a song like the composer never had a father!")

It's possible Sousa was biased because Berlin couldn't sing "oompah oompah."

On the other side of the orchestral spectrum, and many many years later, was a tall, thin, heavy-lipped young man who had a dance band—Henny Youngman. His fiddle at the ready, Youngman was considered to be quite a catch for middle-priced affairs. His reports to us about the previous evening's dance were, already in the early thirties, sprinkled with the jokes he still uses today—"She was such an ugly bride, the fellows got on line to kiss the minister!" "Everybody in her family came over and gave the groom an envelope. There was nothing in them. Her family gave stationery!" "It was a meeting of the Elks—*real* Elks!"

Youngman changed the name of his band to fit the occasion. For a few months he even had a "society" orchestra—"Henny Youngman and his Society Kings!" Matched socks didn't agree with him. Youngman quit the Four Hundred. Asked why by Alan King, Youngman said, "I missed 'Havah Nagilah'!" (The mainstay of Jewish weddings, "Havah Nagilah" is played at least forty times during the wedding, dinner, and reception. The band only goes into "Sorrento" when the chef threatens to quit.)

Youngman gave up the band business for comedy soon after that. Harry Ritz summed it up: "Music's loss is comedy's loss!"

Youngman's desertion from the ranks didn't deplete the society orchestra supply at the Friars. There was always Meyer Davis. Davis probably played for more wealth and nobility than any other man with a tuxedo and two pairs of gold studs. Davis often played in Washington on a sunny afternoon and the Hamptons while the breezes blew at night. Few of the paying customers knew the real Meyer Davis at first, second, or third glance anyway. The leader's tuxedo was pressed, he smiled a lot, and he bowed politely—it had to be Meyer Davis! (In the California Friars we have our own Meyer Davis. Manny Harmon smiles more than Meyer Davis. On a day of real sunshine, his smile has been known to blow out eleven western states. Jan Murray once told us at lunch, "Manny Harmon could spot the Osmonds three teeth!")

Davis had the edge over Harmon in quantity. Davis came in bulk. At a savings of a few dollars, it was possible to buy a Meyer Davis orchestra sans Meyer Davis. The results were the same. Nothing faster than "The Yellow Rose of Texas" was played. No musician dared attempt a jazz lick. Songs more recent than ten years ago were taboo. And the band was polite enough to eat standing up in the kitchen!

Davis never made waves. Society was society and he was Meyer Davis and never the twain mixed. He didn't seem to have the gumption of a Fritz Kreisler. The great violinist was asked to a fancy party in Main Stem Philadelphia. The invitation suggested that he bring along his violin. Kreisler informed the local Perle Mesta that he charged ten thousand dollars to play. The hostess called him and said, "We'll gladly pay you ten thousand dollars, but please don't mingle with the guests."

Kreisler answered, "Oh, if I don't have to mingle with the guests, I only charge five thousand dollars!"

Similarly, Sol Hurok, the impresario, once told us that Marian Anderson, the amazing contralto whose range covered the whole planet, was asked to provide the music for a party in Maryland. The one proviso was that there be no "colored" people in her entourage, the request from a hostess who had no idea of the color of the singer's skin. Through her agent, Miss Anderson said that she had to have her money up front. The money was duly sent. The singer proceeded to send down her last two recordings. They were delivered by an Indian.

One of the dullest individuals ever recorded on the Richter Dull Scale, Meyer Davis had a reputation for being a wit. He hired a press agent, Eddie Jaffe, who flooded the columns with quotes by Meyer Davis. One week Jaffe's secretary, troubled by a family problem, forgot to send out the bon mots for the week, one or two usually sent personally to Davis so he could sparkle at the table too. At lunch Jack E. Leonard asked the orchestra leader, utterly silent and devastatingly dull, "Meyer, did Eddie have a nice funeral?"

Equally dull and cured in part by the power of positive press agents, Arthur Murray joined the table for lunch one afternoon. Let me take that back—the part about Arthur Murray being equally dull. The founder of the dancing school, a branch of which was in every city for years, Arthur was duller than Meyer Davis. Arthur Murray could blend into an empty room. A third blandness at the table went by the name of Ed Sullivan, a man who could light up a room by leaving it. Seeing all three, Red Buttons said, "The first one to fall awake wins!"

Something about playing society music has always attracted our musicmakers. A longtime Friar, one of the outstanding victims at the Round Table, was an ambitious bandleader, Eddie Elkins. He was a good musician, caring about his arrangements and sounds. He looked beyond the one-nighters to the day that arthritis might set in and decided that the best way to keep the wolf away from the door was to marry rich.

Before he played a date, Elkins checked out the number of eligible ladies in the family and ran a Dunn and Bradstreet on them. About to leave for a garden party in Old Westbury, not far from where the Vanderbilts cavorted, Elkins sized up the situation for us: "The daughter is thirty-three."

Jessel said, "Thirty-three isn't terrible. Of course I don't go that old."

Elkins said, "I wouldn't mind thirty-three, but she's the kind of thirty-three you don't see until forty-eight!"

Another potential was: "Pretty enough for the house and maybe the bank, but not enough to eat out with!"

A near miss was stupid. "She's cute, but she thinks Dunn and Bradstreet is an intersection!" (This one would have rated anyway, but her brother was a problem. At a lawn party, the brother entered a running race and was disqualified for skipping!)

We reminded Elkins that the idea was to marry rich, not beautiful or bright. (Or muscular.) The rest of us had all married beautiful and bright and we were in trouble. After a great pep talk as he was about to storm a wedding in Fort Lee, New Jersey, Elkins nodded vigorously. This was it. The lady checked out. The form declared her speed rating and staying power were out of the great mares of the past. Elkins said, "I'll take this one. But stick around the club late. In case I weaken, I'll call!"

We often helped Elkins out with suggestions for pairing. Mimi Baker, a prime choice, was a debutante and glamour girl. By the time she was fifteen she had been in every boozery and gambling joint in New York. We hinted that she was a catch. Elkins was interested until he read that Baker was dating Howard Hughes. Hughes was interested until he read that Baker was soon going to be sixteen. (In those days Hughes seemed to prefer young ladies who had spelling homework. After all, he still liked to play with model airplanes. His latest at the time was the Spruce Goose. Jessel commented on the Spruce Goose one afternoon. It was made of wood, so "it was really a model airplane, but because the kid had a big bedroom it got out of hand!")

When the threat of a Howard Hughes had passed, the Round Table matrimonial agency went to work on Elkins's behalf again. We even had royalty in mind for Elkins. A cousin of the Grand Duchess Marie, herself a cousin of the last Russian czar, and a part-time photographer, was available. Sophie Tucker was her best pal. Al Lackey became interested in putting one and one together when he learned that there was a finder's fee in it for him.

Lackey was unable to bring Russia and Elkins together at the bargaining table. For a long time Lackey lamented the financial loss. At the table he told us, "I had to go crawling to Sophie."

Al Bernie, the comedian, said, "How would she know you otherwise?"

Perseverance paid off for Elkins. He didn't take Miss Fort Lee of the Friday-night dance. It seemed that she was the daughter of an associate of a Mr. Abner (Longy) Zwillman. Longy would have taken a dim view of a marriage not made in heaven. He and his associates often showed their disapproval with cement.

Eddie Elkins did marry royally. Because the young lady wasn't of our faith and seemed to have a bias against those of us of Hebraic persuasion, Elkins was forced to play the WASP. The couple honeymooned at the Burning Tree Country Club in Washington. Our gift to them was a two-week subscription to a Yiddish newspaper. In spite of our largesse, the marriage did well. When last seen, Eddie Elkins was keeping time with his left hand and buying states with his right.

Paul Whiteman came by class without a ceremony or prompting by the Round Table. He looked as if he had been born to the purple, which he wasn't. The legendary horn player Bix Beiderbecke played with Whiteman. Beiderbecke called the leader "Mr. Whiteman." Beiderbecke explained, "You can't call a little fat guy 'Paul'!"

If class lurks in the bank account, Whiteman had it there too. By 1923, Whiteman was making a million dollars a year. When it came to throwing his name around, Whiteman had Meyer Davis beat in spades. Whiteman must have had two dozen right hands to conduct with because at one time in New York there were eleven Whiteman orchestras. Traveling across the country were seventeen more Whiteman orchestras. Whiteman even got paid when other bands played his arrangements.

Jack Pearl, of Baron Munchausen fame, told us at lunch one day about a fast train he'd just taken to bring him from Los Angeles to Chicago and then on to New York. He also mentioned that when he left Los Angeles, Whiteman was playing there. Arriving in New York, Pearl saw a billboard about Whiteman playing in New York at the same time. Actually, of course, it was a "Paul Whiteman" orchestra. When Pearl talked about the speed of the train he'd taken, Jack Durant, ever the comedian, said, "You ought to get on the train Whiteman takes!"

Whiteman lived up to his financial standing. The year new cars with air-conditioning came out, he debated buying a new one. At lunch Ed Wynn told him to spring for a refrigerated special. Whiteman said, "I'm not sure I need it. I keep six cool ones in my icebox!"

Whiteman was in George White's Scandals with a cast that could make the kid who puts up the marquee names shiver—W. C. Fields, Ed Wynn, Willie and Eugene Howard, Ethel Merman, and Rudy Vallee. When George White came downstairs from having blown another bundle at cards, Whiteman asked, "Why do we need so many opening acts?"

Whiteman became famous for "Rhapsody in Blue." Oscar Levant became famous for playing it. For a while Levant played piano in a band led by Friar Ben Bernie.

Slightly less famous than Whiteman, Levant became a great concert pianist, an interpreter of Gershwin, and toward the end of his life admittedly mad. Levant was the gentleman who said, "I knew Doris Day before she was a virgin!" He explained his absence from his usual haunts for a few days by saying, "I got malaria from *Panama Hattie!*" *Panama Hattie* was a show starring Ethel Merman. Levant had a comment for the show, its star, and music writer: "Irving Berlin can't write a bad song for Ethel Merman. If he does, you'll hear it!" Levant came to lunch one afternoon and in his best schizophrenic way told us, "I'm feeling fine and so I am!"

Ben Bernie was a nice man, so nice he was even liked by Billy Rose. Very few men, living or dead, could make that statement. It's not sour grapes on my part. I've been able over the years to put aside the fact that Billy Rose married again and again the same women I married again and again.

Rose feuded with eighty-six percent of humanity. Jackie Miles, another comedian with rare talent, said, "Rose has no prejudices. He hates everybody equally!" Rose had a vicious feud with Mike Todd. Rose would never come to the club if he knew that Todd was around. Mike bribed the receptionist to tell Rose that Todd had just arrived. Mike could be in China. It wouldn't matter—"Yes, Mr. Rose, he just came in."

Ben Bernie liked Billy Rose. Bernie stood up for Rose when the impresario married Eleanor Holm, the swimmer and star of the Aquacade, the show that Rose put on at the New York World's Fair. The show just about paid for the fair.

Rose would have earned himself a blinking light on Broadway for his songs—"It's Only a Paper Moon," "Without a Song," "For All We Know," and others numerous enough to make anybody jealous.

The evening of the wedding ceremony, Bernie threw a party for a hundred people at the Dorset Hotel. The guest list was impressive—Helen Hayes and Charles MacArthur, the Ben Hechts, George Kaufman, Gene Fowler, Paul Osborn, the playwright, and a smattering of Friars. Jessel came with the main dish. Bernie's wife, Wes, was impressed with the guest list and wondered why they couldn't have such fancy friends. Bernie said, "We will, as soon as the band can play *Hamlet!*"

If anybody ran neck and neck with Ben Bernie for the baton of the century, it would be Ted Lewis. Lewis had a band, yet he was much more than a bandleader. He was also a Friar and much more. Like Bernie's, his image had faded. It is doubtless easier to make out because performers still do impressions of Ted Lewis. Most of them weren't born when Lewis worked. He shows up in a movie somewhere between four in the morning and the dawn patrol, and that's about it. Maybe that's the way it should be. There is only room on the top for a few names at a time. However, to forget completely is sometimes to deprive. My son Bill sees an old movie once in a while and wonders why I rave about certain performers. Jolson was no Mick Jagger. W. C. Fields was no Robin Williams. Unfortunately, Bill never saw Jolson in his prime. He never saw any of the great clowns at their strongest. At the end, Garland was an echo. At nineteen she could rip your heart out with two notes.

Ted Lewis was one of those who come up corny today. "Me and My Shadow," which shows up as part of a show-biz tribute to vaudeville on the rare variety show evokes nowadays: "Cheesus Christ. Did you guys really sound like that?"

When Ted Lewis strolled out, top hat, cane, shoes sparkling in the stage lights, he took you for a stroll with him. In a Las Vegas showroom, there was not a sound during his performance. Drunks and unhappy losers shut up. The same respect was shown to Harry Richman, Sophie Tucker, Helen Morgan, and a few other performing giants.

Most of us in the Friars adored Ted Lewis because he had a

thing for the club. During some of the bad times, he housed and fed half the membership. When the big bad sheriff padlocked the front door for nonpayment of rent, he set up card tables in his apartment on Central Park West. Phil Spitalny, famous for his all-girl orchestra, walked the parquet floors between hands, looked out of the window at the sparkling view, and said, "If somebody tries to open the club again, I'll sue!"

Not a notorious wit, Spitalny came in one night, all agog. He'd just come up from auditioning twelve female accordion players. Each one had a fifty-inch bust. Spitalny said, "You never heard such screaming!"

On New Year's Day in 1938, Benny Goodman held forth in a giant swing frenzy that threatened to tip Manhattan. Every bobby-soxer within screeching distance of the city showed up. When we read about the session the next afternoon, Jan Murray said to Lewis, a clarinetist like Goodman, "Are you sure you need your hat and cane?"

Lewis said, "More than ever."

Lawrence Welk had a succinct way of describing the bandleader's plight. Welk owns half of Santa Monica, California—fifty buildings, resorts, banks, and the Pacific Ocean, all the result of waving a baton. Welk says, "It's a living."

Funny Business

They're as Honest as the Days Are Long (But the Days Are Getting Shorter)

Adlai Stevenson did a great job as Attorney General of Illinois. He arranged for the cops in Chicago to wear striped uniforms, so when they went to jail they wouldn't have to change!

Everett Dirksen

One week you're on the cover of Time, the next week you're doing it!

John Mitchell

Why are people picking on Nixon! He hasn't done anything!

Tip O'Neill

Ed Koch has done a lot for people, but so has Kaopectate!

Mario Cuomo

Eisenhower is running for President. What some guys'll do to get out of the army!

Harry S. Truman

On the highway of politics, Fiorello La Guardia is a Nash!

Jimmy Walker

The summer of 1955 had arrived. The last of my Buick shows came and went. While waiting to leave for the West Coast and my new show, I busied myself with the Friars. In the past I'd taken five minutes out every day to work on and rehearse my show. A year and a half before, I'd even allowed myself seven minutes to marry and honeymoon Ruth. We were married on December 9. Ruth wanted to get married on the seventh. That way she'd only have to remember one date for days of infamy. The seventh was a bad day. I had a rehearsal and then I had to rush over to the Friars so the guys could work me over. It was going to be tough enough trying to explain why a honeymoon took precedence over lunch at the Round Table.

Since I stuck my nose into every aspect of Friar life and business from menu planning to the testing of swizzle sticks, as the year's end started to creep up, I got into the gift-giving department, especially the money, liquor, wristwatches, and cash to be dispensed gaily to the many city employees whose paths crossed ours during the year.

The list had eight names on it. The expenditures came to less than two hundred dollars. These were normal gifts. I insisted on seeing the "real" list, the real "real" list. That was it. There was no secret list. Graft and payoffs had come on bad times. What was wrong with all the fire and food inspectors? They weren't even trying. Come on, coppers, don't give New York's finest a "bad" name!

Sitting in the office that afternoon in 1955, I thought back to the good old days—the days of which Damon Runyon said one day at the Round Table, "If we didn't have a big investigation every twenty years, the bridges would be gone!"

At one time the Friars had more city employees on the payroll than the city. We smeared more fire inspectors than the Fire Department knew it had. They did a good job for us. In ten years not one piece of toast burned!

One fireman was signed in at a fire station, but spent days and nights with us. One time he didn't show up at the club. Somebody came up to look for him. After an intensive search, Will Rogers said, "Maybe he forgot himself and went to a fire!"

We had a fireman songwriter whose ambition was to get on Jan Murray's *Songs for Sale,* a TV show from which many hit songs came. Instant fame could be a result for a lucky songwriter. Our fireman songwriter cornered Jan Murray's manager, Harry Morton, and wanted to set up an appointment to audition for Murray. Morton insisted that he had to hear the song first. Taking the dummy into the kitchen, Morton had him do his number for the cooks. It was an unforgettable sight—some dummy singing to four bored

Cuban cooks at eleven-thirty at night. The poor yutz never made it to the show.

At the New York Friars, when the world was new, we had water inspectors, building inspectors, inspector inspectors, and inspectors who went around trying to find things that weren't already inspected. When the mayor was Irish, the inspectors were all O'Brien or O'Malley. An Italian mayor signed on Italian inspectors. When Vincent Impelletieri was mayor an Irish inspector named McKesson surfaced. Lou Holtz explained the discrepancy: "He's of Italian extraction. Ten years ago he pulled out of a Sicilian whore!"

The jobs of police commissioner and fire commissioner were the exceptions from the rule of race. Those positions were always held by Irishmen.

La Guardia was the only mayor who didn't hire by race. La Guardia hardly hired. He was the worst mayor in the history of New York for those who like to feed from a city trough. During his administration no schools, hospitals, streets, or parks were built. La Guardia left no avenues open for graft. La Guardia did favor the Fire Department with the best he could squeeze out of a lean city budget. La Guardia had a special fondess for red trucks and fire hoses. A siren in the distance would bring out the wild man in him and he'd take off to catch the fire. Detained by a political rally in the winter of '39, La Guardia managed to get to a five-alarm blaze when it had been knocked down to a two-alarmer. He congratulated the battalion commander. One nearby fireman said to his hose partner, "We ought to be congratulated. We kept it going till La Guardia got here!"

One politician who should have adored the Friars, La Guardia didn't. Fiorello La Guardia was pure show biz. Politics wasn't even a second love. La Guardia's secret dream was to be the leader of a band much like John Philip Sousa's. (La Guardia came by the urge for music naturally. His father was chief musician at Whipple Barracks in the Arizona Territory. Little Fiorello learned to play several instruments. Then he listened to himself, and decided to go into politics.)

La Guardia had the temperament for the baton. Years later he was to appear as guest conductor for the combined orchestras of the Police and Sanitation departments. Asked if he wanted special treatment, La Guardia said, "Hell no! Just treat me like Arturo Toscanini!"

La Guardia's animosity toward Jimmy Walker colored the Little Flower's feelings about the Friars. "Jimmy Walker," La Guardia told George Burns, "is such a crook his birth certificate is on the back of a subpeona!"

La Guardia was being a little harsh. Jimmy Walker believed in "live and let live well." Walker wasn't the first open-handed public official. Walter C. Kelly, a great comedian and one of my best teachers, ran into Al Smith at the Round Table. Governor at the time, Smith was paying off political debts by the the shovelful and the acre. Kelly said to him, "Governor, don't give away Rochester. I do well there!"

Smith said, "Don't worry. There are some things I'll keep for myself!"

Walker brought greater grandeur to graft. He handed out contracts to anybody who said "hello" to him or who didn't say "hello" to him. (The first time I saw "Jimmy" I was about ten. I thought I was in the presence of a god. My mother and Sophie Tucker both believed that Walker would become the President of the United States. My mother added, "Unless he goes to jail first!")

When I met Jimmy at the Friars a few weeks after my first visit to the Round Table, he told me, "Don't hang around George Cohan. He'll make you bitter."

At the risk of saddening the sanctimonious, Walker pulled stunts beyond mortal comprehension. He okayed the building of a public school between two giant storage tanks in Brooklyn at the edge of Floyd Bennett Field. Repaying a minor political debt, Walker had one of his subordinates order four thousand keys from his cousin, a locksmith. Walker pointed out that keys to the city are ceremonial in nature and shouldn't look like an ordinary house key. He then ordered the subordinate to purchase four thousand large wooden keys in which the other keys could be imbedded.

As far as La Guardia was concerned, his analysis of the Friars came from his evaluation of Jimmy Walker. Walker was a Friar— ergo, we weren't nice folks.

La Guardia came to the club occasionally, once to discuss a giant patriotic rally to be held in Central Park. Eddie Cantor had some jokes for a two-man spot with the mayor and got him up to the club to rehearse. I wasn't jealous. I had a routine with Marian Anderson and Kate Smith.

As we sat around, I asked La Guardia if we could interest him in becoming an honorary Friar. He said, "Milton, don't take this personally. I wouldn't join the Friars if I were offered a million dollars. I wouldn't join the Friars if I were dying of thirst and you had the last drop of water in town! I wouldn't join the Friars if Gracie Mansion burned down and this was the only place to sleep! Never, never, never!"

Eddie Cantor said, "Milton, put down one 'doubtful' for the Friars!"

In the spring of 1947, La Guardia became very ill. Al Jolson suggested that we send a food package up to the hospital, a selection of the club specials. Mack Gordon said, "La Guardia's very sick. What if he goes into a coma or something?"

Danny Shapiro said, "Let's send chopped liver. That lasts?"

That suggestion was voted down. Alternatives were suggested. Alan King said, "Let's go give blood."

Youngman said, "I can't. My blood is too tall!"

The Little Flower pulled through without our blood and our food. And our jokes.

When the Seabury investigation popped up, the Round Table got itself a year's worth of fodder. Ordered by Governor Roosevelt because New York City was slowly disappearing into various pockets, the investigation peeked into every dark corner it could find. No city ever had more dark corners. (When I was five or six, my mother took me to a musical about New York City. One of the songs was about New York graft. It had two lines in it—"When they get through with reform in New York, you don't have a tree with any bark in the park." And so on. I've tried to track down this song for seventy years. Some politician must have stolen it.)

At the Seabury investigation, the borough president of Queens was put on the stand. Mr. Seabury wanted to know what happened to a large sum of money. The borough president explained that the money had been spent for the beautification of the area. He'd had the insides of the sewers whitewashed!

Naturally, the whitewash was water-soluble.

The Friars Round Table gave the borough president an A for that one and considered putting him up for membership. Jack Pearl, the voice of Baron Munchausen, said, "You can tell he wasn't Jewish. He would have taken another hundred thousand for putting down paper till everything was dry!" ·

A district attorney from Brooklyn was asked to explain why and how he had deposited huge amounts of money in a Jersey bank when his salary was only thirty-three hundred dollars a year. The D.A. said that his brother had died and left him with eight hungry mouths to feed. The money was borrowed. The D.A. kept borrowing from Peter to pay Paul. A second question was asked—how come there were no withdrawals? The D.A. blamed the banks' faulty bookkeeping.

H. I. Phillips, a great reporter, was curious about the family. How would it cope with the probability that the D.A. wouldn't have much borrowing power in the future?

Phillips checked up on the starving mouths. There were eight in the family. All eight had city jobs. One, a baby of nine months, was an elevator operator. Luckily, the building had no elevator. When the news came out, Runyon said to us at the Round Table, "A child can only do so much!"

We gave the D.A. an A+ and offered to share his jail sentence. Harry Warren, the songwriter, said, "He'll have a good time in jail. I think his ten-year-old niece is the warden!"

A lady judge in Yonkers was found to have sent her daily work to Wisconsin to be copied by her clerk, who happened to live in Wisconsin. Each day the work would be typed up and sent back.

The lady judge only got a B−. "They must have good ribbons in Wisconsin!" said Harry Richman. He also said, "It must be nice to f—— New York. You don't have to bring a box of candy!"

A gentleman named Chili Anjou was the conversation piece of the Seabury investigation as far as the Round Table was concerned. First, Anjou'd been up to the club several times. None of us knew what he did, but he drove a Hispano-Suisa, which was not a bad car. It cost about seventy-five thousand in those days. Al Lackey wanted to borrow it. Always mindful of Sophie Tucker's money, Lackey wanted to borrow the car and told us, "If I look good in it," he said, "maybe Sophie'll buy me one."

Ben Bernie said, "Carry an empty plate home, maybe she'll buy you lunch!"

Anjou, Mr. Seabury revealed, was a pimp, but a pimp with a difference. Anjou sent male hustlers to the bus and train stations to meet and pick up girls fresh from the farm. Cops on Anjou's payroll would arrest the girls for soliciting. The poor unfortunates would be thrown into the women's detention home on Eighth Street.

Charity personified, Anjou would visit the girls and explain that there were ways of avoiding headlines back home. A month or so of service, and they'd be free to take on the city and become the waitresses and seamstresses they planned to be.

In the evening, the Hispano-Suisa would become a limo for a half dozen men staying at major hotels, men who liked some special kicks. They were driven to the prison, where they entertained themselves with sex behind bars.

To smooth the way, Anjou was partners with the precinct around the corner. On weekends, at times, some of the police were allowed the use of the car.

Years later, Anjou's application for membership in the Friars was found. In the section of comments, Anjou had given three outside references—the police commissioner, the fire commissioner, and the borough president of Queens.

The Friars favorite city employee was Joe Dougherty. He came in one day, flashed his police lieutenant's badge, and became a fixture. For a slight payment, he guarded our bar. Like our fire inspectors, Dougherty did a fantastic job. Nobody ever stole the bar. Dougherty was so committed, he once found two cases of scotch before they were stolen and held them for us in the trunk of his Packard.

Dougherty collected for the vast army of policemen who shared in the payments. It was rumored that Mayor Walker was one of the beneficiaries. Lou Holtz said, "Great! Now Walker can pay his dues!"

Our club manager used to brag that he was putting three children through college—Joe Dougherty's!

Dougherty was worth every penny, if only because he was able to keep us safe from Izzy Einstein and Moe Smith. These two Prohibition agents, whose lives were put on the screen by Jackie Gleason and Art Carney, loved to bust places if a headline was guaranteed. The Friars, well-known and very uptown, would have been a coup. Joe Dougherty was able to penetrate their disguises, warn us, and even keep them from the door. Long afterward, he let us in on his secret. He could read people from their shoes. Prohibition agents, often forced to be long-distance runners because quarries like to take off when accosted, wore clunky brogans.

A smart haberdashery, De Pinna's, was the hot store at the time.

Dougherty arrived at the club one day, De Pinna'd from top to bottom. He modeled his imported brown suit, the tan silk shirt, the blended brown tie, and his cordovan brown shoes. After examining the ensemble, which cost a pretty penny, Fred Allen said, "I must congratulate the police chief on the new police issue!"

Dougherty was by no means the only public official attracted by the Friars. Big politicos showed up for lunch regularly. Al Smith, before he became the chief official of the state of New York and, later, when he was a candidate for President, appeared at every one of our big affairs. Several times he brought a comer named Franklin Delano Roosevelt. Roosevelt loved the food at the Friars. "At Hyde Park," he told us, "the food reflects a basic difference of opinion between my mother and Eleanor."

On the campaign trail, Roosevelt was often forced to eat ethnic foods, obvious proof that he deserved to be elected. He loved the Sunday brunch he attended at the club. He told Raymond Hitchcock, the great actor, "I can eat bagels and lox here without rabbis staring at me!"

Roosevelt was introduced to smoked whitefish by Harry Hershfield and said, "Eleanor has never eaten this, which may account for her dour outlook on life!"

Jim Farley, a deft campaign manager, handled Roosevelt's run at the presidency in 1931. Because money is the root of all good nominations, Farley had an assistant, Fred Brown, an ex-gambler, who walked around with pockets filled with money. Money, especially cash, could work wonders with undecided delegations. Lunching with us one afternoon, Brown anxiously waited for Farley to return from Hyde Park. Definitely not because of our food, Brown, a tall thin man who ate almost nothing, became ill and took off for the bathroom. Farley came in. He wanted Brown to make a delivery. Finally, a worn-out Brown returned from the bathroom. Hearing his boss's order, Brown insisted that he was afraid to leave the building. He didn't want to be more than ten feet from a bathroom. Farley said, "What am I going to do? I promised them the money within the hour."

Eddie Dowling, the actor, said, "If 'insufficient funds' doesn't work, try 'diarrhea'!"

On another occasion, when I learned that Farley, now Postmaster General, was going to be around for one of our affairs, I took an envelope, scribbled an address on it, and put it in my pocket. Lat-

ANNUAL
FRIARS FROLIC

MILTON BERLE
Executive Chairman

Monday, November 29, 1943   Winter Garden

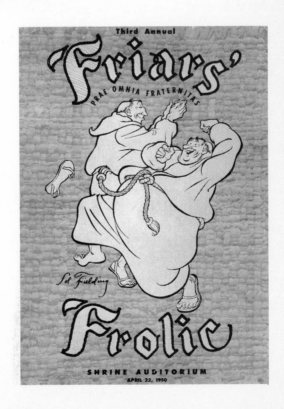

Third Annual

Friars'

PRAE OMNIA FRATERNITAS

Lou Fielding

Frolic

SHRINE AUDITORIUM
APRIL 22, 1950

Bobby Clark and Fannie Brice in a
Frolic special song.

ABOVE: A luncheon for
Sinatra in 1950. (*Mac A.
Shain*)

RIGHT: Danny Kaye, Frank
Sinatra, Groucho Marx, and
George Burns rehearsing a
Frolic number. Burns is the
choirmaster.

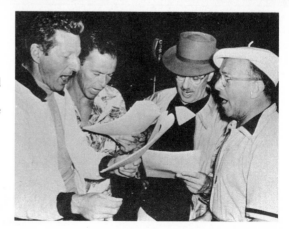

How could I smile at Phil Silvers?
He knocked me off the tube.

ABOVE: Marilyn Monroe and
friend in 1960.

LEFT: Jack Oakie watches as
Sammy Davis, Jr., tells me how
wonderful I am.

Joe E. Lewis, Robert Merrill, and I
managed only forty-one tight-pants
jokes at our affair for Tom Jones.

LEFT: I taught Rocky Graziano everything he knew about the boxing game—bleeding, falling down, hurting . . .

MIDDLE: Jack E. Leonard knocked out Rocky Marciano with a left hook and twelve fast one-liners.

BELOW: Frank Sinatra and Joe E. Lewis toasting the world, each other, and Tuesday.

Betty Hutton and
Erroll Flynn frolicking.

ABOVE: Starting with the
second from the left: Jack
Benny, George Jessel,
Portland Hoffa, Fred Allen,
Mayor Wm. O'Dwyer, Danny
Kaye, Jesse Block, Eddie
Fisher.

LEFT: Hail, hail—the gags
are all here! I'll name them.
You pick 'em: Lou Nelson,
Joe E. Lewis, Lew Parker,
Walter Winchell, Alan King,
Jack E. Leonard, Phil Foster,
Harry Delf, Sammy Davis,
Jr., Lou Holtz, Red Buttons.

LEFT: Eddy Duchin rehearsing Joe DiMaggio, boy tenor.

MIDDLE: Dean Martin being reminded where he is.

BOTTOM: Jack Oakie watching Carroll O'Connor being kept from working alone.

TOP: Don Rickles being as nice as usual during one of my forty-two hundred dinners. (*Richard Stephenson Kee*)

ABOVE: Henny Youngman, Jack Carter, and a third unknown welcoming Neil Simon in 1980.

LEFT: Showing Willie Mosconi, the world's champion for twenty years, some tricks.

TOP: After his stag roast, Humphrey Bogart had to go outside for some fresh air.

ABOVE: Glenn Miller begging for the name of my tailor in 1940.

RIGHT: Barbara Stanwyck didn't want to miss a word I was saying.

LEFT: Mayor Bill O'Dwyer and Mike Todd both knew their way around a dollar. The picture is unique because the mayor has his hands in his *own* pockets.

MIDDLE: Mama flanked by two fair fighters—Barney Ross and Joe Louis.

BOTTOM LEFT: Lyndon B. Johnson offering me a job in his Cabinet.

BOTTOM RIGHT: Muriel and Hubert Humphrey and I trying to outsmile the Osmond family. (*Jules Davis*)

LEFT: A total stranger asked if he could have a nice picture for his mother —Phil Reagan, Eddie Cantor, Benny Fields, and I obliged.

BELOW: George Jessel and George Raft telling Jack Dempsey we were out of bagels.

ABOVE: Harry Delf, George Jessel, and I watching my wife Ruth carry on with Joe E. Lewis.

RIGHT: Vic Damone, Jerry Lewis, and Bob Hope made my dressing room in Vegas a part of the Round Table.

LEFT: Howard Cosell, the mouth that roared, and an admirer.

BELOW: By 1980, the secret between Buddy Hackett and me was out.

From left: Joey Adams, Soupy Sales, Harold Honcho, Pat Henry, Slappy White, and Henny Youngman. The occasion was in honor of Youngman learning a new joke.

Tony Curtis, Janet Leigh,
and Robert Wagner—so
young and beautiful!
(*TriColor*)

Orson Welles and Frank Sinatra—
younger than springtime they were.

ABOVE: From left: Ronald Reagan, Nat
King Cole, and Gary Cooper.

RIGHT: With Carl Sandburg and Groucho
Marx. I'm still impressed from having
spent a few hours with the great poet.
(*Gerald Smith*)

LEFT: From left: Artie Stebbim, George Jessel, Irving Berlin, Al Jolson, and Jonie Taps—dressed for the best food in the West.

BELOW: If you look hard enough you can see Frank Sinatra, Danny Kaye, Desi Arnaz, Jonie Taps, George Raft —and on the extreme right, Harry Cohn, the movie mogul.

LEFT: Marty Allen and I never forgave Norm Crosby for getting laughs.

BELOW: A unanimous note from Myron Cohen, Bert Convy, Jan Murray, Red Buttons, Henny Youngman on "Totie Fields being funnier than anybody."

With Roz Russell.

ABOVE: Cary Grant and Jonie Taps. (Grant is the taller one.)

LEFT: Fred Astaire—a hoofer.

LEFT: Bob Newhart was smiling because his new series was a hit. I don't know why *I* was smiling. (*Las Vegas News Bureau*)

MIDDLE: Sid Caesar and Carl Reiner—together again in 1985. (*Irv Antler*)

BELOW: My date was funny, but Red Buttons' date had something going for her too! Angie Dickinson is the one on the right (just so you don't confuse her with Lucille Ball).

ABOVE: We roasted the Raiders when they came to town. I said only nice things about Lyle Alzado on the left. I didn't even mention Billy Daniels, Jerry Vale, and Tom Flores.

LEFT: Ray Bolger and George Burns.

er, when Farley was leaving, I whipped out the letter and said, "Mail this!"

Farley reached into his pocket and took out two other envelopes. "Milton, you're not the first!"

Standing next to me, Phil Baker, the radio star, said, "Milton, don't tell me you steal envelope bits too!" (Baker once accused me of paying one of his writers to bring me advanced copies of their upcoming script. I told Baker, "I tried that for a while, but after six scripts I couldn't find a laugh!" Another accusation, this one from Bob Hope, was pierced by my mother, who said to Hope, "Milton wouldn't stoop so low. My son stoops high!")

The Friars have always been an equal opportunity club. Huey Long sat with us twice. The king of Louisiana, although he was only a governor, Long hated Roosevelt with a vengeance. Roosevelt had set the tax people on him after promising not to. "Roosevelt," Long swore to us, "can't see a belt without hitting below it!" Long had many cogent things to say about Roosevelt—"Franklin Delano Roosevelt," Long said, "stabs more people in the back than sciatica!"

In New York to search out support for a run at the presidency, Huey Long consoled himself for the lack of it by lolling around with attractive young ladies and with good food. At the New Yorker Hotel on a Friday night, Dougherty told us, Huey Long had gotten into trouble with Trigger Mike Coppola, a gentleman not to be messed with. Frank Costello stepped in and saved Long at the last minute. This was supposed to be the basis of the friendship that turned New Orleans into one big dice table.

At the club for a snack before heading home to the Bayou country, Long was feeling sorry for himself. The young lady who had been his date on the night of his run-in with Mr. Coppola had taken off wisely, departing the scene in the first taxi that showed up. Later, at his hotel, Long tried to phone the young lady. She refused to take his calls. [As far as her switchboard was concerned, she was on the way to Tibet.] "Damn," the passionate pelican said, conceding defeat, "she was a keeper!"

Jack Benny tried to console him. Senator Benny said, "There must be a million beautiful women in Louisiana."

Long said, "There are, sir. There are so many gals in New Orleans, if a man was going at them alphabetical there'd be no man live through the C's. But the trouble is—the gals back home have been bit into. This one didn't have a tooth mark on her!" In emotional anguish, Long summed up his condition with, "And I've got an urge you couldn't bring to its knees with a shotgun!"

Soothed by the arrival of food, Long relaxed. He toyed with a shrimp in the seafood cocktail in front of him. We were proud of our shrimp at the Friars, buying the largest available. Unimpressed and ever mindful of his state's reputation as the home of giant seafood, Long looked at the shrimp and said, "Sure like to see the fella who took this one from its mother."

Soon he went on a different tack. How popular, he wanted to know, was Roosevelt with the people in show business. Most of us liked the gentleman from Hyde Park. Long said, "He'd better not come my way. He wouldn't stand the chance of a loose shoe in a swamp."

I idolized President Roosevelt. I said, "Senator, Roosevelt has done a lot for the people."

Long said, "Sure, Milton. I coulda gotten to like that Dutchman. But you gotta understand—a man can be a lyin', connivin', cheatin', stealin' thief who'd take his sister-in-law from under his brother, but he better be honorable."

Long's last visit came at the time Harvard students were swallowing goldfish. Long was unhappy. "Instead of eating them, we should use them for stocking the Mississippi, then we could all make some handsome money!"

Long asked me and several other celebrities to join him for an evening of letting the good times roll at the dedication of a new bridge forty miles out of New Orleans. He told us the date.

I said, "I'll be in Boston doing a radio show."

"I'm in Chicago," Lou Holtz said.

"A bridge dedication is something in Louisiana," Long said, sorry for us.

Holtz said, "Maybe we can come down a month later, when you put in the river!" (Holtz wasn't far off the mark. Long's brother, Earl, became governor later and put a bridge near Mosca's, the best restaurant in Louisiana. The bridge has no access road and, after you cross it, there's no road leading away. But it's a pretty bridge.)

Seymour Weiss, a Huey Long bodyguard and later the owner of the fabulous Roosevelt Hotel in New Orleans, where most of us headlined at one time or another, visited at the Round Table when he came to New York. One afternoon Eddie Foy asked Weiss what his job was. Weiss said, "Remembering where yesterday's money is!"

Huey Long was shot on September 10 in 1935. Al Kelly, the great double-talk artist, said, "Let's bow our heads for thirty seconds in his honor, while I go around and steal something from everybody!" (Seymour Weiss, luckily, was off on the day of the assassination.)

Only the mayor of Jersey City, Frank Hague, was as much of a czar as Huey Long. Hague controlled New Jersey. Hague was a brilliant politician. Hague could tell you the exact number of votes a candidate would receive. Hague could tell you that three months before the election.

In possession of magical powers, Hague brought the dead to life so they could vote. That gave a new meaning to the notion of "absentee" ballots! Asked once how people who died in 1880 could vote, Hague told the reporter, "Don't talk against the elderly!"

As a guest at a Friars function, Hague was pure gold for the comedians. Bob Hope described him: "Mayor Hague is a lovely man. He has helped six men become senators from New Jersey. And afterwards he helped two of them become American citizens!"

"Frank Hague," Frank Fay said, "promised to get the whores out of Jersey City. He's a man of his word. Last night I saw him driving two of them to Philadelphia!"

Harry Hershfield said, "Let those of you who are without sin, cast the first stone. Frank Hague will pick it up and sell it to New Jersey for a road!"

Hague came to the club shortly before the kitchen was closed. He perused the menu for a long time because he wasn't a good reader. His two bodyguards weren't gifted literati either as literacy wasn't a requirement for public duty in New Jersey at the moment. By the time the group had decided on food, the waiters were just about ready to quit for the night. One waiter, a black man with us only a short time and trapped into service for the mayor, urged the party to make up their minds. I asked him, "Don't you know who this is?"

The waiter said, "No, Mr. Berle. Is he kin of yours?"

The waiter setting up nearby said, "That's Mayor Frank Hague. Unless you have a special liking for harps, you be nice to that man!"

Mayor Hague asked for three orders of Boston cream pie and coffee, got the waiter off the hook with a smile, received what he'd ordered, and started to leave a large tip. I tried to dissuade him. I was willing to sign for the food. The mayor said, "I don't mind tipping. I only come to New York to do the things I can't do in Jersey!"

On another occasion Mayor Hague showed those of us at the Round Table small drawings of places he was having built in Jersey City. One was a huge estate for himself and his family so that his children and grandchildren wouldn't know poverty. A good pal of his, Sinatra said, "They won't even know where the kitchen is!"

The other edifice was a ballpark, constructed at a cost of three million dollars, then a more than ample sum. Tommy Dorsey said, "There must be some mistake. The ballpark is bigger than the house!"

I said, "They're not finished yet!"

The mayor showed his sense of humor and said, "Don't challenge me!"

At the Beverly Hills Friars, we're always holding open house for politicos. Earl Warren, later the head of the Supreme Court, no mean job, was an honorary Friar when the club was formed. Warren and Goodwin Knight, a governor a few years later, took many a steam at the club. Told that they were both in the steam room, Ben Lessy, the comedian, said, "Go in, count the towels, and weigh the sweat!"

A frequent visitor, Alan Cranston, the senior senator from California, comes up to scare people out of dieting. The senator is tall and gaunt. Thinner than the proverbial rail, he's a catalyst for "thin" jokes—"He's so thin his shadow is inside!" "He's so thin he has no sideways!" "He's so thin he turns on the shower water and misses!" The senator is also bald—"He's so bald he has to carry his dandruff in his hand!"

Every four years Cranston makes a noise as if he's running for President. Red Buttons said, "He could make a good President. When other countries see his pictures, they'll send *us* food!"

The mayor of Los Angeles, Tom Bradley, is a proud black man. Bradley has been to many Friar functions and supports our charities. At one dinner he took a verbal bow and thanked just about everybody in the room. He turned to me and said, "Thank you, Uncle Miltie."

I jumped up and said, "You're welcome, Uncle Tom!"

The parade of the politicos never ends. Luckily, the American people manage to elect many who give us matter from which to make up our jokes. As this is being written, Washington is knee deep in material about Iran, the White House, colonels, pretty secretaries, and money that seems to have disappeared. It's at this time that Norm Crosby can sit down at the Round Table and break us all up by saying, "Did you ever dream you'd get up in the morning and miss Nixon?" Or, four weeks after the issuance of the Tower Report, Alan King can offer, "It was just on the news. President Reagan called Senator Tower. He wanted to know when the report'll be ready!" And I can stand up at a Friars' dinner and say, "Washington's a tough town. One day you're on top, one day you're down. I was just telling this to our waiter, Don Regan!"

One thought surfaces—what if our politicians suddenly turned out to be bright, dedicated, and honest? Nah, they would never do that to the Round Table and my act!

The Sporting House

People like to hate Howard Cosell in installments so it'll last longer.

Don Meredith

Bob Uecker's folks refused to have him circumcised. They were afraid of brain damage!

Billy Martin

Georgia Frontiere's been married eight times. Three more and she qualifies for an expansion team!

Pete Rozelle

Reggie Jackson has no enemies. His friends hate him.

George Steinbrenner

Nobody has more respect for John McKay than his players—which is too bad.

John Madden

Bobby Layne would go on the wagon tomorrow...if it had a bar on it!

George Allen

Somebody ought to tell Namath that the pantyhose comes off after the game.

Vin Scully

On the TV screen a short but powerfully built baseball player was seen swinging at a ball. The ball went into the bleachers as the crowd cheered it on. It was the 756th home run, a record, hit by a

Japanese star. Four people sitting at the Round Table in 1977 recognized the player from a close-up. It was Sadaharu Oh. Some Friars at a nearby table also recognized him.

Things had certainly changed.

It's hard to be famous and anonymous today. The faces of the known, foreign and domestic, the unknown, the laid-back, and world-shakers who want the spotlight have become accepted facts of life because of television. We're familiar with hundreds, even thousands, of public figures who could have walked right past us in the past without causing us to blink one hair in one eyelid. In sports this is true with two exclamation marks after it. We can identify jockeys, track stars, ballplayers, tennis stars, and even swimmers. Years ago, only touts and horse owners knew what a jockey looked like. The rest of us only cared if this tiny vague figure crossed the finish line first with a horse somewhere in the neighborhood of where he sat. There was no chance in the world, before television, that any one of us would know a gymnast at sight. Today they all do commercials and we know exactly who they are. In the pre-TV forties, recognition, especially of sports personalities, came tough. At the Friars, where the with-it gathered, recognition came as tough or not at all.

Pie Traynor of the Pittsburgh Pirates is on just about everybody's all-time All-Star list. Coming in to town with his team to play the Giants, he was asked up to the Friars by Bugs Baer, the sportswriter, when we still had the old club on Forty-eighth Street. Almost nobody recognized Traynor. This was a star player whose picture on a baseball card was worth five Lou Gehrigs. Yet nobody at the club knew who the ruddy-faced man at our table was.

Traynor'd just come in from a series with the Boston Braves and Babe Ruth. Recently bought by the Braves and way past his prime, during the series the Babe looked as if he hadn't slept in a week. (This was more than a distinct possibility.) The Pirates ribbed the Babe no end and offered to put a cot out on the field for him. The Babe hit three home runs. Wincing, Traynor told us, "We shouldn't have awakened him."

Ed Wynn said, "You say he hit three home runs?"

Traynor said, "Three big fat home runs."

"Then he was still asleep!" said Wynn.

Babe and the Braves came in four days after the Pirates. Al Schacht, the baseball clown, brought the Babe to the Friars. Jimmy

Savo, a terrific mime who appeared in shows like *The Boys from Syracuse,* found his voice long enough to ask the Babe about the episode of the Pirates and the three home runs. Pursing his lips, the Babe said, "When were we in Pittsburgh?"

The Babe was raised in an orphanage and had nothing as a child. He told us, "We couldn't have pets at the orphanage. I tied a string to my hairbrush and walked that!" After years of starchy cereals and soups, the Babe made up for all the dull meals by eating anything and everything in sight when he started to earn big bucks. The Babe lived high off the hog as soon as he could afford to buy one.

Almost as mellow as the Babe was the great Satchel Paige. In New York for a series between his Cleveland team and the Yankees, Paige was brought to the Round Table by Ed Sullivan, on whose show he was going to take a bow.

Paige told us about a big offer to play baseball in the Dominican Republic. Baseball is a big game in the Latin countries. Trujillo, the dictator of the Dominican Republic, was in trouble and needed some good publicity. Bringing down a team of great black players who'd wear uniforms with his name emblazoned on them would bring him public support. Paige was one of the first players solicited. Josh Crawford, Cool Papa Bell, most of the stars of the Negro Leagues were invited. Paige turned down the offer, telling us, "I suspicioned something. Knowing that those Latin fellars are keen on guns, I asked myself—how come they're running out of their own players?"

By the time the Friars in Beverly Hills was built in the early fifties, the faces of baseball players were all over the tube. Hall of Famers like Joe DiMaggio were selling coffee makers. New ballplayers were selling beer and running shoes. If you drink enough beer, I guess you need running shoes. (Joe Namath's definition of a bastard is "a guy who throws a beer party and locks the john!")

By 1965 a face like that of Casey Stengel was known everywhere. Casey, whose nickname came from his hometown of Kansas City, had a face very few people could forget anyway. Casey looked as if he had been born old. Pat Buttram, Gene Autry's sidekick, the house jester for the California Angels and the Shakespeare of the silo, said to the Round Table, while trying to figure out how to use a knife and fork, "Casey Stengel's face can hold about two hours of rain!" (Autry said about Stengel, "You can't see anything as ugly as him without paying admission!")

Buttram donated pounds of country expressions each time he showed up for real food. Talking about Yogi Berra, Buttram said, "He's got the kind of face that could make a train take a dirt road!"

Describing Jesse White, Buttram said, "Jesse White's so ugly his face could lift a fog!" When Gene Autry's California Angels won the American League pennant, Buttram said, "No matter what Autry touches he comes out fine. The other day he found a squid, squeezed it and sold it as a ball-point fish!"

I think I tied the score for the big-city folks when I introduced Buttram at one of our stag roasts as a man with a black belt in cow flop! I also said, "Pat Buttram was a bottle-fed baby. His mother didn't trust him up close."

Buttram appeared at the Round Table one night after doing a club date. He was still in his wine-colored tuxedo. The subject of Jews came up. Steve Allen said, "Pat Buttram didn't see his first Jew until 1943. That was the guy who sold him the tuxedo he's wearing!"

To celebrate becoming a Friar, for his twenty-first birthday Wally Joyner, a future member of the Hall of Fame with the California Angels, had some family and friends to lunch at the club. Unfortunately, he sat close to the Round Table and had to take the consequences.

The Angels play their home games in Anaheim. Like Azusa and Cucamonga, Anaheim used to be the target of Jack Benny's jokes. To make Joyner feel good, I told him that Anaheim was a great town. "It's a great cultural center. Its new museum was supposed to open recently, but the frame broke."

Tom Bosley added, "It was supposed to publish a newspaper, but they ran out of quills!"

Norm Crosby topped us: "You'll never win a World Series in Anaheim. The town flower is a prune. In Anaheim, cobwebs is a social disease!"

Although none of our comments had anything to do with baseball, the mere defoliation of Anaheim made young Mr. Joyner blush and cry onto his birthday cake.

Feeling defensive, Pat Buttram said, "Wally, don't mind this crowd. They're jealous because Gene Autry has the first dollar he ever made."

I said, "He's got the first dollar anybody ever made!" (Please under-

stand that I'm not jealous of Gene Autry. A man has the right to have
money with his own picture on it. Actually, Autry doesn't have a lot
of folding money. He's got such a wad he can't bend it! Even George
Steinbrenner of the Yankees doesn't have Autry's money, and Steinbrenner, according to what Tim Conway told us at the Round Table,
has water skis that sleep six.)

Although we had an unforgettable stag roast for the Los Angeles
Raiders and, in the past, nights of tribute to the Rams, before they
took the pony express out of town, football players have never stam-
peded to the Friars. It could be that the food portions are too small.

Johnny Unitas was one who did show and brought more fun
than he went away with. His description of his days with the
Bloomington Rams was good enough to eat—we didn't have a team
bus. We had a team bike!

He explained that in semipro football, you didn't always know
you were going to play. You might come out to see a buddy of yours
at quarterback. A vicious tackle might sideline him. Since you were
the only quarterback around and there was money bet, you'd have
to go in. If his shoe size was close to yours, you wore his cleats.
His jersey became yours. You memorized the team's plays while
you looked for somebody to hold your wallet and watch. While on
the Bloomington Rams, Johnny U was rewarded with six dollars a
game, win or lose. Side bets brought in an extra ten.

When Unitas had it made, he came to New York to get the keys
to a car. Because he'd been chosen as the most valuable player in
football, a Chevy Corvette was presented to him on the Pat Boone
television show. Turning from watching the presentation, Gene Baylos
said, "Big deal! Chevy gets them wholesale!"

With us to possibly work out a deal for a painting to be presented to Jerry Buss, the owner of the Los Angeles Lakers and a
very active Friar, Ernie Barnes, the artist, had similar semipro ex-
periences. There was a team called the Anahein Rhinos. The team
meal was at a Taco Bell! Most of the players were collegians taking a busman's holiday, ex-pro players who'd never really made it
out of the trenches with the big guys, and some strong backs who
wanted to maim people on Sunday. Barnes remembers Joe Shimmick, a defensive tackle, who worked for a blacksmith at the Santa
Anita racetrack. Barnes explained, "Shimmick stood around until
the shoe was red hot, then he'd hand the blacksmith a horse!"

Barnes remembers the last quarterback the team had. "He was

a bad quarterback. When he was on the sidelines sitting on his helmet, the other team would intercept it!"

Barnes has come a long way from the Rhinos. After becoming the mainstay of the San Diego Chargers defense for several years, he started to paint full-time. Each of his oils brings more than a whole season of blocking and tackling. Maybe if I keep mentioning his name, he'll throw one my way.

Chuck Bednarik was a human mountain in the Philadelphia Eagle defense. Nobody ran over him. Nobody ran around him. Like Casey Stengel in baseball, he liked to announce his retirement. After pleasing financial adjustments were made, he announced that his wife was pregnant and he'd play another season to cover expenses. The next year he unretired because his wife was pregnant again. Field after field was strewn with warriors from other teams, downed because of his forced returns. Sitting at the club on a Tuesday, unable to practice because he was too battered from the previous Sunday's encounter with Bednarik, Frank Gifford said, "If Chuck Bednarik's wife gets knocked up again, we're all doomed!"

Art Donovan of the Baltimore Colts was a happy Irishman who liked his beer and tackling. Phil Foster gave Frank Gifford a way to beat the Gaelic giant: "As soon as you get the ball, throw Art Donovan a six-pack!"

When anybody at the club saw Gifford, the one complaint was that he was too good-looking to play ball. The consensus was that he was made for tennis or, at worst, yachting. Gifford came to the club early one week. He'd had a rough weekend. Joe Schmidt, the Detroit man-eater, had made Gifford his personal property the Sunday before. Gifford's body was bruised. His handsome face was bruised and scratched up. His limp was more than noticeable. Sid Caesar asked, "What'd you do last weekend, Giff?"

Gorgeous was definitely not the complaint about a gentleman who showed up one day during World War Two. Walter Winchell came in with a wide-shouldered man in a Merchant Marine uniform. The seaman looked to be about fifty. His face was weather-beaten and pushed in. Jack Benny said that he looked like somebody who had tried to board a train from the front!

The seaman's name was Jim Thorpe. Roller Derby was about the only sport he hadn't won medals in, and that was because Roller Derby was still waiting to be invented. In a barrel of great athletes like Ty Cobb and Babe Ruth, Thorpe would have been number one by a mile, two touchdowns, and twelve free throws. On this afternoon, only Will Rogers knew him for sure. I guessed that he was Knute Rockne. Anybody whose nose was pushed so flat he had to breathe from behind his head was Knute Rockne. My excuse was that I was only a baby when Thorpe had made all the headlines. I was still fighting diaper rash when he was battling to keep his Olympic medals.

Whether Thorpe was identified or not really didn't make much difference at the Friars. One of the selling points of the club was the right to privacy no matter how famous you were. Had everybody in the room known the great athlete, he still wouldn't have been pestered.

Winchell wanted Thorpe's permission to launch a campaign that would get Thorpe back his medals, some fame, and maybe a few dollars. Thorpe hadn't done too well. In the late thirties he worked as a common laborer, picking and shoveling dirt out of water trenches. The Olympic medals of which he'd been stripped on a technicality were gathering dust, but not on his shelf. Winchell said, "This would never have happened if you weren't an Indian! What the hell do we have against the Indians?"

Thorpe said, "We got here too soon!"

Will Rogers said, "It was that darn bunch that sold this island, that started it all."

In 1952 some of us met at the club to work on a big dinner for Thorpe. Two years before, the Associated Press had named him as the greatest athlete of the first half of the century. The award didn't bring him a nickel. Our dinner, using the knowledge we had in running these affairs and unable to be a Friars function by our rules, would bring him a decent check. We'd also make sure his medals would be returned.

Jimmy Cannon, the sports columnist, went to see Thorpe in the small trailer he was living in. Thorpe didn't want a dinner held in his honor. Our informal committee disbanded. A year later, Thorpe died of a heart attack. At a somber lunch, Cannon said, "I don't know about the darn money, but it's a good thing we didn't get him back his Olympic medals. The trailer he was living in is so small, there'd be no room for them!"

Jimmy Cannon planned to write some columns on Thorpe, but

decided not to. "Jim Thorpe deserved a happy ending," Cannon said. "There was no way!"

Jimmy Cannon had a terrific story about bigotry that I still use on occasion. It seems that this southern football coach wanted to impress his players with his fairmindedness. Gathering his players around him before leaving to play that afternoon, the coach said, "I want you fellows to know that I don't care about the color of your skin. Some of you may be white, but I don't see you as white. Some of you are colored and I don't see black skin. To me there's no black or white. As far as I'm concerned, you're all green. Now when we get on the bus, I want all you light green guys to sit in the front and you dark green guys sit in the back!"

Sharp student of all sports, Cannon wasn't a bettor. His opinion was never sought out. One afternoon he started to analyze a coming fight for us. Phil Silvers silenced him, "If you didn't bet, you have no opinion!"

A pretty good judge of fighting ability, I don't like to bet on the sport. Fighters are too childlike for exploitation in that way. From Slapsy Maxie Rosenbloom, the light-heavyweight champ who played at being a fighter to Rocky Marciano, a pure fighting machine, they all have a little-boy aura about them. In the early fifties Rocky Graziano and Tony Zale knocked each other's heads off with both faces blood red, yet they were always two neighborhood kids with no idea of adult responsibility.

Like a kid, Rocky Graziano was proud of a brand-new car he'd bought. He made everybody at the club come down and look at it. A few weeks after buying the car, Graziano received a good offer to fight in Australia. Although it would have been for a big purse, he turned it down, telling us, "I don't want to go to Australia. Somebody told me you can't drive there!"

Slapsie Maxie Rosenbloom, a great light-heavyweight champ, did accept an offer to work Down Under. At the time he had an act that purported to be comedy. To make sure he had the wherewithall to get to Sydney, he gave his paid-for ticket, sent by the booker, to Harry Gelbart, his barber. Under no conditions was Harry to part with the ticket until boarding time.

Such precautions were necessary in the case of Rosenbloom because he wasn't overly bright. After one fight, he said, "I think I got a conclusion of the brain."

Came a moment of truth. An inveterate baseball bettor, Rosenbloom received a fat tip on the New York Yankees to sweep a doubleheader from the White Sox. Broke, he tried to pry his trip ticket from Gelbart. Gelbart didn't listen. Rosenbloom screamed, threatened, cajoled, and offered to settle for the sale of the return half of the ticket. Gelbard refused to budge. Rosenbloom invoked the greatest punishment he could come up with. He said, "Gelbart, I need a haircut. If I had the money, I'd go to another barber!"

Playing along, Gelbart asked, "How much do you need for another barber?"

Rosenbloom said, "Two hundred bucks if I bet only one game!"

Sad and as wise as ever, Rosenbloom came up to the club and ran into Pat O'Brien. He told his unhappy story to Hollywood's Knute Rockne. O'Brien said, "You told Gelbart not to give you the money under any circumstances."

Rosenbloom said, "That's not what friends are for!"

Harry Gelbart has several other claims to fame. A songwriter at heart, he wrote some numbers with one of his customers, Ned Washington. In addition, Harry Gelbart has a son named Larry, who, among other things, brought *MASH* to television.

Larry Gelbart lived in England for a number of years. After his return, he came to visit me while I was rehearsing my show. It was a rough day. Hal Kanter, my producer, and I were not playing the same chords that day. Larry Gelbart asked Kanter, "How come you're his producer?"

Kanter said, "I get paid a lot of money for it. How come you're his friend for nothing?"

At the Friars, friends are sometimes for challenging to a round of golf or a card game. Any discussion about golf, whether it starts with a comment about Jack Nicklaus or the announcement that so-and-so has won this week's pro tour tournament, is followed by an offer to go eighteen holes because the man making the offer is on his game. A foursome is arranged quickly and it heads for the Hillcrest Country Club. Hillcrest was the Plymouth Rock of Friars coming west. Friars stopped at Hillcrest and quenched their thirst and sated their appetites. Many of the Friars never left Hillcrest. Some have been sitting there for thirty years and are dusted once a week. Once in a while, a gentle busboy turns a member toward the sun.

The founder of Paramount, Adolf Zukor, was a daily visitor to Hillcrest. Irv Brecher, the creator of *Life with Riley*, said that "when Zukor becomes a hundred we're going to split him two for one!"

At ninety-nine, Zukor was aware of his advanced years but couldn't believe that others had immortality going for them. Seeing a seventy-four-year-old Jack Benny in the dining room one day, Zukor asked, "Are you still around?"

Into this center of youth, a foursome from the Friars ventured one day. Jack Benny, George Burns, Norman Krasna, the only serious player, and I were about to challenge the famed course. Benny teed off first, Norman Krasna, a fine writer, once said that "Benny had a swing like Don Loper." And this time Krasna had it pegged exactly right. Benny's swing was mighty. Looking down the fairway, Benny asked, "Where's the ball?"

I said, "It's behind you!"

Benny'd missed on the upswing, but as he brought the driver down, the club had tapped the ball back.

Krasna smiled. Tonight he'd have a good reason for drinking.

Benny tried again and tricked the ball twenty feet down the fairway. Krasna was even more impressed. He'd heard that Benny had been taking lessons; now he was sure of it.

After Benny swung at the ball, Burns said to Benny, "Does your husband also play?"

A little too eager himself, Burns hooked his ball into some nearby trees no more than fifty feet away.

Krasna was not ecstatic.

Having given up the game five years before, I proved why, by hitting just about as far as Benny. As I turned to join Burns and Benny at the golf cart, Krasna turned toward the pro shop and yelled, "Hearse!"

Krasna strolled off. I was back in the Friars in an hour.

The Write Stuff

*Sidney Sheldon isn't himself today. It's almost
noon and he hasn't written a novel yet!*

Steve Allen

Abe Burrows is a legend in his own mouth!

Cy Howard

*Cy Howard has often been compared to great
writers of the past...and very unfavorably too!*

Abe Burrows

*Goodman Ace has an even disposition—always
rotten!*

Selma Diamond

*Some writers write for posterity. I have four that
write for oblivion!*

Eddie Cantor

*Mel Brooks is one of the funniest writers of the
day. That day was October 4, 1972.*

Sid Caesar

We comedians like to pick on them a lot—"Do you call yourself a
writer? You couldn't dot the 'i' in the word 'shit'!" "I wish I had
another writer like you. The trouble is I have six more like you!"

"You did to this script what Nixon did to the country!" My personal favorite was to Neil Simon—"Your first gag bombed, but after that it was downhill!"

You see, most comedians don't need writers. We ad-lib everything we say. (If you believe that, I'd like to talk to you about some swampland I have in Florida. That's a joke. I have great property in Florida. The other day they found land on it!)

Naturally, writers attempt to justify their existence by heaving a few epithets of their own—"Comedian X couldn't ad-lip a belch after a twelve-course Hungarian dinner!" "Comedian Y couldn't come up with an 'ouch' during a prostate attack!" One of the writers on my Tuesday night television show listened to Jack E. Leonard deliver some homemade jokes and said, in kind, "Your material's great. You should have a suit made out of it!"

The fact is that the Round Table has always welcomed writers—joke writers, script writers, playwrights, anybody with a pencil or word processor—because if we didn't the welfare rolls would double and the population of skid rows all over the world would go up.

A comedian is a patsy. With the possible exception of Bert Lahr. When the Home for the Aged came for a donation, he gave them his mother and father!

The best example of a soft touch is Bob Hope. A few years ago, the Writer's Guild honored Hope for being a one-man employment agency. The men and women who have written for him over the years were brought onstage, one by one, two by two, and, at one phase, to keep the evening from running over into the next season, eight by eight. The list was impressive. There were slews of Emmy and Oscar winners and a good representation of Friars. Hope, after all, was early in the Friars and had material shipped to him between courses at lunch. One of Hope's writers, Gig Henry, was asked to join the club. Henry said, "The Hope writers are starting their own club."

Tim Conway said, "You could start your own country!"

Safety in numbers wasn't a tactic limited to Bob Hope. Announcing the winners of the Emmy for writing one year, Johnny Carson read off the names of each of the writers of *Saturday Night Live*, adding, after the last name read, "And the Writer's Guild of America East!"

The barb may have been deserved but it's rumored that writers aren't among Carson's favorite people anyway. Pat McCormick, the author of many of Carson's wildest routines, told us at the Friars, "The writers come in every day and each one puts a quarter in a kitty. The first one Carson says hello to gets the money. The kitty is now up to three hundred and seventy thousand dollars!" That was the day McCormick, unusually insane, told us about seeing a "maidmer" at the beach. That's like a mermaid, but the top half is a fish! In addition, he mentioned that it was so hot, he'd seen a Dalmatian with its spots on the ground! McCormick blamed his mental condition on his failure to pay a utility bill. He said, "The electric company came in and turned off my shock treatments!"

McCormick came in for lunch one afternoon looking absolutely grim. I asked him what was wrong.

"I just came from the doctor," McCormick said. "He gave me three days to live. But not consecutively!"

McCormick's madness may be due to the fact that he wrote for Johnny Carson for so many years and the disdain got to him.

Garson Kanin, the writer of *Born Yesterday,* had a choice Universal story he shared with us one lunch. Kanin told of a writer-director who was brilliant with fast cheap pictures. He made ten-day pictures that grossed a fortune. After dozens of them he walked into the office and insisted on a thirty-day picture. He was tired of writing them in three days and directing them in ten.

Edward Muhl, the head of the studio, said, "Listen, you're a three-day writer and a ten-day director."

The director said, "If I don't get a thirty-day picture, I'm going to quit."

Muhl's assistant told his boss, "He makes a fortune for us. Give him one thirty-day picture. He'll be happy."

Muhl acceded to the demand. The director was given a bigger picture. He wrote it in three days and brought it in in ten days!

Come up with any Hollywood mogul and you'll almost certainly come up with an anti-writer. The Lord High Executioner of MGM, Louis B. Mayer, qualified easily. Mayer hired great novelists and playwrights, paid them gigantic salaries, but spread the word that the producers' dining room was not a healthy place for them to lunch.

Visiting with us at the Round Table, L. K. Sydney, a major figure at MGM and certainly a good mirror of Mr. Mayer's feelings, said, "We should hire more women writers. They type faster!"

Mr. Mayer must have squirmed on his heavenly cloud, if he made it up there, when a writer, Dore Schary, became head of the studio.

In due time to author *Sunrise at Campobello*, a brilliant play about Franklin Delano Roosevelt, Schary tried to sell me jokes when he was struggling in the East. I didn't buy. Later, I didn't get into many MGM pictures either. You'll notice they picked Gable for Rhett Butler! (I was in the running until they dropped the idea of having Martha Raye play Scarlett O'Hara.) Politics play an important part in the movie business. A moment in the shooting of *Gone With the Wind* got Abe Burrows, a radio writer then but a Broadway show doctor later, a huge laugh at the table. In for a brief stay with us, Errol Flynn mentioned that when he'd left Hollywood, they were burning Atlanta. Burrows asked innocently, "For the insurance?"

Dore Schary wasn't the only about-to-become-somebody who tried to sell me material. Almost daily large envelopes were left at the desk for me. Some were from would-be young writers I'd met outside theaters or in restaurants. I was willing to look at all material submitted, so if they'd leave it at the club, it would be read. Other new writers, aware, from items in Broadway columns, that I spent my free moments at the Friars, submitted material by the pound without prompting.

In one batch I found some very funny parodies. The subject matter was a little too fancy for my barefoot tastes and following. If I'd ever used the word "egregious" onstage, my mother would have fainted and taken the whole sixth row with her.

The writer did come up for lunch one afternoon. He was as classy as his parodies. His name was Alan Jay Lerner. His family had a number of ladies' specialty shops, a business he was determined to avoid. I introduced him to George Raft, who told him, "Silk panties made your family rich. They busted mine!"

· When Arthur Miller's play *The Crucible* opened, many of us were in the opening-night audience. At lunch the next day we discussed this powerful drama of witches on trial in Salem. Jackie Gleason said, "That's nothing. Did you ever try to beat a traffic ticket in New Haven?"

Miller wasn't one to emit one-liners with the intensity that he had in making dramatic phrases, but his wife, Marilyn Monroe, came up with some beauties. We even entertained the thought of making her a Friar. In the locker room we'd know immediately she wasn't a man, but who would tell!

Garson Kanin knew Monroe well and swore to us that she had actually told him the line coming up. Invited to the home of Arthur Miller's parents a number of times, Monroe was always served chicken soup with matzo balls in it. Returning to work after a weekend of matzo-ball soup, Monroe said, "I wonder if Arthur's mother knows how to cook any other part of the matzo!"

In 1960 I did *Let's Make Love* with Monroe. Because she was often a few minutes late for work, a few minutes sometimes lasting two days, Norman Krasna, the writer, and I lunched at the club together. We often had three lunches a day. When the director, George Cukor, couldn't shoot around his blond star, another "lunch" would be called and off we'd go. If and when Monroe arrived, Cukor would blow his stack quietly but firmly. This would cause Monroe to be even later the next day. One morning, lo and behold, she was all set to go on time. At our one lunch that day, Krasna and I talked about the miracle. Krasna said, of the director, "Poor Cukor must be losing his lack of grip!"

I share the Round Table's affection for writers. As noted before and often, I don't need writers. When he dubbed me "The Thief of Badgags" Walter Winchell agreed that I didn't need writers. I had everybody else's writers. But like Mark Twain said when a rumor spread that he was no longer among the living, "The extent of my stealing jokes has been greatly exaggerated."

Proof positive of my innocence is the fact that the Bishop Fulton J. Sheen came on against me with *Life Is Worth Living*, got a lot of laughs, and I never once took a line from his writer! (Steal one line from his Writer and a bolt of lightning hits you where you sit!)

In 1953, not happy enough because he had God on his side, Bishop Sheen hired Shakespeare. In one show he read the burial scene from *Julius Caesar*, putting in the name of Russian leaders instead of the Romans. As if on cue, Stalin had a stroke. A week later Stalin was dead. We heard the news at the club. One of my writers, Jay Burton, said, "Why can't you do something like that!"

Hal Collins, another of my writers, said, "What for? They'll say Milton stole the bit!" Roly-poly, not overly handsome, but with a merry twinkle in his eyes, Collins spent most of his money on whores. As he was walking out of the club one night, he saw a young lady of the evening, off duty, trying to hail a cab. Collins started to talk to her and eventually convinced her that she was what he'd been looking for all of his life. The young lady was willing to service him but she was hungry and wanted to go eat first. Collins said, "Come up to my place. I'll make you a steak."

"Fine."

Once in Collins's apartment, the young lady sat down. In the light the essential shabbiness of her apparel became obvious. There were rips in her skirt. A button was missing from her blouse. Collins walked into the kitchen, opened the refrigerator, and hid the steaks in the vegetable bin. Returning, he said, "Somebody ate the steaks. How about a TV dinner?"

On the other hand, Jay Burton will have nothing to do with play for pay. He told us at lunch one afternoon, "I'll never go out with anybody who has to gargle as part of her job!"

Jay Burton is the nervous type. When he goes to the doctor, for example, he shakes like a leaf in the wind. One time he told us, "I was shaking so much at the doctor's office the X ray missed!"

Having saved his money and invested wisely, Burton has a better stock portfolio than I do. Still, he panics. He bought a stock at twenty-two dollars that climbed to a hundred and forty dollars a share. One morning it went down an eighth of a point. Sweating, Jay said to us, "I saw it coming!"

Every comedian has taken a line from somebody else. Years ago you could go into a magic store and buy a pencil in the shape of a fingernail. Watching other acts or shows enabled you to write down key phases or lines without being noticed. Magicians loved to steal jokes for their between-trick patter. Bob Orben, the joke writer for President Reagan and, before that, President Nixon, compiled a dozen books of one-liners and bits that are still being used. It's comforting to know that the President uses the same gags as a three-dollar magician.

My affection for writers is obvious from the fact that my payroll for a writing staff on the first *Milton Berle Show* was almost two hundred dollars. The head writer was the guy who could change a twenty. Hal Collins insisted that he was the head writer because the show owed him for a new typewriter ribbon!

Woody Kling, the son of Ken Kling, the racing cartoonist who kept me broke for years, asked for a fifty-dollar raise. I offered ten. He said, "If I took the ten, I'd hate myself in the morning!"

I said, "Sleep late!"

I moved on to bigger and better, or at least bigger. Goodman Ace became my head writer. Previously he had earned ten thousand a week writing for Perry Como. Ace didn't have to do much for Como. "Perry," he explained, "used to fall asleep between 'but' and 'if.'"

Ace described himself: "I am the funniest thing to come out of Kansas City, Missouri, since the statement that there's a good restaurant there!"

Ace had a radio show, *Easy Aces*, with his wife that lasted for years. To use up some of the class he was dripping with, he wrote a column for *The Saturday Review of Literature*. While we were discussing an article about Lincoln, Jack E. Leonard said, "I don't read that fancy stuff. *Boys Life* gives me headaches!"

Just beginning to tear down the barbed-wire fences around comedy's subject matter, Lenny Bruce, fair-faced and young, chided Ace for playing it safe with his jokes. Old values, many of them bad, had to be questioned and altered. Comedy was the best weapon. Ace agreed, but reminded Bruce, "'Tristan sat on a log, expelling and picking boogers out of his nose' isn't necessarily literature!"

Ace showed up at the club once or twice a week. We discussed our sketches and sometimes monologues. I had a hot nut for a Columbus sketch toward the end of the season. Ace didn't want to write it. I said, "It's funny."

He answered, "Columbus would have turned back if he had known you were going to do that sketch."

Ace wouldn't have agreed with me even if he agreed. He was one of those pussy cats who was fond of almost nothing. Joe E. Lewis asked me, "Does anybody ever agree with Goodman Ace?"

I said, "Not if Ace knows about it!"

There must have been an eavesdropper in the room. A line much like it was said about a senator a few years later. Senator Borah.

Among Ace's biggest enemies were phonies and liars. We had an opera star on the show one week who believed that he was beautiful. The star, a basso, wanted Max Factor to do his makeup personally. He wanted to rehearse at his whim. He asked Ace if a certain kind of water had been brought in from Hot Springs, Arkansas, for him to quench his royal thirst with. Ace said, "We've done everything you've asked. We've even arranged an elevator to take you down to your low notes!"

I told Ace that I'd be just as happy dumping the guest. Ace said, "Think of it this way—while he's here, we're saving the Met!"

Some people must like abuse. When the basso was offered an hour special on educational TV, he asked Ace to write it for him. Ace turned him down, explaining, "I'm helping my aunt prepare jams for the county fair!"

Obviously, I enjoy writing about Goodman Ace. You can see that from all the space he's gotten. But he was something.

Ace had an endless supply of hates. After he'd gotten through berating one of our writers for bad pickles, I said, "Goodie, you must have a list of hates longer than my arm."

Ace replied, "I have a list longer than your arm. I also hate midgets who are *shorter* than your arm!"

Among the lowest of Ace's lows were agents. All agents. He dismissed them as people who come to work Tuesday morning and say to their colleagues, "Have a nice weekend!"

One agent, high up with an agency that sold mostly variety acts and, in one case, water-skiing elephants, was an inveterate liar. Ace came from a brief confab with him at the bar and told us, "I just caught Al in the truth!"

Al was almost proud of never having told the truth. His favorite clincher was to raise his hand and swear on his mother's life. Eddie Cantor once asked him, "How could you swear on your mother's life?"

Al said, "I was never crazy about my mother."

Al was put on the witness stand. Raised arm, he was asked if he promised to tell the truth, the whole truth, and nothing but the truth. Al said, "For how long?"

(Fred Allen had a similar dislike for those who fibbed. He believed that Jessel often toyed with the facts and said, "When last seen, Jessel was racing with the truth. The truth was leading by twelve lengths!")

Al died in the mid-1960s. After the eulogy we all passed by the open coffin. I whispered an aside to Joey Adams: "I don't believe him!"

Agents, mendacious or otherwise, are not the world's favorites. John Byner, a comedy gift from Canada still going strong, and I were at the funeral of one half of a team of agents. Byner said, "Let's take up a collection and bury his partner too!"

The creator of *You'll Never Get Rich*, the real name of the Bilko show, Nat Hiken, did penance with me too. At lunch he was telling me the trouble he was having in assembling a staff. "I won't hire a writer who doesn't believe that he's the greatest writer in the world. He must feel inside of him that he's the greatest writer in the world. But I know he's wrong. Because I'm the greatest writer in the world."

In 1958 I was lucky enough to get Hal Kanter as my head writer and producer. Brilliant, a smooth southern gentleman from Savannah, Georgia, whence came Johnny Mercer, Kanter isn't easy to argue with. I objected to the wording of some monologue jokes. Kanter likes to be clever. I like to lay it right in their laps. I said, "They won't understand these jokes in your hometown."

Kanter said, "They don't watch you in my hometown. You're on opposite a debate on the philosophical implications of Neo-Existentialism."

I did the jokes his way. They worked. I'll never know who won the other debate.

When the New York Friars roasted me three years ago in New York, they allowed me to choose my master of ceremonies. I chose Hal Kanter. He accepted and was a smash. My request, more than a hedge because I knew how well he would do, was my way of tipping my hat to the craft of writing.

A wise man once said that the blank page is God's way of showing how hard it is to be God. Though we've belted them and flayed them, by the living God that made them, writers are more than okay in my book.

Vices I Never Indulge In

Get Along, Little Stogie

DUMMY: *What are you smoking there?*
VENT: *This happens to be a White Owl.*
DUMMY: *Well, take the feathers off!*

Paul Winchell

*I got this cigar from the cigarette girl at the
Latin Quarter. She also gave me a dose.*

Jack Osterman

*To Enrico Caruso, who smacked his lips when he
inhaled: Caruso, I love to hear you smoke!*

George M. Cohan

To forgive George Burns for his lack of couth around a panatela doesn't mean that some of us are afraid to be counted, even in this day and age, as lovers of the leaf.

Comedians and cigars always go together for me. Maybe it's because so many were and are puffers of the royal weed—George Jessel, Groucho Marx, Alan King, Danny Thomas, Bill Cosby, Ernie Kovacs, Lou Costello, Jack Benny, and anybody else with lips and two bits.

I love my cigars. I had a go at my first one when I was eleven. My brother Phil had wangled it from the ice vendor who serviced our neighborhood. Although it cost only two cents in the store, Phil had to fork over three cents for it. That was just about his yearly allowance.

The cigar was an Italian job, long, thin, shaped like an "I" written by a nervous hand. It was cured in wine. The wine made it lethal. During World War One, I heard, Bronx Italian stogies were used instead of poison gas. Six healthy breathers puffed smoke at the enemy and shortened the war by a year. The Italian ropes are still sold in certain cigar stores. You know it's Italian because you have to put the smoke through a blender before you can inhale.

Brother Phil took the first puff, a second one, then proceeded to upchuck his first and second meals of the day. In his anguish he offered the culprit to me. I said, "I'll take a puff, but I don't know if I can throw up."

The episode of the trombone was a lot like that. Always eager to be involved with music, one day I was lent an old trombone by a musician. I brought it home and spent hours blowing into it for the entertainment of my brothers. I didn't play music. I made noises. I went upstairs. My Uncle Charlie was visiting. He asked me if I played well. I took out the instrument and started to blow in it. I'd been blowing it so hard and often for my brothers that my lungs were still protesting. On the second exhalation of air, I heaved all of my cookies. Uncle Charlie said, very sincerely, "Is that how you play it?"

I learned how to play cigars with more deftness and much less esophageal anguish. Jessel showed me some of the finer points. He prided himself in the perfection of his smoking. He never blasted away into somebody's face. He never downed a cloud of tobacco so that his face turned white. He was a smooth smoker.

Jessel and Groucho Marx, another Class A cigarist, wouldn't talk to Ken Murray. Ken was a chewer, not a puffer. When he got through, his cigar looked like a swamp. Groucho caught him chomping away one night and said, "Ken, how fast can you dice a carrot?"

Benny once said, "Murray drools so much he's going to die of cancer of the vest!"

Books have been written about the wit and wisdom of Groucho. His life is a lot of open books, yet I think I own this story about him. In 1922 a young hoofer came to the club to meet with the Parker of a trio soon to be called Parker Rand and Cagney. Cagney asked Parker why they wanted the third man out. Parker explained that the soon-to-be ex wasn't a good dancer and had an annoying dimple. From the bar three feet away, a young and feisty Groucho said, "Take the job, fella. If you grow a dimple, we'll pound it out!" Laughing, any doubts erased, Cagney joined the act and slowly started his climb.

The old act was soon forgotten and also the name of the third man, Archie Leach. He became a stilt-walker and changed his name to Cary Grant.

After the premiere of *She Done Him Wrong,* Groucho ran into Lowell Sherman, the director of the film, and said, "You've got me to thank for that Grant fellow. I put him in pictures."

Nor have I seen much about the epitaph of Groucho he wrote for himself—"Here lies Groucho Marx, who lies and lies and lies. P.S.—He never kissed an ugly girl."

Second-team smoker though he was, George Burns had a patented Round Table lecture about cigars. He believed that the prop cigar was as important as the performer. Certain cigars were automatic hits no matter who smoked them. Some cigars were flops. Any cigar that came in a box with a girl dancing on the lid was a loser. Cigars under a quarter with a caballero on the lid were a smash in Altoona. Burns never lit his stage cigars. "No long ash ever closed at the Palace!"

Jack Waldron, a comedian who did me before I knew I was doing me, was one of my cigar instructors. He taught me what to look for in bouquet. He showed me how to pierce the tip of the cigar delicately to allow for a thin cool flow of smoke. "Don't stab the damn cigar! It hasn't killed anybody! Be gentle. Pretend it's a virgin on her wedding night. Although I've never been with one." He taught me a great deal. He even taught me how not to wince when Dunhill's sent the bill. Most important, he showed me how to make friends of very rich men who smoked good cigars. A mournful look got you a box in the next mail.

Waldron was more than a cigar freak. Onstage he was one of the first masters of the one-liner. Until then it was par for the course to come out and tell stories. If you were a real sneak, you'd throw a one-liner into an introduction, and then lose it in a glowing description of how great this girl danced or that juggler juggled.

Playing to an empty club, he'd say, "Good evening, tablecloths!" and "Better fill up the tables. I'm getting snow-blind!" The few slow nights aside, he showed some of us that "brash" and "topical" could be funny.

At the Round Table, Waldron was pleasantly vicious. After an hour of a dull lunch in which nobody had said anything mildly witty, he said, "Fellows, I'm warning you, I'm gonna get even for this lunch!"

One afternoon, Sime Silverman, the founder of *Variety,* the show business bible, started to tell a long story that had no punch line. For the last endless minutes of the telling he kept looking around for somebody to say something that might get him off the hook. Waldron shrugged his shoulders: "Sime, there's no way to save you!"

Gertrude Ederle swam the channel in 1926. She was greeted here with bands, ticker tape, roses. Waldron said, "Nobody thought to bring a towel!" *Ben Hur* reached the screen the same year. Waldron was the architect of the phrase "Loved him, hated Hur!"

Cigars were more than props. They also indicated that you had arrived. Or were faking it. A feeble comic walked in one afternoon and started puffing on a solid import. Harry Hershfield, another aficionado and top man in my list of storytellers, said to him, "Lou, if your wife didn't have a kid today, you threw away ten cents!"

John F. Kennedy, a friend since 1946 when I was at the Carnival nightclub, wasn't faking it when he smoked cigars. I sent him some cigars when he was turning the White House into Camelot. He must have liked the cigars, because he called a few weeks later for the name of the tobacconist. Blushing, I told him they were from a two-man shop in Havana. Months later, the Cuban crisis arose. On the day the Bay of Pigs invasion took place, Harvey Stone, who did the best army routine since Johnny Burke after World War One, said, "If Kennedy wanted cigars, why didn't he ask Berle?"

To make up for some promised cigars, I placed an order one morning with a Swiss dealer for a box of Romeo and Juliet "torpedoes," the huge cigar made famous by Churchill. President Kennedy loved them. Two mornings later, he left for Dallas.

The cigars never came. I never checked up on the order.

When I light up a Romeo and Juliet now, a memory starts to surface. I don't mind. A single tough memory in a lifetime of pleasant ones associated with cigars isn't a bad deal. Also, a recent happening comes back to mind. Joe Vitrelli, a Friar who could have posed for the club's logo, was talking about buying cigars. He couldn't think of the brand, saying, "They were the Shakespeare things…uh…uh… Romeo and…uh…uh…what's that broad's name?"

Like I say, one tear in a carload isn't bad.

My Kingdom for a Horse

I bet on a horse at ten to one. It came in at five-fifteen!

> Henny Youngman

The race is not always to the swift. But that's the way to bet!

> Joe E. Lewis

I had some horse. The jockey kept a diary of the trip!

> Fred Astaire

My horse is a good mudder. He kept eating it all race!

> Eddie Arcaro

I like to follow horses—who like to follow other horses.

> John Forsythe

My horse misjudged the finish line. When he left the paddock he thought that the race was over!

> Willie Shoemaker

You can't win them all...but One?

> Henry Slate

On New Year's Eve of 1979, I resolved to stop betting the horses. I quit cold turkey. It was the two hundred and eleventh time I quit. In my early twenties, having learned much about the birds and bees, I picked up a few items about the ponies. On the road I'd find tracks hidden in swamps. I bet on horses at tracks that didn't have a starting gate. The horses used to line up a man with long fingernails. At one track the record for six furlongs was held by the man with the long fingernails! When I played New Orleans, I actually found a small track in the bayou country about an hour from the city. A race was held when two horses showed up. When daylight started to go, a race was held if a horse and a chicken showed up. Or two chickens.

The great quitting of 1980 time was going to be different. Filled with dedication, I swore off with industrial-strength determination. Other forms of gambling were to be equally taboo, but there were a few football bets made in the past that I'd honor. I was down on six bowl games, the pro Superbowl, three All-Star games, and a quoits match in Liverpool. Those bets would help me numb my passion for the ponies.

I haven't made a bet since!...And if you believe that you also believe that someday there'll be a Boy George, Jr.

But I did get the reader's attention. That's important, because those of us at the Round Table who love the four-legged creatures love even more the literature of the degeneracy. We love to tell about those who are in worse shape than we. I sometimes think that there is a special relish to be found nowhere else than in recounting the sorry lives of other losers.

Jackie Miles, a comic taken too early by the jealous fifty-dollar window in the sky, said many memorable things on many subjects. I can think of only the material, biographical to the hilt, in which Miles talked horse talk. Of all his great one-liners, one pops up at first asking—"I'm very interested in the improvement of the breed. I give half my money to the horses!" (Miles fibbed. He gave *all* of his money to the horses.)

Miles told hysterical stories. Under the threat of death, I can come up only with his classic racetrack tale:

Herman was a track bum. Herman had just put his last twenty on a long shot. As the horses started to enter the gate, Herman talks to his maker. "God," Herman said, "I never asked you for much in my life. Just this one time be good to me. When the gate opens, let three of the horses remain stuck in their stalls! Do that for me, God, and I'll give up all my evil ways. I'll get a job. I'll stay home with my wife. Three horses stuck in the gate, God. Then as the race starts, let my horse jump out in front. At the half-mile pole let him be twenty lengths ahead. Do that, God, and I'll turn over a new leaf. I'll be good to my children. I'll start going to the temple every Friday night. Please, God."

The race starts. As luck would have it, three of the horses get stuck in the gate. Herman looks skyward gratefully. At the half-mile pole, Herman's horse is leading by twenty lengths. Herman says, "God, let him increase his lead by another ten lengths. Do that and I'll pray every morning, every afternoon, every night!"

By now the horses are at the sixteenth pole. Herman's horse is leading by fifty lengths. Now sixty. Seventy with a hundred feet to go. Herman looks up and says, "Okay, God, I'll take it from here!"

Because they were rampant in show business, breed improvers weighed in by the ton at the Friars Round Table. One act alone, the Yacht Club Boys, came in at eight hundred pounds and thousands of dollars. When the act broke up, one of them, Billy Mann, became a stockbroker. Jimmy Kern became a director. Charlie Adler and George Kelly, the final two, ended up making book. Adler and Kelly made a good living booking Mann and Kern.

"Joe and Asbestos" was a popular comic strip that ran in the New York *Daily Mirror*. It was required reading for all horseplayers because Ken Kling, the man behind the strip, gave hot tips. Ken Kling was a Friar. People returning from the track with him waxed eloquent about his ability to choose winners. After each race he came up with a winning ticket. His uncanny ability could have been exposed with careful study. Before each race he bought a ticket on each horse. Starting with his shirt pocket, going clockwise, he put one ticket in each pocket. The race over, he knew from which pocket to extract a winning ticket. The system served him well for years, especially with out-of-town editors he wanted to impress.

Even though the veterans among us knew that he had a system, no day went by without our begging him for a real hot tip. One Saturday, Sid Gary, a headliner but far removed from our gambling virus, was faced with the prospect of having to attend Belmont Park with Harold, his brother. Gary asked Kling for assistance. Kling offered him none and went back to the *Daily Mirror* to work. Gary was slightly put off, so we explained that our tipster, Mr. Kling, bought a ticket for every horse in a race when he went to the track. He really knew no more than we did. Gary said, "Then we'll do that. That's not a bad system. You win every race."

I said, "That's not a system. You have to be crazy to do it."

Joe E. Lewis said, "You're throwing away your money."

"You're betting against yourself," Ben Bernie said.

Sid Gary and his brother went to the track. True to his word, Gary bought a ticket on each horse in the first race—seven horses. The winning horse won at thirty-to-one odds. In the second race the winner paid twelve dollars and change. Long shots swept the rest of the card. Two of the horses paid over fifty dollars for the two invested. The Gary brothers each won a bundle.

At the club several days later, Sid Gary gloated at this score. He said, "Ken Kling's system is fantastic."

I said, "It's not a system."

Gary said, "You guys'll never learn!"

The following week I went out to Belmont Park. I bet on every horse in every race. I lost my shirt.

Tips from the horse's mouth didn't help much either.

A guest one day was Sol Rutchick. Rutchick was a horse trainer. Sitting around with us, he gave no sign of being a man whose horse was going to win the Kentucky Derby. Rutchick had made a lot of money selling candy. He was a natty dresser. In the right light he looked like George Raft.

Seated next to him was the owner of a horse he trained. Jack Amiel was pleasantly plump. ("Jack Amiel," Joey Adams said, "could get up in a bus and give his seat to four ladies!" Morey Amsterdam didn't quite agree. "Jack Amiel is just a little short for his weight. He should be nine foot three!")

While pretending to run his eatery, the Turf Restaurant at Forty-ninth Street and Broadway, Amiel read the *Racing Form* and imagined himself to be a genius at bloodlines. At the Friars, once his food was served, he never looked up from his plate until it was glisteningly clean. Today it was the turn of a chicken pot pie.

The discussion came around to the upcoming Kentucky Derby. Our eyes begged for a tip. Rutchick didn't want to discuss the race. It had caused a big rift between the two men. Rutchick was violently against running the horse. "The horse has absolutely no right going to Kentucky!" Rutchick said.

"We'll win it," said Amiel.

"Not with me around," said Rutchick. "I'm not going to Kentucky!"

Since the horse, Count Turf, was at best questionable, we started to ask about other horses in the race. Rutchick didn't like Battle Morn, the certain favorite. He wasn't too high on Fanfare or Ruhe. Amiel was sure he could beat Big Stretch, Hall of Fame, and Timely Reward.

"You can forget the Whitney horse, Mameluke," Rutchick said. "The whole entry can't win it."

After hearing so many horses wiped out, Jay Burton, one of my writers, said, "Is there a place you can bet the track veterinarian?"

Rutchick was almost violent about not wanting Count Turf to be shipped to Kentucky. Amiel disregarded his protests. Part of the "field" in the race, Count Turf won by four lengths.

Happy and sad at the same time, Rutchick sat with us at the club several days after the race. Spud Chandler, the great Yankee pitcher, asked, "How come the horse won?"

Rutchick said, "Horses are stupid. This one didn't know he wasn't supposed to go to Kentucky!"

"Is he going for the Triple Crown?" Chandler asked.

"He hasn't told me his plans!" said Rutchick.

Conn McCreary, the great jockey, sat at the Round Table with us once. Conn and I were close, as I had already lost several hundred thousand dollars on him and was heading for a cool million. A tiger, McCreary was a come-from-behind specialist. Once he saw an opening on the rail, he went through it. But the openings started to close quickly. The magic disappeared. Few mounts came his way, and even fewer winners. I'd invited him to lunch to cheer him up. Things were going slow for him so he'd started to gallop horses in the morning. He was on a hate against horses. "I don't care," he said, "if I never see another nag in my life. I hate every horse I ever rode, win or lose. I'd give my eyeteeth to do something else. Any darn thing!"

I said, "If you really mean it, you might think about doing a comedy act with somebody. There's a lot of funny jokes you could do."

McCreary said, "Could I do them on a horse?"

When I was headlining at Miami's Royal Palm in 1939, Conn McCreary was riding at Hialeah. I kept badgering him for tips. Finally, he found himself on an interesting card. He had six mounts, he loved five of them. The sixth wasn't a lock, but he felt that it had a good shot.

Since all gamblers like company, I talked Abe Lyman into playing with me. We each put in fifty dollars. At the end of three races we had four hundred dollars in the kitty. Lyman demanded his half. I begged him to stick it out. Lyman said, "The miracle is over. He's not going to win four. God can't sweep a card!"

I said, "McCreary felt good. Let's go one more."

Lyman nodded and we bet the next race. Our horse was the favorite so we won only seven thousand at the end of the race. Lyman asked out again. I begged again. We bet. We won. We won five in a row. We had twenty-two thousand dollars. Lyman asked out. I begged. This time he was adamant. In spite of my threats to have him deported to Cuba, Lyman took his share and disappeared. I plunked my half down. If there's a position worse than last, that's where my horse ended. After the race, McCreary tiptoed into the stable so he wouldn't wake the other horses.

I didn't see Lyman for the rest of my stay in town. When I got back to New York, I saw him at the Round Table. I said, "You're one lucky bastard!"

Lyman said, "Look, I begged you. I showed you why the horse didn't have a chance. I told you you were crazy. I told you you were an idiot!"

"Talk isn't enough," I said. "Next time, let a guy know you mean it!"

Of course I didn't need to be spurred to any kind of action when a horse named after me ran. Milton Berle, the horse, made a lot of people rich—hock-shop owners, shylocks, bankruptcy lawyers, and undertakers who specialized in suicide cases.

The jockey never had to hit Milton Berle, the horse, because there were never any other horses behind it. In sixteen races he never saw the front of another horse. We listened to a replay one afternoon—Milton Berle is trailing, Milton Berle is trailing, Milton Berle is trailing. Pat Henry said, "Milton Berle can't win unless Ruth is in the saddle!"

Earl Wilson, the columnist, came in for lunch one afternoon, put three fingers right into my face, and asked, "How many fingers do I have up?"

I said, "Three."

Wilson, "You can see? The way you ran yesterday, I thought you went blind!"

Pat Henry was not one to throw stones because he lived in a pretty shaky glass house when it came to the enrichment of the breed. One afternoon Pat was paged at the club. The call was from Florida. The voice at the other end indicated that there was a good thing in the fourth at Hialeah in Miami. Pat said, "Put two hundred down for me."

Jilly Rizzo jumped in, "Let me get in on it. I want a hundred!"

Pat said, into the phone, "Make it another hundred."

The bets were accepted. An hour later, the Florida contact called back. "You ran third."

Pat and Rizzo were unhappy. Rizzo asked, "What was the name of the horse?"

Pat said, "I don't know."

In due time, Florida checked in again, thanked the bettors for sending the money, and announced that another sure winner loomed the next day.

Pat said, "Give me three hundred."

Rizzo said, "I'll take a hundred, but what's the name of the horse?"

Pat asked Florida, "What's the name of the horse?"

Listening for a moment, he turned to Rizzo. "He says he deals with a hundred people. We're the only ones who asked the name of the horse!"

Rizzo said, "The hell with him!"

Pat hung up and said, "Jilly, I'll kill you if that horse comes in!"

Neutral until then, I asked, "How will you know?"

Henry said, "I'll look in the *Racing Form* tomorrow!"

Shaken in his suspicions, Rizzo said, "If he calls back, let's bet something!"

This kind of brilliant thinking is what let B. S. Pully, the gravel-throated comedian whose initials summed up the hygiene of his act, came over to me at lunch and smiled down at me as if he didn't know that he owed me money. I said, "Where's the two hundred you owe me from yesterday?"

Pully said, "You mean three hundred."

I said, "I only lent you two hundred."

Pully said, knowingly, "It's gonna *be* three hundred!" (To lend more stature to his act, Pully worked with a partner named H. S. Gump, and then added a girl they called M.S.)

Bud Abbott of Abbott and Costello was close to being the classic loser. Already a victim in 1938 when he and Louis came to New York to star in Michael Todd's *Streets of Paris,* Abbott mulled over a bad streak in both cards and horses, concluding, "I'm going to quit while I'm behind!"

Some people thought of Joe Frisco as being the perfect model for losers. He stuttered his way to a lot of laughs with statements like "If you s-s-see a white f-f-flag over the track, that's my s-s-shirt!" Or "I had a g-g-great d-d-d-day at the track. The b-b-bus got a f-f-flat!"

At the New York Friars, Frisco came in with a tip on a sure winner. He tried everybody in the card room with no favorable results. Finally, he came over to us, the court of last begging. "Valdina George wins," he swore. "I'll give you the fifty for now and I'll pay you back what I owe." This was a blanket offer, as he owed everybody at the table. We turned him down. A little anxious, however, we all bet a few dollars on Valdina George. With so much on him, the horse tired quickly and ran seventh. The result in, we confessed to making a bet. Phil Baker, the radio star, said, "Give us a good excuse."

Frisco said, "The h-h-horse didn't t-t-trust you!"

As in any human endeavor, there are those who excel. For the brotherhood of the beaten, two pennants fly higher than any others. They deserve the introduction of this great story:

A women is berating her husband, "You're a schmuck. You've always been a schmuck and you'll always be a schmuck. If they had a contest of schmucks and there were only one entry you'd come in second."

The husband said, "Why would I come in second?"

The wife answered, "Because you're a schmuck!"

Our prizewinners were far from schmucks, but in a contest to find the all-time loser with only the two of them as candidates, they'd both come in second. Possibly even third.

Belly-Laugh Up to Bar, Boys

Jackie Gleason knows that he can't drown his troubles in drink, but he sure makes them swim for it!

Red Skelton

Dean Martin doesn't know the meaning of the word "defeat." There are also about a million other words he doesn't know the meaning of!

Frank Sinatra

The ten funniest drunk jokes?

Billy Barty, small but talented, said, "Any three minutes from Joe E. Lewis's act!"

Red Buttons said to Robert Merrill, "You'll hear the ten funniest drunk jokes at the Joe E. Lewis dinner, just in my twelve minutes. What else are we going to talk about—his underwear?"

I said, "I have two good underwear jokes." (One was about the old man who went to the doctor. The doctor asked for a specimen of the man's urine and his bowels. So the man gave the doctor his shorts! The other joke has even less socially redeeming qualities so I won't even mention it!)

Buttons said, "This is a joke I heard at Dean Martin's birthday party—Dean doesn't drink unless he's alone or with somebody!"

I said, "That's not one of the biggies."

Buttons said, "I always start slow. It gives me somewhere to go."

I said, "I wasn't invited to Dean Martin's party anyway so the hell with him!"

Jan Murray said, "Milton, you can't afford to lose friends!"

I said, "This is the grandfather of them all—Joe E. Lewis only drinks to steady his nerves. Last night he got so steady he couldn't move!"

Barty said, "That's one of the first jokes I ever heard."

Jan Murray chimed in, to Barty, "That's because all the others went over your head!"

I said, "Barty, I wouldn't stand for that. And if you do stand, how will we know?"

Merrill said, "What are the ten funniest midget jokes?"

I said, "We're still on drunk jokes—Joe E. Lewis's eyes are so bloodshot, he's got to close them or he'll bleed to death!" I carried on, "Joe E. Lewis only drinks at certain times of the day—two, four, six, ten."

Murray said, "They named a forest after Joe E. Lewis—Petrified!"

Barty said, "Joe E. Lewis went to a blood bank and donated a fifth!"

I said, "This is a standard too—Joe E. Lewis saw a sign that said, 'Drink Canada Dry'—and he did!"

Murray said, "The other day the cops stopped Joe E. Lewis and gave him a balloon test. It melted!"

I said, "Another standard—I never knew Joe E. Lewis drank until I saw him sober!"

Merrill said, "You take this list seriously, don't you, Milton?"

I said, "At the Round Table, a request for a list must be honored."

Buttons said, "Yes sir! In that case, I offer my masterpieces—the way Joe E. Lewis drinks, when he eats something it makes a splash! Nobody makes Joe E. Lewis drink the way he does. He's a volunteer!"

Barty said, "This is a standard too—Joe E. Lewis loves flowers. Every night he locks himself up in his room with Four Roses!"

Merrill said, "I don't have to go to the dinner anymore."

Murray said, "You'll miss the ten funniest gambling jokes."

I said, "Wait. Wait. I just thought of a story about a drunken performer."

Buttons said, "Oh boy, and I was going home early."

I ignored him. "Do you all know the Jim Thornton story?"

Murray said, "Would it do us any good if we said we did?"

I said, "Jim Thornton was a vaudevillian. He loved the juice and before each show he put away a fifth. He was playing this theater in Bethlehem, Pennsylvania. The boss was a real dry. He couldn't stand whiskey. He sneaked into Thornton's dressing room and spilled out every drop that Thornton had hidden there.

"Thornton walked in toward the end and saw what the boss had done. To hell with the engagement! Thornton started to pack. The boss barred the door. 'You're not going anywhere! You're going to finish this engagement!'

"Thornton said, 'I'm walking out of here.'

"The boss said, 'You are not walking out of here!'

"Thornton scowled at the boss and said, 'If Jesus Christ could walk out of Bethlehem, so can Jim Thornton!'"

A List for Lust

*Errol Flynn must be with the Secret Service. He
spends all of his time undercover.*

Red Skelton

*John Barrymore comes from a sexy family. His
grandfather died at 102. He was shot by a
jealous husband.*

Gary Cooper

*Of all his relations, Harry Richman liked sex the
best.*

Tommy Dorsey

Joe Franklin is so easygoing. Why doesn't he?

Leonard Lyons

*On his honeymoon with Liz, Mike Todd kept
looking out the window. The guys had told him it
was going to be the most beautiful night of his life.*

Orson Welles

*Tony Martin has women by the score—and
always does.*

Charles Coburn

Inevitably, a discussion of actors becomes a discourse on sexual
prowess. The mention of Warren Beatty doesn't evoke an immediate fanfare for his brilliance as an actor. Instead, somebody hap-

pens to mention that Warren Beatty was seen in the elevator of the Beverly Wilshire Hotel with two stunning ladies. This is followed by a mention of somebody else having seen Dudley Moore at Nicky Blair's restaurant with some Swedish knockout. Simple bookkeeping over, the conversation turns to more lurid details. (The steps taken don't reflect the Round Table's being a haven for dirty old men and dirty young men. It is a haven for such fortunates, but the Round Table shouldn't be held responsible.)

One scenario followed an opening gambit by Sid Kuller, a local historian and a fine writer of special comedy material. Kuller's version of Shaw's great play and later incomparable Broadway musical, renamed *My Fairfax Lady*, played a local club in Los Angeles and was funnier than either of its antecedents. (Fairfax Avenue is a street in Los Angeles that looks as if it was shipped lock, stock, and bagel out of the downtown New York of fifty years ago. It is doubtless the last street west of the Lincoln Tunnel where old-fashioned girdles can still be bought. It also has a podiatrist who does his work, according to a sign in the window, "while you wait.")

The Bandbox, where *My Fairfax Lady* took shelter, was a club the size of a phone booth. It was, during the sixties, a popular spot because it remained open until the dawn came up like thunder across the bay. Major stars often dropped in at the Bandbox for the last of many nightcaps.

Joe E. Ross, the star of *Bilko* and *Car 54, Where Are You?*, was one of the players at the Bandbox. Not overly handsome and hardly endowed with a purring voice, Ross swore that he had made many conquests at the Bandbox. Among them, his proudest achievement, was a ménage à trois with Lana Turner and Ave Gardner in his tiny dressing room. Admitting that both ladies were well out of their gourds by the hour of conquest and didn't know him from Montgomery Clift, Ross described the pleasures in intimate detail to all who listened. One of the listeners was Sid Kuller. Since Ross wasn't much of a liar, when he showed up at the Round Table to recount the experience, most of us believed him. Aware that doubters might appear, Phil Silvers said to Ross, "You should have taken a picture to show us."

Ross answered, "I thought of that, but it wouldn't have been nice. Neither girl had makeup on!"

Relating the story again last year, Kuller got a few memories started. No face for a theatrical Mount Rushmore, Joe E. Ross was special enough to merit some attention.

Joe E. Ross measured his life in hookers. At his death, street corners in Hollywood were draped in black. We had fun with his "girlfriends." Red Buttons said, "Joey's latest girl has spent so much time on Sunset Boulevard they just gave her a street number!" "Joey's new girlfriend," Jesse White offered, "spends so much time walking the street, her panty hose have curb feelers!" Ross himself had a comment about one of his lady friends: "She's trying to stop screwing everybody, but she's not good at it!"

We wanted Ross for a tiny benefit once. I phoned him. The phone was answered by a sweet feminine voice. She said that Ross was in New York for a commercial. Who was she? Or, she was his fiancée. They were getting married when he returned.

The following week Ross came up to the club. We congratulated him on his impending marriage and asked the name of his intended. He said, "I think it's Doreen."

Harry Ritz asked, "Aren't you sure?"

Ross said, "You know these hookers. They never use their real names. But I think it's Doreen."

I said, "Did she tell you that?"

Ross said, "No, she wants me to call her Mary. I think she's Doreen because that's the name on some of her medicine bottles."

Sadly, the wedding never took place. One day when Ross was out, Doreen/Mary rented a U-Haul It. She and her boyfriend cleaned out Ross's apartment. The police were called. The only photos of his lady love were French postcard Polaroids. Ross asked the police, "Can I keep the ones with me in them?"

These tales prompted a Round Table discussion of sex and the actor. Anthony Newley told a rather lurid tale about an escapade in Las Vegas with three English ladies of the chorus. Phil Foster said, "With Newley every broad is a British Open!"

I told my harrowing tale of the Stroud Twins. Claude and Clarence Stroud worked as a comedy team for some years, got their share of polite laughs, and finally ended up in Hollywood. One became a character actor, the face you see in a hundred movies but you can't place the name. The other picked up a high-back chair and became a director.

In their glory days both were dedicated to wenchery. A woman unsullied was a mark of shame on the Stroud family name. They managed to sully many damsels, but with a difference. To provide a base of operations once in San Franciso, they took a large suite with a sitting room on the other side of the ample bedroom door. Each brother dressed similarly, thus their robes matched. Fortunately, their bodies were a matched set too.

A young woman was invited to the suite by Clarence. After a brief interlude in which the state of the nation was discussed, Clarence managed to suggest a more intimate activity. There being no objections, soon a coupling was effected. Clarence was at least an adequate lover so the coupling wasn't hurried. When it came to an end, Clarence put on his robe, whispered a momentary farewell, and sauntered to the sitting room.

Now it was Claude's turn. Within a minute, a Stroud returned to the bedroom. A little love play, to the obvious surprise and delight of the maiden, and again a romantic pairing took place. Since only five minutes elapsed from the first, the young lady attempted to test her companion's stamina. She found it remarkable. These pleasant moments passed. In time, Claude arrived at completion. He kissed his passion, put on his robe, and walked into the sitting room.

Rejuvenated by a half hour's rest, Clarence was ready again to take up the battle. He did so with much vigor.

When they were in their twenties and well into their thirties, the Strouds were able to manage enough matings to keep any lady happy. More than happy, the damsels had to believe that they had discovered perpetual motion and eternal pleasure.

Before Tommy Lasorda, visiting the afternoon of the telling of the Ross saga, and Richard Moll, the giant from *Night Court*, could add episodes of their own, Kuller asked, "Who are the great studs of the business?"

I said, "The game for the day is—the ten biggest studs."

Phil Foster said, "At lunch?"

Tony Newley said, "Milton likes games where he can win."

Lasorda said, "I'll give you ten ballplayers who belong in the record book."

I said, "Show business, but no Sinatra. He's on too many lists for too many things."

Moll said, "I don't know any in television."

Foster said, "Just sit there and keep eating from the top of our heads!"

Newley said, "I know he was English, but the top man had to be Chaplin."

Lasorda said, "He went for little girls."

I said, "Little girls, big girls, fat, thin. When he was fifty, he swore to me that he'd had two thousand women!"

"That's only six hundred a year," Jack Carter said, breaking a two-minute silence. "Warren Beatty does better than that on a Thursday."

I said, "Don't he wish! Let me tell you about Chaplin. When he was hanging around with Thelma Converse, the one who married into English royalty—" Newley interrupted, "She became Lady Furness. Her husband had just gotten out of a lot of trouble, so the papers said. He just got out of the fire and into Lady Furness!"

"I never knew that," said Foster.

I tried to go full steam ahead. "Chaplin was faking going with Converse, she was like a shill so he could hang out with Lita, the kid actress he married when she finally got to be sixteen. But there were two other reasons. Converse had a sister and a twenty-year-old cousin. He was manhandling them too. In between, he also went after Pola Negri and Mabel Normand. This was his steady routine."

"In England," Newley said, "the newspapers used to publish Chaplin's exploits. I remember one article about his being at Hearst's place. It said Charlie was made of iron."

Moll said, "I didn't know the gentleman, but I'll accept him in the race for number one."

"Gary Cooper belongs up there also," Foster said.

"Definitely," I said. "Two days before she left for Hollywood, Tallulah Bankhead called me at the club. We were doing something for flood relief in the South somewhere and she had to back out. She swore she was going to the Coast for two reasons—'I want some of those divine lemons. And then I'm going to f—— that divine Gary Cooper!' "

Moll said, "That gives us two for the list."

Foster said, "This tall dummy is counting!" He grabbed at the paper Moll was writing on. "You don't write it down. We don't want a record—five grown men playing pishy-cocky games with 'Who's the biggest stud?' "

"I like the game," Newley said. "It turns me on!"

"RyKrisp turns you on," Foster said. "The trouble is, you marry the broads! I'll give you a name for the list—Errol Flynn!"

"Don't get vicious about it," Newley said.

"Why shouldn't I get vicious? We're talking about men who did what we just talk about!"

"Speak for yourself," I said.

Lasorda said, "Put Berle on the list. If we don't, he'll put his name on himself!"

"You talk brave for a man whose team is gonna lose again!" I said.

"All of the men you've mentioned are well-known womanizers," said Moll. "Who are the secret studs?"

I said, "I'll give a batch—Fredric March!"

"The actor?" Lasorda asked.

Foster nodded along with me. Foster said, "When March did a play in New York, the rest of us could have stayed home!"

I said, "March holds the record for extras at Paramount!"

"He was so square," Newley said.

I said, "Watch out for those. Look at Herbert Marshall. Walter Pidgeon."

"Do you want a sneaky Englishman?" Foster asked. "Try Peter Lawford. He didn't miss anybody."

"Rubirosa," Newley said.

"He's not in show business," said Moll.

"He went with Zsa Zsa."

"Now we're into groups," said Foster.

"Okay, no Rubirosa," said Newley. "I'll give you the all-time winner—Jimi Hendrix!"

"The rock guitarist?" Moll asked.

Newley explained, "I knew him a little in London. He was wild. The women were wilder than he was. He used to love to take girl-friends away from other rock stars."

I said, "Should I tell you about Elvis Presley?"

Lasorda said, "Of course you will."

I said, "Presley was doing pictures for Joe Pasternak at MGM. One a day. He'd break just before noon and take a stroll. No body-guards circled him, because he was on the lot and nobody both-ered him. When he got outside, he played Cops and Robbers with some writer. They'd hide behind cars, with their extended fingers, duck, pop up, and shoot again. Two little infants. Presley never spoke to the guy, only Cops and Robbers. Presley would work himself to the two-story building in which some of the TV shows were put together. There was a secretary for one of the companies waiting for him. Next to her woud be a girlfriend, a different one each day if possible, and they'd go into a nearby office with a couch and have a quick trio. Then Presley would zip up and head back to his own office. This went on day after day and didn't slow Presley down one second in his close friendships with the three women who were always hanging around, the handful of women who paraded in and out of his portable dressing room near the stage, and whatever female visitors showed up of an afternoon. This was the same Presley who did my show in 1956 when he was eighteen. Offered a wild time by some of the other guests, he passed on it. He had to get his sleep for the show."

Foster said, "I have nice Billy Eckstine stories just like that. Billy didn't come in second to anybody!"

Lasorda said, "We must have forty names already."

"We have ten," said Moll.

Foster said, "Add Guy Marks, the comedian—a real legend!"

"He's not famous," Moll said.

"He should be!" I said.

"How many do we have now?" Lasorda asked.

"If we add us, we've got enough."

"Add us," Newley said, "but put an asterisk after my name!"

Kuller said, "How about women?"

I said, "Just say—Tallulah and Mae West! That's ten already!"

Lasorda said, "Hey, you forgot old George Raft!"

I said, "Kuller, we're grown men, we don't have time for such foolishness." Then I suddenly remembered the greatest oversight of all. Opening the meeting for further nominations, I had to offer up the name of Harry Richman.

Mae West didn't know what she was unleashing on the world when she took this honky-tonk piano player and put him in her act. Or maybe she did. The other option, one she almost took up, was a bulbous-nosed Italian named Jimmy Durante.

One way or the other, Mae soon learned that her piano player had other talents. Harry Richman displayed them in the dressing room at every opportunity, in closets, on floors, in trains, cars, and more than once in the street. West, the star who personified sex, could hardly contain her paramour.

A big star in a few years, Richman went on to conquests of his own, conquests too numerous to count. He was beyond being a satyr. He was a machine. In three big Broadway shows, not one woman in the cast, star or chorus girl, escaped Harry Richman's attentions.

Richman wasn't merely a taker of favors. He lavished gifts on his ladies. He owed the world. One time he and Errol Flynn were comparing minuses. Flynn counted off debtors in twenty countries and every corner of the globe. Richman looked at him with disdain. "You owe money? You're *rich* enough to be my banker!"

Richman didn't think of money or, for that matter, women in the same ways most of us do. Money and women were to be used. When you reached down, money was supposed to be there. When you started to unzip, a woman was supposed to be there. Most of the time, a woman was.

Toward the end Richman was a basket case, supported by old friends. Yet nobody felt that it was charity. You took care of Richman because he was the king bee. The job of the drones, as famous as or more famous than he, was to keep him going in the style he was accustomed to.

Without a few endorsements for George Burns before he married Gracie, a list of romantic figures would be horribly incomplete. Burns's liaisons were beyond count. After he married Gracie, he told us humbly, "I threw all my phone numbers in the garbage. I had to make three trips!"

We made a good list that day at the club. It would stand the test of bed and time. Yet, I can hear Richard Burton's words to us after returning from the shooting of *Cleopatra*. "Sometimes I think," Burton said, "lust is a step too far."

Ladies Be Seated

Phyllis Diller

Lily Tomlin loves to redecorate the house all the time. That way she doesn't have to dust!

Carol Burnett

Phyllis Diller almost didn't marry Fang because of the difference in their ages. She was twenty-two and he was poor!

Dolores Hope

Sophie Tucker made an honest man of her husband. She kept watching him!

Sandra Berle

Carol Channing is a health nut. She takes so many iron supplements, when she gets up in the morning she slowly starts to face North!

Mary Martin

My husband makes love to me almost every day of the week—almost Monday, almost Tuesday, almost Wednesday...

Ruth Berle

I drove my husband George to drink, and that's not the only nice thing I did for him!

Alice Gobel

In 1985, Phyllis Diller infiltrated a Friars' stag roast. Dressed in men's clothes, with a mustache added to hide the face that launched a thousand ships, Diller felt that she was setting a precedent. She was seventy-five years too late. The sanctity of the club itself had been de-filed by one of the greatest actresses of another day.

Sarah Bernhardt's leading man in many of the sketches she did on the vaudeville stage, Lou Tellegen, a future matinee idol, swore that he brought Bernhardt to the Friars for lunch one afternoon in 1913. Draped in the latest men's fashions, her hair up and covered by a dark felt hat, and walking slowly to hide the fact that she had a wooden leg, Bernhardt, Tellegen told W. C. Fields, fooled Al Jolson and Rennold Wolf, the critic of the *Telegraph*, completely as they sat innocently at the Round Table. (In addition to his inability to separate the sexes, Wolf was a terrible critic, but he was the best toastmaster the club had until Jessel came along. As far as I know, Wolf was the first to use the line—"Ladies and gentlemen...if that's what you are." I know I was second, third, fourth, and fifth.)

Tellegen introduced Bernhardt as a Parisian moviemaker in the States to put together a deal for the French film comedian Max Linder. Eating fast-food lunches Linder made five hundred pictures in one year. Half of them would get big laughs today.

W. C. Fields told the Bernhardt story to Carlotta Monti, his companion for years. Monti told the story to a close friend, Frances Kemp, an Earl Carroll show girl and dancer, who told it to me. That's as close as I come to firsthand with a Sarah Bernhardt caper.

Bernhardt's sneaky attack on the Friars would have been very much in keeping with her way of thinking. She was an original. She requested, and received, her money in gold at the end of each show. Animal acts were forbidden to come within a mile of any bill she headed. Blackface acts were taboo. Jugglers were her pet hate.

However, she bought W. C. Fields. Explaining, years later, Fields said, "She was afraid of me because I had it bruited about that I carried a beaver in my luggage."

Bernhardt's demands were slightly exorbitant in the face of a slight language problem. No American in the audience understood a word she said. Martin Beck, her booker, sat down at the Round Table once and after setting the scene involving contract negotiations said, "That bitch is lucky. She has no idea of how close I came to setting her leg on fire."

Jerry Cohan said, "She has ten like it."

Beck said, "I was thinking of the *real* one!"

At the rule-breaking lunch, Tellegen reported further, Jolson shifted around to become comfortable. Accidentally, he kicked the wooden leg and was a little puzzled by the firmness. In fractured English, Bernhardt explained, "It is no problem. I am unfortunately damned with a permanent erection. I must strap it down to get around!"

Years after the Bernhardt raid on the male stronghold that was the Friars, I told Jolson about how he had nudged elbows with Sarah Bernhardt. Taking center stage at the Round Table, Jolson said, "It's a good thing I didn't know. I would have been obliged to ask her for a date. Dinner would have been followed by a romance. I would have been forced to lie next to her, kiss her passionately on the neck, and then say, 'Spread your leg!' "

Lumber didn't come up after Phyllis Diller pulled her stunt. Many at the Round Table didn't want to believe it. William B. Williams, in New York, asked, "How could Phyllis Diller look like a man?"

Joey Bishop said, "Just by changing her sneakers!"

A fitting punishment was decided on. To get even, the mighty Friars would roast her. Diller said, "I thought you'd never ask!" She insisted that no special treatment be given. No kid gloves. She wanted the works. Buddy Hackett said, "Phyllis, you heard. The guys get pretty raw. Somebody could call you a nymphomaniac, a whore...somebody could come at you how you like whips and chains and sodomy...somebody else, Phyllis Diller loves orgies... Phyllis, it gets real raunchy."

Diller said, "They can call me a nympho, let them say I'm into S&M. Let somebody say I'll take on anybody. I don't care if somebody gets up there and also tells *lies* about me!"

Paul Anka said, "You still keep putting yourself down. I can't understand that. Since you had that work done, you look sensational!"

Diller said, "Anka, you really know how to hurt a lady!"

Not one to miss a shot at an audience, Diller went into a rehearsal of some of her latest plastic surgeon jokes—"I went to this plastic surgeon. He took a look at me and just wanted to add a tail!" "He said my face looked like a bouquet of elbows!"

"You know something," William B. Williams said. "If Milton Berle was here in New York now, he'd call for a list of 'ugly' jokes."

Diller asked, "What do you mean by 'list'?"

Anka said, "When Berle's at the Round Table, any noun brings on a list of the ten best, worst, the ten something."

Diller said, "I love to play games. That's how I got Fang. I took a chance on a blanket!"

William B. Williams said, his voice firm and commanding, the voice that made him such a powerful radio personality and disc jockey, "The ten best 'ugly' jokes."

Diller started it off, "The only way I could get to a plastic surgeon is on a blind date!"

Anka said, "That's ugly."

Diller went on, "I have a great birth-control device—my face!"

Seeing that there was a little frivolity about, the executive director of the Friars in New York, Jean-Pierre Trebot, joined the group. In an accent that still hadn't left Paris, Trebot asked, "What's going on?"

Williams said, "List time."

Trebot said, "Without Milton?"

Williams said, "Jean-Pierre, please don't tell him."

Having gone through the files in his mind, Red Buttons said, "Will Rogers had a good one—She was so ugly she could make a mule back away from an oat bin!"

Paul Anka said, "She was so ugly her parents put out a contract on her!"

There was a sudden pause, then, after a moment, Trebot said, "It's no fun without Milton."

Diller said, "I'm having fun. Here's one I adore—The last guy who gave her a hickey got fur in his mouth!"

The biggest laugh of the meal. Hard to follow, it brought the contest to a halt. (William B. Williams went home and put as much of the lunch meeting as he could remember on a tape, which he sent to me. At first I was furious that somebody had tried a list without me. Thinking about it, I decided it was an honor. However, I could never put the matter to rest until I aired a few of my favorite "ugly" jokes—She was so ugly she tried out for a hooker at the Mustang ranch and she was beaten out—by a mustang!" "He was so ugly he always wore a mask. Except when he robbed a bank!" One more: "She was so ugly, Customs wouldn't let her enter the country without a crate!")

The jokes at the Phyllis Diller roast in New York were a little rougher than our prime-time "uglies." The smash affair served as a good tune-up for a second Phyllis Diller Friars frying on the West

Coast. To make preparations for the second roast, this one to be held in Beverly Hills, and possibly to play "ugly" jokes with us, Diller joined us for a basket of hot bagels. Redd Foxx reminded us of an all-time classic—"Women like her don't grow on trees—they swing from them!"

Fang, Phyllis's former husband, was a guest speaker at the Round Table several times. Brought in by Tom Korman, a major agent in Hollywood, Fang acted the Fang part. Melvin Belli asked if Phyllis Diller was anything like the character she portrayed. "Is she really a terrible homemaker? A bad cook?"

Aware that Belli spends much of his time on a large yacht, Fang said, "Put Phyllis on your boat for three days. Her dust would sink it!"

Then came the roast. It has been many months, but the Beverly Hilton Hotel has never recovered.

A week after the affair I was at the Diller house. After dinner our hostess played the piano for us. She was wearing a light-blue print dress. Her hair was bound in a white and blue scarf. Her eyes were closed as she played. Ruth and I looked at one another. We were watching a lovely lady.

Sophie Tucker

Phyllis Diller wasn't the first lady to whom the Friars paid an X-rated tribute. That honor would have to go to Sophie Abusa, a little lady born in Russia who changed her name to Sophie Tucker. Called "The Last of the Red Hot Mamas," Tucker learned early that suggestiveness and innuendo were a girl's best friends. A wink, a hint of something forbidden, and cogent pauses made audiences forget that the little lady was a few pounds overweight and didn't have the best singing voice since Jenny Lind. Ever aware of milady's fashions, Julian Eltinge reported to the Round Table after seeing one of Tucker's performances, "Sophie was wearing a dress with feather highlights. In her hand she had a big feather fan and on her head a band with a feather in it. She looked like she'd flicked a chicken on the way to the stage!" Eltinge was just about this kind to everybody. Seeing me in new plaid knickers once, Eltinge asked my mother, "Why do you shop in Wilkes-Barre?"

Approval by Julian Eltinge always pending, Sophie Tucker laughed all the way to stardom without it.

By the time her fiftieth anniversary in show business went into the books, Sophie Tucker was a synonym for sex. She could say "ketchup" and the audience would hear something almost obscene. (A fairly good parallel exists with the smash TV show *The Golden Girls*. Because the show revolves about elderly women, the audience tunes in to hear "dirty.")

Tucker's being a women presented a problem to those of us who had broiled every kind of male under monsignor. Was this a nice way to salute a nice lady? Could we get away with it? How far could we go? Would she even go for the idea? I called her from the club. I said, "Sophie, this is Milton."

Sophie said she knew who it was. Eight four-letter words later,

she slowed down enough for me to explain I was calling from the
club. She started again. A dozen four-letter words later, all brand-
new ones, she slowed down again and asked me what I wanted.
Or had I called because her husband was dead? "If he's dead,"
she said, "okay. If he's alive, don't lend him any money."

"Sophie, we'd like to roast you. A stag."

"A stag? Did you run out of schmucks?"

Right then and there I knew we'd have no trouble roasting Sophie
Tucker.

The affair was sold out in two days.

As the show grew closer, Tucker started to play Ziegfeld.

Every day she called with new suggestions. *The Kinsey Report*
was published at this time. Because it was an early version of Masters and Johnson's famous book on sex, it had to come to Tucker's
attention. "Let's get that Dr. Kinsey on the dais."

I said, "What if he doesn't perform?"

She said, "That would explain why he had to write a book!"

The sex manual prompted her to force me to write a song with
her. It is printed here for the first time. And probably the last:

Take it easy, Mr. Leader.
Don't let the musicians cavort.
While I tell everybody about
My own Kinsey Report.

My first love was an artist.
Of the Louvre he could boast.
But he wasn't hung where it
Mattered the most!

My next was a jockey.
Up the creek with a paddle.
My gentleman jockey couldn't
Stay in the saddle.

The song had a thousand choruses.

The phone call after the Kinsey matter was prompted by the
climbing of Mount Everest by Hillary. "I've been thinking, Milton.
Let's get the Englishman from the mountain."

I said, "Sure. He'll come ten thousand miles for a bow."

"If he doesn't want to take a bow, let him teach my husband not to fall off so much!"

(My mother told me that Sophie Tucker has had a bedroom headache for eighteen years! A sharp soul, I retorted, "Yeah—Al!")

When I reported Tucker's comment about the lesson the English climber could impart, Abel Green of *Variety* said, "Al Lackey doesn't fall off. He jumps!"

In spite of Tucker's outward obsession with the pelvic playground and her apparent calm during the show, the roast made her a little sad. Later she told my mother, "For years I dreamed of somebody whispering dirty words in my ear. Now I get twenty men screaming dirty words and I can't hear half of them."

I called Tucker from the club to let her know how much of a sport she'd been. She answered, "Milton, if all that filth got one Friar excited enough to go home and get laid, the roast was a success!"

I reported her words to Charlie Dale, sitting at the Round Table with us. Dale said, "Tell Sophie she's gonna get her wish. Sinatra's dirty parody is beginning to work on me!"

Jack E. Leonard said, "If Sophie calls back next month, Charlie will know for sure."

Buddy Arnold and I wrote the Sinatra parody, as we did many others for stag roasts. They can't be offered here because of our modesty, the Mann Act, and the Meese Commission Report on Obscenity. Our last parody, for Phyllis Diller, is being used as a school song by Masters and Johnson.

The hell with modesty! Here's the parody Sinatra sang to the tune of "Mother":

S is for the sweetness that is in her.
O is for the oldies that she sings.
P is for the people who adore her.
H is for the happiness she brings.
I is for the ideals that she lives by.
E is for the endless curtain calls.
Put them all together, they spell Sophie
The only Friar without balls
And we're not certain!

Mae West

Although for some years before going to the Friars I'd been reading about Mae West, the "Nell Brinkley Girl," so-called because of the styles like the Gibson Girl, I wasn't ready to sneak into theaters to see her. (How was I to know that in my TV wardrobe I would end up with two Nell Brinkley outfits and a silk Mae West gown? I don't wear them much anymore. True story: Before leaving to emcee and appear in a taped show with the stars of the Las Vegas revue *La Cage Aux Folles,* I was looking through the wardrobe closets for some outfits. Ruth pointed to one aqua gown and said, "You spent so much for that dress. How come you never wear it?")

Mae West became a topic for conversation at the Round Table, as far as I was concerned, in 1921, about a year after Eddie Cantor brought me to the club. A piano player around town, Harry Richman, was sipping a drink and telling about an audition he'd had that midmorning. Mae West needed a piano player quickly. The choice was between Harry Richman and an Italian kid, Jimmy Durante. Richman said, "I think I got it. The Italian boy loused up the ballad and the third hump!"

Richman got the job. A month later Richman told us, "We've been rehearsing ten hours a day. Next week we start with a piano!"

Richman brought us a new Mae West saying each day and reported on surprising Westian innovations. Richman swore that they'd made love through two innings of the first radio broadcast of a baseball game. Announced by Graham MacNamee from the Polo Grounds in New York, the game helped West concentrate. "I need something," West told Richman. "Music makes me drowsy."

In spite of glands ever-pumping, Mae West knew what was going on in the world. When President Harding commuted the sentence of Eugene Debs, the Socialist, West sent a congratulatory note to the White House. Doubtless, she was sensitive to people going to jail for their words. Her words had been arrested more than once. West also was aware of a tiny fact like the invention by a fellow named Harwood of the self-winding watch. West was, however, unable to resist highlighting the event with a little sexual reference. The invention, she felt, would leave us all more time for other things.

Mae West was aware all of her life. She knew her philosophy, medicine, and even politics. Although ten White House cabinets sitting in conference for ten years couldn't explain the invitation, Mae West was asked to join President and Mrs. Ford for dinner with Anwar Sadat of Egypt. West begged off. George Raft, still her buddy, told us at the club, "Mae thought it seemed like a long way to go for one dinner!"

George Raft took over when Harry Richman decided that familiarity is bad for a working musician. Raft was close to Owney Madden. They'd been pals since childhood, so when Madden needed a courier and Raft a job, the twain met. Madden owned a chunk of *Diamond Lil,* West's big hit of the season. Raft came to pick up Madden's share of the profits and stayed to brunch with Mae West. (West was responsible for Joe Louis becoming the heavyweight champ. At the time, boxing wasn't eager to give black fighters a shot at the heavyweight title. West called Madden, the informal fight czar at the time, and begged for a favor. Madden granted her desire to have Louis get into the ring with James Braddock, the champ.)

Raft wasn't one to brag about his prowess, but West spread the word around, and it got to the Round Table sooner or later. The word was—frequent, all the time, and anyplace. Raft and West made love in cars, closets, on the floor, kitchen tables, under canopies, and like the word said—anyplace.

On one occasion, after Broadway had gotten the report from West that she and Raft had made love nine times the previous day, Ben Bernie asked Raft if it was true. Raft nodded and explained simply, "She don't ask for much!"

The Raft years were interrupted by Mae West's discovery of Gary Cooper. Then along came Steve Cochran. And along came, et cetera, et cetera.

The Friars' tribute to Mae West was more than an acknowledgment of her sexuality. This great lady was much more. She was a star and an institution. Her movies helped to save a studio. Her plays tested the strength of the First Amendment. Mostly, she was a truly funny lady—"I'm a gal who works at Paramount all day and Fox all night!" "Come up and see me sometime. Come up Wednesday, that's amateur night!" "Between two evils, I always pick the one I've never tried before!" "Trust me. Thousands of men have!"

She wrote the lines, fought police commissioners, mayors, studio heads, and censors for them, and made us laugh with them. (Give me the floor and I'll do two hours on Mae West. I said that at the Round Table once. The owner of the Lakers, Dr. Jerry Buss, said, "Milton, you can do two hours on onion rings!")

So overwhelming was Mae West's aura, she didn't have to set up sexual premises. On a radio show she once told the story of Adam and Eve, each word from a clean-scrubbed Bible, and the shock waves almost destroyed a network.

On a television variety show Mae West was supposed to act in a kitchen sketch about the Mae West Cooking School. At the first reading West started to recite a recipe for scrambled eggs. She got as far as "Take two eggs. Break them..." The sketch was erased by the network. West erased the show and went home. West didn't come near the studio again until Rock Hudson got her to do a duet with him on the Academy Awards.

At the roast Mae West accepted the final ovation gracefully. She concluded her remarks by paraphrasing H. L. Mencken, the smartest man this side of a typewriter: "I had to fight the Puritans. I don't like people who have the haunting fear that someone, somewhere may be happy!" Then, controlling the crowd as usual, West looked at George Raft, her escort for the evening, and said, "Now if you don't mind, George is going to take me home now so we can continue what we were doing thirty years ago when Gary Cooper interrupted us!"

Some Choice Ones

The search went on for more ladies to have fun with. Since each had to be the right lady, the search was diligent. It seemed that Tallulah Bankhead was a good choice. There's nobody today like Tallulah. A magnificent actress and the granddaughter of the Speaker of the House of Representatives, this Alabama beauty was at once a southern belle and a foul-mouthed free soul with little respect for morals and rules of behavior. She was a flower child in a Coco Chanel suit, uninhibited, basic, and bent on self-destruction. Having had breast surgery about the time that we considered her as a roastee, Tallulah was proud of what could be done with Silly Putty. A little bored and starved for a headline while sitting in the Stork Club, Tallulah reached in and pulled out one of her new jobs so that Otto Preminger could see the results of modern medicine. That half of upscale New York could also see didn't bother her.

During a Las Vegas stint, her claustrophobia real, Tallulah refused to close the dressing-room door. Nor would she close the bathroom door. As a result, her ablutions were almost public. The singer on the show, a young man named Merv Griffin, told us at the club, reminiscing about the experience, "I spent the whole engagement walking around backstage with one eye closed!"

Goodman Ace wrote Tallulah's big radio show. Her nightclub act, a successful one, was filled with Ace material. The Round Table sent Ace to check on Bankhead's attitude toward the roast idea. Ace reported back. "We were in," he said. "You could have sent out circulars to the membership. You could have taken out ads. She didn't say one cross word. Not one expletive."

Sonny Werblin, then an MCA agent, said, "What happened?"

Ace said, "I got to her place!"

I said, "Stop clowning around. This could be a big affair."

Ace said, "No, it couldn't."

Werblin said, "She turned us down?"

Ace said, "She'll do it if we can get Richard Burton to make mad passionate love to her on the stage."

I said, "She didn't say that."

Ace said, "Yes, she did. Of course those weren't her exact words."

Werblin said, "We'll get Burton!"

Ace said, "I don't think so. He's already turned down the same request from her for a Sloan-Kettering dinner!" (At that time the Richard Burton express was just leaving the station. *The Robe,* the biblical epic he starred in, was still in the first-run theaters. But the train was beginning to pick up speed. Talk about strange quirks of fate—the only person at the Round Table the first time Burton came to the Friars was Eddie Fisher.)

Walter Winchell tried to get Tallulah to reconsider our kind offer. We would be very gentle and make no unkind sexual references. Tallulah said, "Walter, that would be even worse. You ought to know, all I have going for me is my lack of dignity!"

At the Round Table, we mulled on. If not Tallulah, who? A roast for Lena Horne was suggested. The suggester was almost thrown out of the club. Lena Horne was not roast material. Till this day I personally will challenge to a duel any man who even leers at Lena Horne.

Finally, we came up with another winner for the roast derby. The discovery came about because Nick Condos returned back from Florida. One half of a sensational dance act, maybe the best in the business, Condos was also a Greek charmer who had tapped his way into Martha Raye's heart. Raye today is seen ten times a night in some commercial for a denture cream or cleanser. When seen in public, she's recognized pretty much as that nice gray-haired lady who talks about shining teeth.

Time sure do go by. Once upon a time, like it says in the fairy tales, Martha Raye was one of the great singers, somewhere between Judy Garland and Lena Horne. She was far from being the croaking singer she often pretended to be—"I have the face of a vulture and the voice of a crow. If you threw a rock at me, you could kill two birds with one stone!"

Raye was always putting herself down—"When I finish carrying a tune, you can see fingerprints on it!" "My mouth is so big I can sing duets!" After a tempestuous fight with Raye, Condos complained to us, "That goddamn wife of mine has a walk-in mouth!" Raye told me the reason for her divorce from Condos: "He got sore the other day. I made a nice dinner and he broke his tooth on my coffee!"

The day before his return from Florida, Condos had a real fifteen rounder with Raye. Unaware, we asked Condos, "What are the chances of getting Martha for a stag luncheon?"

Condos said, "Why don't you honor another broad and you could hold the affair in Martha's mouth!" (Condos pulled out all the stops only after a squabble. In times of peace, Condos was a gentleman and supportive. Unhappily, the truces were short. Eddie Cantor once told him at lunch that the secret was to count to ten before throwing an insult. George Jessel said, "I took Cantor's advice many years ago. I think I'm on my fifth wife!")

A goodly portion of Nick Condos's epithets mentioned the size of Martha Raye's mouth. The strange fact was that the notion of Raye's big mouth was the result of a snow job. Tell an audience something often enough and it'll believe every word. Martha Raye had a cute mouth. Moreover, Raye had a sensational figure, legs to match, and was amply endowed. Once during a rough flood that had wiped out half of the roads of Tennessee and Kentucky, a food shortage seemed imminent. At the club, Joe E. Lewis had a great solution: "Let's fly down Martha Raye. She could breast-feed both states!"

The joke wasn't all poetry. If Martha Raye had felt that she could be of help where the water was cold and deep, she would have paid her own way or paddled a canoe down the Mississippi. The next day she'd be found on the levee helping to stuff sandbags.

When this country went to war in 1941, Martha Raye went too. Years later, when we were bogged down in Vietnam, Raye sang and ad-libbed her way up and down Asia. One outfit named her "the funniest man in 'Nam."

The idea of having a stage for Martha Raye preceded our involvement in Southeast Asia. Saigon, as far as most of us were concerned, was one of those places Alan Ladd went to in Paramount movies. Indochina was a country lit by one candle. Saturday night there was nothing to do. General Yang had the ricksha.

The world was a more peaceful place at the time we heard that

Martha Raye was willing to be roasted. Naturally, we couldn't pick on her because she was a massive talent and a hell of a patriot. We were lucky in that Martha Raye had, among other characteristics of course, many major roastable qualities. First, she was a lady whose sexual interests, historians reported, put her right up there with Catherine the Great. Maybe even a length or two ahead of Catherine the Great. This might have been reflected in the large number of beaus and husbands who filled her diary.

For a while Raye was married to David Rose, the composer. In additon to marrying singers, with Judy Garland being another one, David Rose liked model trains. Checking with us to see how the roast was coming along, Raye told us a David Rose anecdote that might fuel a run for some comedian. This one afternoon, Raye was in the house minding her own business while her new husband was outside tinkering with a new engine. Suddenly, Raye felt a need for some extremely personal contact with her husband. Raye called to Rose to come inside. Rose said, "I want to wait till this engine comes around. I don't want to miss the train."

Raye yelled out, "If you don't come right in, you're gonna miss better!"

Martha Raye wasn't bashful about her appetites. "For me," she confessed, 'How do you do?' is an aphrodisiac!" At one of the Friars' annual dinners, my wife kiddingly asked Martha Raye to spell "aphrodisiac" for a dollar. Raye said, "I just learned how to spell 'douche' Thursday!"

If spelling wasn't one of Martha Raye's strong suits, her ability to cuss was. Martha Raye knew words truck drivers hadn't learned yet. No guest at the roast would need to worry about offending Martha Raye's tender feelings. The luncheon went off as planned and was a highlight of obscenity for the year, maybe even for the century.

One of the Friars at the post-mortem later in the day was Doc Mumble. An actor who didn't do much work, Doc Mumble was hard of hearing. Because we're a fraternal group, some of the club members chipped in and bought Doc Mumble a hearing aid. During the Martha Raye luncheon, Doc Mumble had actually heard a roast for the first time. He told us, "If I'd known you guys had such filthy mouths, I never would have joined this club!"

Afraid that the previous stag roastings of great female stars couldn't be topped, we took a long hiatus. We wore kid gloves and silken tongues when we honored Dinah Shore, Barbra Streisand, and Lucille Ball. (We were much more refined than Johnny Carson on the *SHARE* show, explaining that there would be no obscene four-letter words to shock the elite gathering, so here she is—Lucille Testicle!)

We have class. As Mae West said in her rebuttal after having been maligned for two hours, "I love the way you guys use all that filthy language. You use it with such good taste!"

His and Her Towels

To roast the ladies with no holds barred is one thing. To hand them the Friars Club—lunch menu, sauna, and card room—is another. That's what we did in May of 1987.

On May 22, in California, we took in our first dues-paying female member. (Actually our rules never precluded woman members. Had that discrimination been in effect, I and the club would have heard from Ruth Berle. Ruth was a women's libber before she could spell ERA. Rumor has it that her pediatrician had to salute her before an examination. I do know that her gynecologist has to say "please" a lot.)

No woman had ever applied for membership until early in 1987. Gloria Allred, a pretty, dark-haired, petite attorney, came to lunch and stayed to make out a membership application. Eight hundred and twenty Friars sponsored her. She even got support from the young men in the parking lot, nine busboys, the chef, and a deliveryman who happened to be in the neighborhood. (Of course when Ruth heard that Allred was our first female applicant, she said, "Why did you have to start with a young pretty one? You could have chosen an old bat with arthritis! I answered, "We have enough arthritis in the club. Motrin could be our club logo!" Ruth didn't think that was funny. It was one of those days.)

Because the Friars of California was the first so-called men's club to welcome a lady member, the club received national publicity and made every major news telecast. I was interviewed eighteen times, most often by somebody who felt that our motives were suspect. Sorry, but there was no duplicity. Show business is always ahead of popular sentiment—singers protested wars long before politicians, and moviemakers debated moral issues long before the courts. Because the Friars is flavored with show business, it too is ahead of issues. We welcomed Gloria Allred because we recognized that her time had come. Moreover, as Henry Slate, the actor and bon vivant, said at the table, "From now on we'll have a hell of a locker room!"

The issue may have been summed up when Marshall Berle, my handsome nephew, who manages the top rock group "Ratt," heard Tom Bosley say, "Now we're all equal in the steam room, and answered, "Wanna bet on it?"

The number of female members will grow and will always be welcome. Before long it may be larger than the male membership. That a lady president looms in the future isn't mere whimsy. I have my ideas as to whom that lady will be. I won't reveal the name of my candidate until Ruth Berle is under discussion.

Parting Salvos

A Few Jokers in the Deck

*Lou Walters is Mr. Bad Luck. He could get a
paper cut from a Get Well card!*

Earl Wilson

*Mike Todd never did a thing in his life and he
never did that well!*

David Merrick

If a man thinks he can win, he might not!

Harpo Marx

*Back in Oklahoma we got a game—you deal four
cards up, two cards down, one in the middle,
then you get up, go find a bootlegger and get
drunk!*

Will Rogers

*I've been taking bridge lessons for a month now. I
already know there are three suits!*

Rocky Graziano

*If Chico Marx made a better mousetrap, he'd only
end up with better mice!*

George S. Kaufman

My lack of character in the early 1980s was sorely tried by my partial
abstinence from trying to beat the odds. (Ruth was thrilled when I
burned my little black book. In it were the names of a slew of book-

makers and fifty doctors, most of them proctologists. Luckily, I had copies of the important numbers—four of the bookmakers and all of the doctors. The contrast was sharp between this black book and the last one to which I'd set fire after my marriage to Ruth. Don Juan went up in smoke with that one. I was grateful to Ruth for ordering the arsenous act as I was already at the age where I couldn't read most of the phone numbers without squinting.)

To help overcome the shock to my system and my wallet brought on by the abstinence of the eighties, I ventured into the card room of the Friars. Early in my days as a club member, I played poker. I wasn't allowed to take my turn as a dealer because I'd learned too many card tricks from magicians while we waited to go on in vaudeville. (Harry Houdini told me that I had good hands. He also told me not to become a magician. The magician's life must end in tragedy as there is no last illusion, no point at which he can stop trying to top himself. Being a perfectionist, Houdini believed that someday he would actually walk through a wall. In 1925 he made a statement I found repeated years later in a Felix Aylmé short story: "The man who has a reason," he said, "could walk through walls.")

My foray into the card room at the Friars was a dismal failure. I could find no one to play with me. Some knew of my card prowess. Others, to whom the card game is a religious venture, thought I was clowning. Also, most significant, was a sudden awareness that the Friar card room had nurtured stories and men of matchless achievement. I'd never be able to compete with them in future myths.

How could I reach the heights of a Lou Walters? Walters was the owner of a top New York nightclub, the Latin Quarter. Greater was his siring of a daughter, Barbara, who grew up to be a charming woman and a premiere lady of television. (Every time I hear what Barbara Walters earns I look at Ruth and cry. Come to think of it, I never did find out why Ruth stopped working when we married. She did mention that she wanted to devote herself to me fulltime. I've seen her a total of nine minutes in thirty-six years.)

Lou Walters found an idle Mike Todd this one afternoon. Todd was also of epic proportions. A brilliant impresario and entrepreneur, he produced Broadway shows. He later went on to produce the movie *Around the World in Eighty Days*. To demonstrate his idea of subtlety, Todd threw a tiny party for the movie at Madison

Square Garden. His greatest accomplishment, history will report, was his wooing of and marriage to Elizabeth Taylor. (Todd's love for his bride was so intense, she was the only one he never bankrupted. An earlier wife complained to Todd that she couldn't understand why he was cashing all of her bonds. He answered, "You don't keep enough cash in the house!")

A fresh deck blessed by Al Lackey, acting as head kibitzer, Walters and Todd went at it. This was not to be Walters's luckiest day. By six Todd had a hefty mortgage on the Latin Quarter. By seven Todd owned it, unless Walters could come up with an impossible number in the next twenty-four hours.

Nine o'clock found Todd playing with George Meyer, the songwriter. As good as the cards had been earlier for Todd, they turned twice as sour. By eleven Meyer had won a bundle.

Soon after midnight Walters showed up again. Within two hours Walters won back his club.

Taking a well-earned break with us downstairs, Walters was told that he was a lucky man. Walters said, "Why am I lucky? I broke out even!"

Eddie Cantor asked him, "Don't you worry when you lose?"

Walters said, "I never cry over spilt milk. I figure it has enough water in it already."

After another *mano a mano* with Todd, Walters found a silver cloud somewhere. "I wasn't lucky today," he explained. "I wish I'd had yesterdays' cards."

Todd said, "Yesterday you lost twelve big ones."

Walters said, "Big deal."

"You've lost nine days in a row."

Walters said, "Do you know anybody who's lucky *every* day?"

Walters had the victim's disdain for other victims. During a lull, Walters sat with Ed Wynn. A bad player who'd been Walters's partner in bridge a few days before joined them. A few minutes later, Chico Marx showed up and said to the bad player, "What's your game?"

Walters jumped in, "Not even dealing."

For a short while Walters attempted the gentlemen's game of bridge. To bring him up to par with the other players, many of whom, like George S. Kaufman, had been playing for years, Walters started to take bridge lessons. After his second lesson he felt ready for the big time and got into a fairly steep game. On the third hand of the night, Walters's partner bid four no trump, a bid that has a special significance in most bridge systems. Walters responded, "Can you bid something else? We're not up to 'no trump' yet!"

Lou Walters did become a decent bridge player and, sitting with us in the neighborhood of a tongue sandwich, was paid a typical Kaufman compliment by the playwright: "Walters is a pretty good bridge player. He's never lost his home!"

Sime Silverman, the founder of *Variety*, was another card freak, but his game was poker. Only rarely did the publication of *Variety* interfere with Silverman's poker game. One issue was in danger of having some jumbled copy on page two. A call was put in to Silverman, who told the typesetter, "Bluff!"

Joining the Friars because the *Variety* office was too small to accommodate a decent poker game, Silverman soon got into a regular game with George M. Cohan, Jack Lait, the columnist, and Billy Rose. (Cohan liked to borrow amounts from other players during the game, so that at the reckoning he could challenge their figures and possibly save himself a few dollars. When a failproof system with chips was introduced, Cohan quit the game. At the Round Table, Cohan said, "I only play poker with people who trust me. I never cheated a man in my life!"

Jack Lait, probably there for the defense, said, "Yesterday you snookered me out of twenty-five dollars."

Cohan said, "You thought I owed you another twenty-five."

Lait said, "So did the four other guys."

Cohan said, pointing to himself, "It wasn't unanimous!" (His urge to be numero uno at everything stronger than his fear of eternal damnation, George M. Cohan wasn't above some unethical maneuvers. Many times at the beginning of play, he'd manage to drop a card on the floor. His knowledge of what the card was gave him an edge. The ploy worked until another player floored a card that woud equalize the odds. Sitting down for one session of old-fashioned seven-card three-handed gin rummy, having joined Cohan and Jesse Lasky, the movie mogul, Robert Ripley said, "Are we playing house rules for 'floor'?")

Silverman and Lait believed that their luck didn't turn good until two in the morning. Because they kept testing their theory until the dawn came up like thunder every morning over Broadway, they, along with the other dedicated players, were suspended by the Friars. Law demanded that the club be closed each day for a few minutes to allow the smoke to settle.

Putting on sandwich boards, the eleven suspended Friars picketed the premises—all-night poker was protected under the First Amendment. A nation that denies a game to a poker degenerate is a nation in chains. (Julian Eltinge, a man of rare sexual appetites, came upstairs one afternoon after seeing the pickets and asked, "What's wrong with a nation in chains?")

The suggestion was lifted by the house committee acting out of a desire to be fair and a fear of bad reviews in upcoming issues of *Variety*. The sole stipulation in the bringing of democracy to the card room was that the room would have to be closed at a decent hour. Somehow, the big hand seldom got to the moment of truth. (The comedian Joe Cook had a watch that always read two minutes to twelve. Cook claimed that the reading was in honor of the last total eclipse in Passaic, New Jersey.)

The poker games went on, bringing joy to many. Yet it was the absence of a poker game that gave Irving Caesar, the songwriter, two of his biggest hits. Caesar lived for lobster and poker. One afternoon, too early for the lobster he dreamed of devouring, Caesar was standing in front of the club awaiting the arrival of some poker players. An earthquake or tornado had put an unfortunate ending to the game of the night before, which, of course, would also have been today's game. (Lew Brice, Fanny's brother, who, like Al Lackey, had dedicated his life to proving that money was thicker than family, once walked into a Monday-night game and said, "I can't play after Thursday!" Brice was another born loser and knew it.)

As Irving Caesar waited, Otto Harbach, the librettist, happened by. A pious man whose range of tastes allowed for neither poker nor lobster, Harbach lectured Caesar on the twin evils, especially poker. On the way to a rehearsal, Harbach said, "Come with me to a rehearsal. You'll be better off."

Because Harbach was a Broadway patriarch, Caesar joined him at the rehearsal. The play being worked on was *No, No, Nanette*. The loss of the poker game got Irving Caesar together with Vincent Youmans so they could write "I Want to Be Happy" and "Tea for Two."

A few days after the rehearsal, Caesar managed to sneak back to his old haunts. Taking a breath from his ingestion of a two-pound Maine lobster, Caesar told us the story of his great assignment. Bobby Clark, the vaudevillian and one of the funniest men ever to grace Broadway, waved off Caesar's so-called good luck and said, "You have no luck. If it's the day I'm thinking of, you missed a helluva game!"

Although Damon Runyon played cards, especially with Ken Kling, he didn't like the ducats. Card players were wastrels. In the time it took a good card player to play a hand, a true gambler could lose two races at Bowie. (Runyon may have been the prototype for the great joke about the gambler who bets a fortune on football and loses every game. He then bets basketball and loses ten more games. At the track he goes down the tube with all nine races. That night, avid to get money down somewhere, he looks for some ballgame. A friend says, "You can bet hockey tonight." The gambler says, "What do I know about hockey!")

Runyon bet on every sport. On my eighteenth birthday, Runyon took me to a dance marathon in New Jersey. He was planning a story on the phenomenon. As a tinny quartet played, couples struggled to keep dancing. Some, it looked to me, were fighting to keep alive. Runyon looked at one couple that showed signs of perking up and said, "I wish I could get a bet down!"

In 1934 the world was pleasantly stunned by the birth of the Dionne quintuplets. When somebody brought up the news, Runyon looked up from his drink and said, "I bet on triplets!"

While the honor of misfortune was being held up in the Manhattan Friars, others were attempting to balance things in the West. Tony Martin needed no forgiveness for being a shorn sheep. Martin himself confessed to us, "I lose like clockwork and then I lose the clock!"

Martin came in one day with a severe case of laryngitis. Passing the Round Table, he whispered as best he could, "I lost my voice."

Steve Allen said, "Pass the word—they're taking throats in the card room!"

Walter Matthau put it all in perspective for the rest of us, however. After a half dozen jokes about Martin's ability to lose floated through the air with the greatest of ease, Matthau mused, "Tony Martin can lose a thousand, ten, twenty." Matthau sighed. "But at the end of the day he goes home to Cyd Charisse!"

Hal Linden, just starting out as Barney Miller, said, "If *she* loses, what does Cyd Charisse have to look forward to?"

Eddie Cantor never understood the finer points of winning and losing big. Saturday nights, Cantor played poker with Sophie Tucker, Joan Davis, the comedienne, and anybody else who wouldn't go to pieces if he or she lost two dollars for the night. When Cantor moved to California, a substitute game was arranged. Californians being a wild bunch, the stakes were raised slightly. At the end of an evening's play, Cantor counted up and found that he'd lost forty dollars. At the club the next day, he talked about some of the odder hands. He was thrilled that he'd won the last hand, bringing his losings down by ten dollars. Steve Allen said, "It's a good thing you won that last hand or you would have moved back to New York!"

Cantor, the richest man in the Western hemisphere, said, "With what?"

The western intermediate class had many luminaries like Bud Abbott, Paul Small, the agent, and Henry Slate, but at the top of the pyramid had to be somebody like Harry Karl. The husband of Debbie Reynolds at the time and owner of a large chain of shoe stores, Karl became a size 12 triple E patsy during an ugly gambling scandal at the club. After a big loss one day, Karl sat down with us for a few minutes. Tony Martin said, "Hang around, Harry. The Red Cross has been notified!"

For a while Harry Karl was married to Marie MacDonald, a gorgeous actress whose working title "The Body Beautiful" told only about half the magnificent story. The marriage, one of two the lovebirds waged against one another, was, to understate it, stormy. Bob Hope once told that Harry Karl's house was a stop on the USO tour!

Marie MacDonald often complained that Harry Karl was trying to make her something she wasn't. At the table, Red Buttons asked, "What is Harry Karl going to do with a boy?" Similarly, another afternoon, Karl plopped himself down and said almost helplessly to the rest of us, "She won't change!"

Danny Thomas said, "If she's not broken, don't try to fix her!"

These Slipped Through the Cracks

Some dine at the eternal table,
Their names recorded in History's book.
But some escape History's long register
And eat in the kitchen with the cook.

Grantland Rice

Al Lackey, a Friar out of pity and Sophie Tucker's husband out of a moment of madness on the star's part, was a sentimental sort. He summed up his marriage and wife by stating proudly, "She never gave me a bad check!"

Some time after a marital separation, one of many, Sophie left to play a club in Atlantic City. Pained by the absence of the women he loved, even though he had made himself absent when she wasn't absent, Lackey rushed to the beach city. He was driven by a need to make up with his wife and, as a sign of affection, put a touch on her.

Lackey took a suite at the Ritz Carlton Hotel. Within the hour he had charmed Sophie to his chambers and started to enter into connubial bliss. As they were in the midst of a passionate embrace, to show the extent of his repentence, Lackey started to moan, like a priest recognizing that he was betraying his trust with a virgin. "What am I doing to you? What am I doing to you?"

Kicking him halfway across the room, Tucker said, "You're stealing all of my goddamn money, that's what you're doing to me!"

Ever sentimental, Lackey reported the event in all of its gory detail. Jessel asked, "Did you get any money?"

Lackey answered, "Nah, but she split the price of my suite with me!"

That history in its inexplicable way has chosen to submit Al Lackey to oblivion is unfair to both Lackey and the legions who still today search for heroes. (The Round Table has been blessed with many who deserve fame. In part, my exercise here is to present their credentials and allow mankind to judge.)

I, for one, believe that we zero out too many potential evergreens. Who among us has said one word in recent years about Deczo Retter, a man who came out onstage and wrestled with himself for ten minutes? He often came to the Friars when I was a youngster and sat off in a corner, wrestling with himself until his food came. I have dedicated much of my energy to the revival of the great unsung who deserve a melody.

Al Lackey was as unsung as they come. He was of the stuff of which the unsung are made. Lackey had no profession or trade.

Al Lackey spent between eight and ten hours a day, holidays included, trying to raise money. The number of people east of the Mississippi from whom Lackey hadn't borrowed money could be counted on somebody's missing finger. The amount wasn't important. What counted was the mere success of Lackey's efforts. Harry Hershfield summed up Lackey's method in a short dissertation between cocktails at the Round Table. Hershfield explained, "Al Lackey has three methods—a 'borrow,' a 'loan,' and a 'lend.' A 'borrow' of fifty dollars means that Lackey has no intention of paying back the money. The debt is canceled upon receipt of the money. Within five minutes, Lackey no longer remembers that the money was 'borrowed.'

"A 'loan' has the intention to repay behind it. Lackey will honor the debt if somebody dies and leaves him Arizona. A 'loan' also stands a chance if Lackey's claim to the czarship of all the Russias is accepted by the Comintern.

"A 'lend' is tricky. When a 'lend' of fifty dollars is made, the transaction isn't final. Lackey reserves the right to get more out of his affluent victim with either a 'borrow' or a 'loan.'

"For extreme emergencies, Lackey has a special—'Gimme fifty till I cash a check.' The 'gimme' is a sign of real desperation, often signifying that Lackey needs milk for his ulcer or cab fare. The threat to 'cash a check' sends shivers through the banks of North America. No Al Lackey check ever went through. Lackey checks were made of an unusual compound. They didn't bounce. They'd hit the ground, go up, and never come down again. Also, Lackey never explained why he needed fifty dollars for milk. He did have an explanation, untold till now, that might have helped—his ulcer required milk from one special yak in Tibet. The container was made of rare Venetian glass hand-blown by the last living Murano milk-bottle blower."

One afternoon Lackey saw Mike Todd sitting with us at the club. Lackey hadn't put the touch on Todd for a day and was worried that the impresario wouldn't appreciate the neglect. Todd was no mean "borrower" himself, except that he started at fifty thousand dollars. Somehow Todd got what he asked for.

Working on Todd this one afternoon, Lackey mentioned that his ulcer was really acting up. (Ben Blue, the comedian, told us once that Lackey's ulcer came from a dream. Lackey had dreamed that he was working! Hearing of the affront, Lackey approached Blue and said, "If you don't stop making jokes about me, I swear I won't come near you no matter how much I need the money!")

Todd handed the desired fifty to Lackey, who went up to the card room to check on the next yak milk shipment from Tibet. A little later Todd went to the card room to promote a game. Todd didn't have to wait long. The writer of "Margie," and one of the club champs at gin, Benny Davis, appeared. Todd and Davis linked up. Kibitzers started to gather, among them, standing behind Davis, Al Lackey. Todd asked Lackey, "How come you're hanging around? You were going to get some milk."

Lackey said, "With what? I got fifty on Davis!"

Todd picked beautiful cards and beat Davis handily. Some time later in the afternoon, Lackey was with us downstairs when Todd appeared. Todd asked Lackey, "How are you feeling?"

Lackey said, "With the way you picked cards, how could I feel?"

Todd went on, "Do you want another half a hundred?"

Lackey said, "Nah, with your luck today, you'll only beat me again!"

One afternoon a young messenger came up to the club and asked, "How can I find Al Lackey?"

Al Jolson happened to be with us that day and said to the messenger, "Open your wallet!"

Lackey spent no sleepless nights worrying about his need to replenish himself daily. Consistently a loser, Lackey no doubt felt that he was merely helping to circulate money and thus stimulate the economy.

Lackey never panicked. Lackey was always able to pick up a few somewhere. Brandishing one of Sophie Tucker's unsigned checks one day, Lackey tried to milk Mike Todd again. If Todd gave him money, Lackey would hand over the check. Todd said, "It's not signed."

Lackey said, "Sophie won't sign it for me."

Todd said, "So how do *I* get her to sign it?"

Lackey said, "She respects you! Maybe she'll do it for you!"

Hit with a "borrow" of two hundred one afternoon, Todd laughed and asked the world in general, "Al, why do you keep coming to me?"

Jack E. Leonard said, "He can't help it. You're on his route!"

Chevalier summed up Lackey beautifully, saying, *"Le rôle est détestable mais quelle performance!*...The part is detestable, but what a performance he gives!"

A Hungarian Goulash

There's never been a dull moment in Violinsky's life. Years, yes!

Billy Rose

Solly never wanted to get married because he was born that way.

Jimmy Ritz

When somebody drops his name they leave it there!

Jack Pearl

Solly Violinsky used to be very humble. But he broke himself of the habit!

Tommy Dorsey

Solly Violinsky came up from upstate New York. He took his name from his act. He came out onstage and sat down to play a piano to which a violin was attached. With his left hand he played chords on the piano. With his right he bowed a melody. At rare moments rhythm and melody came together to form a whole.

Had Violinsky been a master musician, the moments still would have been rare. His act was one of the shortest on record. His opening number, sweet, short, and fast, was one of his obscure songs.

As was the custom for all songwriters who performed, Violinsky then went into a medley of his hits. Having had only one hit, "When Frances Dances with Me," Violinsky played a three-minute medley consisting of "When Frances Dances with Me" played in two tempos, one of them with a violin solo that would make Isaac Stern cry. The audience his, Violinsky moved on to a stirring rendition of "The Stars and Stripes Forever." This got him an ovation. A tight act Violinsky's was, with no fat or lulls in it. For some unfathomable reason, Violinsky was seldom booked back.

At the Round Table, Violinsky was always rebooked. He'd walk in to the room, his body at full slouch, his shoulders rounded. Asked once why he was so round-shouldered, he said, "That's from trying to make hookers come." Another time he explained, "It's from trying to fit into ready-made suits." He was known to blame his hometown for the condition. Pushed by Charles Atlas, the muscle king, to pull his shoulders back and stand proud, Violinsky said, "This is as far as you can go when you're from Binghamton."

Aware of his minor physical faults, Violinsky had great faith in his songs. In 1955 a young man named Elvis Presley appeared on my show. He was already well on the way to becoming a giant star. As Elvis sat with me early in the evening after the first day's rehearsal, Violinsky sauntered over to the table. Shaking hands with Presley, Violinsky told the youngster that he was great, would be the biggest star since Jolson, and that he, Solly Violinsky, had a great number for the kid to record.

Presley said, "Most of my material is picked out by my manager, Colonel Parker. I couldn't even look at your song."

Violinsky shrugged his shoulders. "Okay, kid, you're still going to be big, but it's going to take you longer!"

Violinsky wrote "When Frances Dances with Me" in 1926. A few years later he wrote another song and was admitted to ASCAP. As proof of his membership he was sent a button to be put in the lapel of his coat. He wrote back, "Have a button already, please send coat!"

Married, he summed up his life by saying, "I get a lot of ass but it's all on one broad!"

His wife sent him out for a loaf of bread one afternoon. A few hours later he found himself on the train going to California. In Los Angeles he checked into a hotel and loafed around with the comics. After two weeks, a cab pulled up and his wife emerged. Solly said to her quickly, "The bread's up in the room!"

Caught jaywalking one afternoon, he asked the ticketing cop, "How fast was I going?"

Violinsky finally settled down to write such great songs as "Moonlight Hasn't Seen Daylight" and a brilliant book, *I Laid Off Under Four Presidents*.

Violinsky's talents didn't go unrewarded. Once he received a royalty check of a few cents from Robbins, Feist, and Miller, a major publishing conglom known as the Big Three. Coming over to the Round Table, Violinsky held out the check and asked, "For this the Big Three went to Yalta?"

Violinsky's most glorious moment came during the celebration of the end of World War Two. New York went crazy. Tons of paper were thrown from windows. Walking by the Brill Building, Solly picked up a piece of paper and said, "Hey, this is the first time one of my songs ever saw daylight!"

Violinsky's proudest moment came two days after the death of Albert Einstein. Violinsky cried as if he'd lost his closest friend. The world, he felt, would never recover from the death of this great man, this genius, this architect of America's strength. Finally, I said, "Why are you carrying on like this? You didn't even known Einstein."

Violinsky said, "No, but do you know how long I've been using relativity!"

When Solly Violinsky himself died, there wasn't nearly as much carrying on. Some of us felt a keen loss. It would be hard to explain to anyone who hadn't known the short violinist from upstate New York who spoke with a slight Hungarian accent.

Almost in Closing

I have always found Ruth Berle to be warm,
friendly, considerate, kind, and compassionate.
She is a wonderful mother and wife. She spends
almost her entire day doing good deeds. She has
given blood to the Red Cross and food to all the
poor people in Beverly Hills. I would be proud to
call her my daughter and I do because she is.

Sophie Rosenthal

As the eighties wind down, the notion of an all-male Round Table is fast becoming an anachronism. Before long, witty women will trade lines with us and utter enough cogent remarks to fill a second book. It won't be long before Goldie Hawn, Lily Tomlin, Whoopi Goldberg, and Liz Taylor sit at the Round Table and make us wonder how and why we ever bothered to play male chauvinist.

The ladies will probably come up with "lists" too—the ten dumbest things my husband says when I ask him to take out the garbage, ten things I want to do with Robert Redford, and, one day after they take over, ten reasons why we shouldn't allow men into the Friars.

Whatever the agenda and the personnel at the Round Table when the women rule, I'd like to offer my wife, Ruth, as the Mother Superior. My choice is honestly objective. Ruth is a very funny lady. (Half of my ad-libs come from Ruth. Most of the other half comes from Ruth's mother. One or two come from listening to the Larry King Show.)

Ruth is almost a member of the Round Table already. I quote

her about five times a day. I have to. If she finds out she's gone unmentioned, I have to sleep with the torn patio furniture. I may even be forced to eat her cooking. I won't say Ruth is a bad cook, but Betty Crocker once threw a rock through her window! The other day I came home and Ruth was defrosting the stove! These jokes may be proof of the need for new blood at the Round Table.

Ruth recognizes her culinary deficiency. She brags that her idea of a hot meal is when the house is on fire. She even told me that one evening when I'd expressed the feeling that I'd like to eat home. I repeated my desire. Ruth felt at the wall and said, "The wall is cool. We're eating out!"

One morning I had a writing session planned for the day. The night before a performance I lock myself in a room with Buddy Arnold and lay out my ad-libs. On these days Buddy lunches with us, the lunch almost invariably a simple turkey sandwich. The eternal hostess, Ruth will ask, "What do you want for lunch?"

Buddy will ask, "What have you got?"

"We have turkey."

Lunch, therefore, becomes a turkey sandwich. It has always been and will always be a turkey sandwich. (On a banner day in 1986, Ruth offered us a sardine sandwich. Buddy and I accepted quickly. Ruth returned from the kitchen two minutes later and said, "Somebody ate the sardines." Buddy and I ate turkey.)

The day of the writing session under scrutiny, Buddy was delayed and didn't arrive until after two. Ruth said to him, "You beat the turkey today, huh?"

Two nights before leaving for Las Vegas to do a show with the performers of *La Cage aux Folles,* we held a last script-polishing session in the house. The writers and I sat around the dining-room table and made minor changes in the script. Leaving for a Share charity meeting on the other side of town, Ruth said, "If you want a Coke or coffee, call me."

Last winter, the football season in full swing, Ruth was in the den watching two football games at the same time. In order to cure me of gambling, Ruth took up the hobby to help cure me. She has cured me out of all of our stocks, bonds, and my gold cuff links. An astute student of football, Ruth manages to handicap four losers a weekend. Proof of that is the fact we keep moving into smaller and smaller homes. Between the two of us, we have proved that it's possible to gamble and be poor.

Ruth sat this day watching the two games on television and praying for her teams to make a comeback. I'd been out to a long and tiring meeting. I was exhausted. Plopping into my leather chair, I said, "Ruth, can you bring me a glass of water?"

"Cincinnati is on the eight-yard line, are you crazy?"

"I would like some water."

"If they go for a field goal, I'm dead!"

"If I don't get water, *I'm* dead."

"When did I become your slave?"

"I'm not asking for a lot. I work pretty hard. I deserve a glass of water."

"Leave me alone. I need twelve points on NBC."

"I slave seven days a week. I should get water."

"Go in and get some water!"

Sadder and wiser, I struggled to my feet and went into the kitchen. Returning a minute later, I said, "Where do we keep the water?"

Ruth topped me, "How do I know? I'm not the Sparklett's man!"

Ruth busied herself with the games, worked her way even, and, rooting with some indelicate phrases, managed to snatch defeat out of the jaws of victory.

Away from home, Ruth is an incomparable blast of fresh air. At a fancy Beverly Hills restaurant, Ruth was served a tasteless cream of asparagus soup. The maître d' joined us and asked how the soup was. Ruth answered, "My condiments to the chef."

At Chasen's, the world-famous restaurant, we generally get fine food. An exception occurred one evening when we were out with the Modells, Art, the husband and the owner of the Cleveland Browns, and Pat, his wife. Our salads were placed before us. New to the restaurant, the waiter asked if we wanted fresh pepper. On request he ground pepper into each of our dishes. Ruth's salad received a storm of pepper. It covered the lettuce like a blanket. Tasting a fleck of pepper, Ruth said, "It needs salad."

That Ruth would make a strong honchette at the new Friars Round Table needs no massive corroborating evidence beyond what is her most oft-quoted line. Ruth was at the Friars to pick up some papers that had to be signed and sent away. John Forsythe and Tony Bennett were sitting with me, looking at pictures of a party Ruth and I had attended the week before at the Sinatra house in Palm Springs. Barbara Sinatra had gone all out to give the affair a western flavor. Looking at a photograph of an area that had been set up to look like a hay barn, Forsythe said, "I don't get this. Do they really have a barn down at Rancho Mirage?"

Ruth glanced at the picture and said, offhand, "Oh, that's just the manger Frank was born in!"

Then there was Ruth's simple retort the day I proposed to her. I said, "Will you marry me?"

Ruth said, "Milton, don't put me on the spot!"

Ruth knows no fear. The Round Table would be in good hands.

Quote Unquote

In 1987 spring came to the Friars with more than seventy-six trombones and a big parade. We held our annual Life Achievement Award dinner. A big event in a city of giant galas, this year's dinner honored Liza Minelli. Bowing along with twelve hundred guests was a dais of stars—Gregory Peck, Burt Reynolds, Lonnie Anderson, Charles Bronson, Buddy Ebsen, and a few other beginners. As the master of ceremonies, I did a monologue about Liza that was fourteen minutes longer than her life. The entertainment lasted three hours.

The day after that event I appeared at the club to carry out my responsibilities as President. I was the Abbott of the Friars in the East and have been since time immemorial the President of the western Friars. As honcho, I've learned that my first duty is to come around and be bawled out the day after one of our events. I'm to blame for bad seats, wilted salads, and a bad note played by the third trumpet. There is one Friar who still is unhappy because he had a bad seat at the Julius Caesar knifing.

I have learned how to protect myself. When I come in I say, "I'm sorry." That covers me for the whole day. (I picked up this technique at home. In the past, Ruth has blamed me for World War Two, five flu outbreaks, the Iran problem, and, last year, the failure of the L.A. Dodgers. So I learned to awaken, say "I'm sorry," and go into the bathroom to brush my teeth. Unfortunately, with Ruth, one "I'm sorry" lasts only thirty minutes.)

Sitting at the Round Table, I was surprised at the paucity of complainers after the Minnelli dinner. Mr. Bad Seat wasn't even in the club. He showed up later and complained about his urologist. I won't accept blame for an insensitive urologist.

There were a few rumblings at the Round Table. Danny Thomas said, "Milton, why do you work so hard? You emceed a show for three hours. You don't need it. You have nothing to prove. You've done it all—you were a huge television star, movies, radio, books, stories. You even did a *Fantasy Island*."

Tom Bosley said, "Nobody else at this table ever did a *Fantasy Island*."

Dick Shawn said, "Nobody at this table would *admit* doing a *Fantasy Island*."

Thomas went on, "Milton, you should relax now. At big dinners, sit back, let the rest of them struggle. You relax, sit there, let the waiter bring you oxygen as your entrée. But, no more working. Enough is enough."

Bosley said, "It's time the younger guys took over. Let Richard Pryor work, Chevy Chase, Jay Leno. You deserve a rest."

Shawn said, "Milton, Tom's right. Once and for all, you should step back."

Bosley said, "Milton, please promise us you'll never do another show after December. Promise?"

I said, "Why December?"

Bosley said, "Because *my* dinner is in December and I want you to emcee."

Shawn said, "Make that January. I have a dinner too!"

"Another thing," Bosley said, "stop with your tape recorder and all those notes you take."

"They're for my book."

Thomas said, "Forget your books, the stories. Let other people write them. Let Sidney Sheldon write them."

Alone later, after the ribbing and lunch were over, my mind drifted to a special evening with Sheldon. I'd just told him some of my Caruso memories. Sheldon said, "Milton, you have to put that into a book."

"I have a million stories like that."

"Put them down. They deserve to be kept alive."

"It's a lot of work."

"You owe it to Cantor and Jessel and Kaufman and Welles and everybody."

I owed it to the Round Table too.

I sat down to write.

This book was started hundreds of pages and six thousand memories ago. Hopefully, the hundreds of pages have been filled to the satisfaction of the reader. I like what I wrote. Ruth likes what I wrote. My son likes what I wrote. The mailman didn't like it, but he likes the cleaning lady and she liked what I wrote. The gardener is non-commital. He becomes my friend only for six days before Christmas when the Christmas gift is imminent.

With the mapping of memories I feel that I've done a better than average job. I worked from key words on paper, guttural comments on tape, faded letters, some of which I wrote and others that were written to me. One Eddie Cantor story was brought to mind by a weathered news clipping on the other side of which is a grocery-store ad selling a pound loaf of white bread for eight cents.

Many of the lunches were revived by sitting with and hearing out men who remember just about everyone and everything that ever happened in show business. My gratitude to contributors is limitless. In fact, if everybody who gave a line or thought to this book were given a free copy, we'd never break even. Since I intend to give a free copy to each donor, I'll be broke by next winter. I don't care. I didn't write this book for money. I wrote it because I was tired of having all those wonderful secrets.

Now if you'll stand and join me in "The Friar's Song," I'll be able to start collating all the little pieces of paper, junk, and tapes I have in many other drawers. I only covered two thousand lunches, dinners, and cocktail hours at the Friars. There are eight thousand of each left to be recalled for Volume II.

Of course the first part of Volume II will be taken up with my declaration of eternal love for my Ruth. I may have neglected to mention my adoration in the book of which this is the curtain line.

Index